Theatre as a Weapon

Theatre as a Weapon

Workers' Theatre in the Soviet Union, Germany and Britain, 1917–1934

Richard Stourac and
Kathleen McCreery

Routledge & Kegan Paul

London and New York

To Rosa.
To those who forged the weapon
and to those who will continue to sharpen it.

First published in 1986
by Routledge & Kegan Paul plc

11 New Fetter Lane, London EC4P 4EE

Published in the USA by
Routledge & Kegan Paul Inc.
in association with Methuen Inc.
29 West 35th Street, New York, NY 10001

Set in 10 on 12 pt Linotron Plantin
by Input Typesetting Ltd, London
and printed in Great Britain
by The Thetford Press Ltd,
Thetford, Norfolk

Library of Congress Cataloging in Publication Data

Stourac, Richard.

Theatre as a weapon.
Bibliography: p.
Includes index.
1. Workers' theater—Europe. 2. Theater—Political
aspects. I. McCreery, Kathleen. II. Title. III. Series.
PN3307.E87S76 1986   792'.094   85–28087

British Library CIP data also available.

ISBN 0–7100–9770–0

Contents

Illustrations

Part Three Theatre of attack: Workers' theatre in Britain
(between pp. 269–78)

Sources

We are most grateful for the help received from the following people and institutions: Illustrations 1, 2, 5, 6, 11, 12, 16 to 30, and 35 were provided by the Akademie der Künste, Berlin, GDR. Illustrations 31 to 34 were provided by Edith and Maxim Vallentin. The photographs for illustrations 38 and 39 were taken by Carlos Guarita. The photograph for illustration 41 was provided by Ray Waterman. Illustrations 46 to 50 were provided by the National Museum of Labour History, London, with the permission of Bram Bootman. Photographer: John Vickers. Terry Dennet of Photography Workshop gave unstintingly of his expertise and creativity in helping us prepare the photographs.

Acknowledgments

We would like to express our gratitude to all those who have given advice and practical assistance in researching and writing this book, in particular to the veterans of the theatre movements we have interviewed. In Britain they were Bram Bootman, Fegel and Philip Firestein, Andre van Gyseghem, Alice and Jack Loveman, Charles B. Mann, Philip Poole, and Tom Thomas; in the German Democratic Republic Edith and Maxim Vallentin. Not only did they share their memories with us but they and their families often generously provided us with historic and photographic material.

We are also indebted to Genya Browning, Ruth Kisch, Stanley Mitchell and Brian Reeves for translating the Russian material so kindly lent by the Lenin Library, Moscow. The Akademie der Künste in Berlin, Marx Memorial Library and the National Museum of Labour History in London were also extremely helpful in providing us with photographs and allowing us access to their collections. Angela Tuckett's hospitality, inspiration and willingness to lend material from her personal collection must also be mentioned here, along with Bram Bootman whose unique collection of Unity Theatre material was invaluable in writing the British section.

We should also like to thank those with whom we had a fruitful exchange of ideas and written material: Genya Browning, Leonard Jones, Kevin Mundy, Raphael Samuel and Ian Saville.

Finally, we'd like to thank Ted Braun of Bristol University who was Richard Stourac's academic supervisor for the research that provided the basis for this book. His encouragement, advice, help with Russian translations and with the search for scarce material was crucial to the realisation of this project.

Richard Stourac and Kathleen McCreery

Introduction

> Unfortunately, no real collection of . . . agitprop plays from pre-
> proletarian epochs exists, nor is there a systematic précis of the current
> material. . . . This is . . . an important task for historical materialist
> research and for practical application. Without this historical
> knowledge our present workers' theatre can be understood as little
> as the political struggles of the working class can be understood
> without a knowledge of bourgeois or feudal social systems.[1]

This statement by Friedrich Wolf, playwright and leader of Performance
Troupe South-west, Stuttgart, was written in 1933. It could just as easily
have been made today. Although there has been a tremendous revival of
interest in workers' theatre since the late 1960s, very few of the contemporary groups performing plays for working class audiences have any
knowledge of the large popular movements which existed in the 1920s
and 30s. This broken tradition has meant learning lessons all over again.

In some cases the history remained hidden because of overt censorship.
The rich documentation *German Workers' Theatre 1918–1933* (in German)
could only be pieced together (by Ludwig Hoffmann and Daniel
Hoffmann-Ostwald) after the liberation of Germany from Fascism and
the founding of the German Democratic Republic. After all many of its
sources were police reports. A book called *Theatre of the Mountains* (in
Greek), whose author G. Kotzioulas worked among the partisans in World
War II, had to wait for publication until the fall of the last military
dictatorship in Greece. The actor Pericles Korovessis, imprisoned and
tortured by the junta, saw the discussions he and his wife had painstak-
ingly recorded in their theatre in Piraeus impounded by the police. These
are only a few examples. There are many other countries with repressive
regimes which fear progressive artists, particularly if they address themselves to working people.

But often persecution is not necessary. Just as women have been
ignored by historians, so revolutionary working-class artists are swept
under the carpet by the chroniclers of culture. They are members of a
dominated class and subject to the cultural domination, however subtle,
which expresses and reinforces the rule of capital. This book is a contri-

bution towards mending our broken tradition.

But just what is workers' theatre? Is it merely theatre by workers or for workers? The movements we have analysed had both these characteristics in common but there was another definitive dimension to their activities. They saw the working class and its organizations as the main historical force for bringing about a radical social change. For this reason they chose to perform mainly for working people on their own ground and focused in their plays on the problems of their audiences in the light of the struggle for change. The workers' theatre movements consciously aligned themselves to this struggle and became part of it.

In the process they had to find forms which could express these new subjects, forms which were appropriate to the new venues, and which made possible a different kind of relationship with their audiences. The problem of play-making, of a dramaturgy which could meet all these requirements, especially that of taking the audience through a differentiated learning process, became the main theatrical challenge faced by all these movements. From our own experience with Red Ladder and Broadside Mobile Workers' Theatre here in Britain as well as with the Portuguese migrant workers' theatre Alem Fronteiras (Beyond Frontiers), and to some extent with Die Komödianten in Austria and Theatermanufaktur in West Berlin, and from our knowledge of groups in other countries, we are certain that evolving techniques and structures which can help alter an audience's world view is still the central artistic problem facing workers' theatres today. We have therefore not attempted a complete history of three movements, but have concentrated on the theatrical methods contributing to the formation of class and revolutionary consciousness which they developed.

Theory is too often the province of those with little or no grounding in practice. The women and men with practical experience are usually preoccupied with the work at hand and often lack the confidence to step back and analyse what they are doing, to generalize from their own and other's experiences. And yet without a theory that is alive and at the same time rooted in an historical understanding and analysis, action can be blind, the artistic weapons blunted and the over-riding purpose ultimately lost.

We hope that this book will prove useful to film makers, musicians, visual artists, writers and teachers as well as readers with a special interest in theatre. But we also believe it is important for all those who are interested in politics to consider the role of art and culture (in the broadest sense) in shaping consciousness, and to understand the problems facing those working in the cultural field, sometimes independently, sometimes in relation to a political party or organization. Fegel Firestein, veteran of the Yiddish workers' theatre in London's East End, expressed this simply but eloquently when she said, 'from the theatre and from culture I could learn how to build a better future'. Workers' theatres and workers' movements are needed 'to look after the revolution'.[2]

Abbreviations

R.S. and K.M.: the initials of the authors, used in explanatory notes within texts and quotations.

ATBD	Arbeiter-Theater-Bund Deutschlands (translated as Workers' Theatre League of Germany or Workers' Dramatic Union of Germany)
CC	Central Committee (mainly referring to the Workers' Theatre Movement)
Co-op	Co-operative Society
CPGB/CP	Communist Party of Great Britain, often referred to as the Party
DAThB	Deutscher Arbeiter-Theater-Bund (translated as German Workers' Theatre League or German Workers' Dramatic Union
IATB	Internationaler Arbeiter-Theater-Bund (translated as International Workers' Theatre League or International Workers' Dramatic Union)
ILP	Independent Labour Party
IRDU	International Revolutionary Dramatic Union
IRTB	Internationaler Revolutionärer Theaterbund (translated as International Revolutionary Theatre League, or International Revolutionary Dramatic Union, or International Union or Revolutionary Theatre/International Revolutionary Theatre Union)
IRTU	International Revolutionary Theatre Union
IURT	International Union of Revolutionary Theatre
IWDU	International Workers' Dramatic Union
IWW	Industrial Workers of the World, often referred to as 'Wobblies'
KAPD	Kommunistische Arbeiterpartei Deutschlands (Communist Workers' Party of Germany)

KJVD	Kommunistischer Jugendverband Deutschlands (Communist Youth League of Germany)
KOMSOMOL	Kommunistitchesky soyus molodyoshy (Communist Youth League)
KPD	Kommunistische Partei Deutschlands (Communist Party of Germany)
Narkompros	The People's Commissariat for Education
NEP	New Economic Policy
NUWM	National Unemployed Workers' Movement
Proletkult	Proletarskaya Kultura (Proletarian Culture)
RAPP	Russkaya Associaciya Proletarskich Pisately (Russian Association of Proletarian Writers)
RFB	Roter Frontkämpfer Bund (Red Front Fighters' League)
RGO	Revolutionäre Gewerkschaftsorganisation (Revolutionary Trade Union Organisation)
ROSTA	Russian Telegraph Agency, equivalent of TASS today
SPD	Sozialdemokratische Partei Deutschlands (Social Democratic Party of Germany
TRAM	Teatr Rabotshy Molodyoshy (Theatre of Working Youth)
TUC	Trade Union Congress
USPD	Unabhängige Sozialdemokratische Partei Deutschlands (Independent Social Democratic Party of Germany)
WTM	Workers' Theatre Movement
YCL	Young Communist League

Part One

We are the Blue Blouse . . . Workers' theatre in the USSR

1 · The roar of the dynamo

October 1923, Moscow:
Three students from the Institute of Journalism . . . made an
appearance at the third anniversary evening of the Institute . . .
where they put on a then quite new amateur living newspaper.
(Blue Blouse, Moscow 1925)[1]

The amateurs soon became professionals. A number of playwrights, directors, composers, and designers, mostly from the revolutionary avant-
garde, joined the first Blue Blouse company. Inspired by their example
other groups sprang into being. By 1927 the ranks of the Blue Blouse
included up to 7,000 workers' circles as well as four or five professional
groups with names like 'Model', 'Shock', 'Fundamental' and 'Variety
Vaudeville'. These professionals served workers' clubs in Moscow. But
they were also responsible for providing the workers' circles with up-to-
date material on the questions of the day, via a bi-weekly journal *Blue
Blouse* (Sinyaya Bluza). This is how the movement defined itself and its
work:

1 The Blue Blouse is a dramatic living newspaper which emerged
   from the report (the spoken or oral paper).
2 Blue Blouse is a form of agitation, a topical theatre born of the
   revolution, a montage of political and general phenomena
   presented from the point of view of the class ideology of the
   proletariat.
3 Blue Blouse is a flexible, vivid, juicy, hard-hitting and mobile
   theatre, performing under any conditions.
4 Blue Blouse is . . . a kind of variety platform, a special form of
   amateur art in the workers' club.[2]

In 1925 the editors of the journal were to claim that 'As far as new
artistic forms for ideological influence on the working masses are
concerned the *Blue Blouse* is the only movement of social significance'.[3]

In 1927 for the Four Year Celebration Conference they wrote that the *Blue Blouse*:

> put the question of a new theatrical form on the agenda. It organized an active nucleus of young workers in the clubs around questions of artistic and agitational work, it served as a constant booster in the struggle against negative phenomena and for the propaganda for new social habits in everyday life . . . a mass audience exists, a workers' audience which loves it and impatiently awaits the chance to see it.[4]

But by 1928 this extraordinary movement was fighting for survival. There is poignancy in this defiant account of Blue Blouse triumphs:

> In 1918 the enemies of Soviet power were shouting, 'Another two weeks and the Bolsheviks are finished!' The enemies of the Blue Blouse movement were saying in 1923, 'Another month or two and there won't be any Blue Blouse'. Both . . . were bitterly mistaken'. . . In five years Blue Blouse has travelled a long way, from a nameless living newspaper working in local tea shops all the way to the Berlin Piscator Stage; from the beer shops of the Moscow trade associations to its own theatre on Strasthaya Square; from a collective which served workers' clubs as far as ceremonial evenings in the House of Soviets, in the Bolshoi Theatre, in the Conservatoire. The Blue Blouse has travelled over the whole of the vast multi-faceted Soviet Union, from the Caucasus to the shores of the White Sea, from the Ukraine to the Siberian Taiga. The work of the Blue Blouse is equally well-known to the Tartars and Usbeks, Kirgis and the other Russians.

Wherever the Blue Blouse had been it had left not only enduring memories but new groups:

> They are perhaps the most eloquent summary of the living quality and fruitfulness of the Blue Blouse.[5]

Although it was not the only workers' theatre movement in the Soviet Union during the tumultuous 1920s, the Blue Blouse was undoubtedly the largest and most influential. It was also most clearly conceived of as a tool for raising consciousness, for deepening and widening the revolutionary process of a society in transition from capitalism to socialism.

At first glance it seems incredible that such an impressive movement could flourish in a country like the young Soviet Union. Capitalism had arrived late, the industrial proletariat was tiny, illiteracy was widespread, a series of wars had devastated the country. In order to understand the Blue Blouse phenomenon we must look at its roots.

2 · From the reformers to the revolutionaries: sources and influences

The democratic heritage – popular or pure art?

> The Blue Blouse has been occupied with precisely this work of tearing down the exterior of apparent well-being, of laying bare the truth underneath, the faults, the negative phenomena of our life today.
>
> (*Blue Blouse*, 1927)[1]

The 1905 revolution led to an upsurge in literary production by proletarian writers. In response to an appeal from the publishing house Pribej 450 works were submitted in three months, including 300 poems and eight dramatic plays. This output, although often 'clumsy and naive',[2] is particularly remarkable in view of the authors' total lack of leisure time, a basic prerequisite for creativity. 'One of the best known worker-writers A. Bibek wrote his novel *To the Long Road* at night and in exile, his play *Black Birds* was written during an illness, and the short story 'On the Black Strip' in prison.[3] In spite of such prohibitive conditions, proletarian cultural activity increased as the class struggle intensified and the middle-class intelligentsia tended to fall silent.

As far as workers' theatrical activity before the revolution is concerned little is known. Pavel Markov mentions the existence of nineteen workers' clubs[4] and Frantisek Deak refers to 'an estimated 5,000 workers' theatrical clubs . . . in 1905'.[5] Their activity was probably oriented towards the critical realistic tradition associated with the writers of the bourgeois democratic revolutionary movement which dominated the political thinking of the working class from the 1860s until the turn of the century.

The new aesthetic developed by the realists was summed up by Chernyshevsky, whose novel *What Is to Be Done?* provided Lenin with the title for his famous pamphlet:

> Art does not limit itself only to the beautiful. . . . It embraces the whole of reality. . . . The content of art is the social aspect of

life. . . . The beautiful is that in which we can see life as it ought, in our understanding, to be.[6]

Such ideas influenced painters and composers as well as writers. The Wanderers took their exhibitions to the common people whose lives inspired their canvases. The Academy accused them of having taken 'the false path of tendentiousness' producing 'not so much a picture as . . . a protest'.[7] The Mighty Group of composers formed by Dargomyzhsky together with his followers Balakirev, Cui, Mussorgsky, Rimsky-Korsakov, and Borodin also looked to the masses for themes in their attempt to escape from the salon via the Free Music School. Mussorgsky echoed Chernyshevsky in defining his art:

> Artistic depiction of beauty alone is grossly infantile, childhood art. . . . You cannot get by with just pretty sounds. That is not what the modern man wants from art, nor does it justify the artist's efforts. Life, wherever it manifests itself; truth, however bitter; boldness, sincere speaking . . . that's my taste, that's what I want.[8]

In the professional theatre the main advocate of realism was Stanislavsky. He aimed to 'respond to social currents, explain them to the public, and be a teacher of society'.[9] In 1898 he and Nemirovich-Danchenko founded the Moscow Popular Art Theatre. Its repertoire was based on Chekhov, Ibsen, Lev and Alexei Tolstoy, Hauptmann and some of Gorky's works. The Art Theatre broke with the petrified, declamatory acting of the nineteenth century state theatres based on a star system with clichéd villains and heroes. Instead ensemble playing, the expression in artistic form of the inner life of a character through Stanislavsky's system of emotional memory, and the detailed reproduction of reality were stressed.

Within a few years this progressive approach had proved remote from the increasingly harsh reality as experienced by the masses of the Russian people. Incensed by the St Petersburg massacre of 1901 the audience interrupted Stanislavsky's production of *An Enemy of the People* to shake his hands. They had interpreted Dr Stockmann's rhetoric as a call to arms. His response was dismay:

> That evening I found out through my own experience what power the theatre could exercise. From that evening on many attempts were made to drag our theatre into politics, but we, who knew the true nature of theatre, understood that the boards of the stage could never become a platform for the spread of propaganda, for the simple reason that the very least utilitarian purpose or tendency brought into the realm of pure art kills art instantly.[10]

In 1905–6 only one play in the Moscow Art Theatre's season (the word 'Popular' had been dropped) was of political significance: Gorky's *Children of the Sun*. Then, at the first staff meeting of the Art Theatre's new Studio

Stanislavsky warned that 'theatre cannot and does not have the right to serve pure art alone'.[11] Had he changed his mind? This speech was made in May 1905 only a few weeks after the Bloody Sunday massacre which left the liberals, his main audience, outraged. Gorky had been imprisoned for revolutionary activity and strikes had shaken the country, even threatening to involve the Art Theatre's own company. But there were other forces at work. Stanislavsky's pupil Meyerhold was to take over the directorship of the Theatre-Studio. He had openly stated his intention of aiming at a stylized or conventionalized theatre. In this context his warning against pure art may well have been an expression of Stanislavsky's fear that the Studio would abandon naturalism for a more esoteric approach.

Meyerhold – breaking the mould

There is art and art. One art impartially depicts and adorns life, masks, covers over the shortcomings and negative sides of real life, or simply states them, incapable of showing ways of reconstructing. Another art organizes life, takes part in the day by day building of society.   (*Blue Blouse*, 1927)[12]

Meyerhold was certainly aware of Stanislavsky's desire to keep the Studio tied to the Art Theatre's apron strings. He was glad in retrospect when its opening was cancelled under the pretext of the armed rising in Moscow on October 14, 1905. Behind the closed doors of the Studio the pupil Meyerhold began to question his teacher's methods in earnest and to search for new dramatic techniques. His realization that some of these techniques had revolutionary political potential came much later.

The years of repression following the 1905 rising led to a retreat from reality in the arts and a preoccupation with dreams, illusion and transcendence of the real world. In keeping with this trend, the Symbolist poet Valery Bryusov was made head of the Theatre-Studio's literary committee. The disintegration of a once homogeneous world view was expressed in fragmentary poetic forms predating 1905 which in turn demanded new forms of theatrical presentation.

Meyerhold believed that Stanislavsky's rejection of the superficial clichés of the state theatres had led him to oversaturate audiences with naturalistic detail:

the stylistic method presupposes the existence of a fourth *creator* in addition to the author, the director and the actor – namely the spectator. The stylized theatre produces a play in such a way that the spectator is compelled to employ his imagination *creatively* in order to *fill in* those details *suggested* by the stage action. In the stylized theatre 'the spectator should not forget for a moment that an actor is performing before him, and the actor should never forget that he is performing before an audience, with a stage beneath his feet and a set around him.'[13]

In stark contrast to Stanislavsky Meyerhold rejected the idea that art could convey the sum of reality. In his own discussion of the grotesque he quotes with approval the Symbolist poet Bely:

Art dismantles reality, depicting it now spatially, now temporally. For this reason, art consists either in images or in the alteration of images: the first yields the spatial forms of art, the second – the temporal forms. The impossibility of embracing the totality of reality justifies the schematization of the real.[14]

But this did not mean empty posturing:

With the word 'stylization' I do not imply the exact reproduction of the style of a certain period or of a certain phenomenon. . . . To 'stylize' a given period or phenomenon means to employ every poss- ible means of expression in order to reveal the inner synthesis of that period or phenomenon, to bring out those hidden features which are to be found deeply imbedded in the style of any work of art. . . .[15]

Nothing but the most important . . . 'the quintessence of life' as Chekhov put it.[16]

As early as 1910 Meyerhold began to restructure the plays he directed to achieve an episodic, even montage-like effect. He was influenced by Blok, Sologub and Wedekind:

The realism of these dramatists . . . is such that it forces the spectator to adopt an ambivalent attitude towards the stage action by switching the course of the action with strokes of contrast. The basis of the grotesque is the artist's constant desire to switch the spectator from the plane he has just reached to another which is totally unforeseen.[17]

Such theories led Meyerhold to radically redefine virtually every aspect of theatre from the very architecture to the actor's expressive powers. He believed that the stylized theatre was leading to a revival of the Greek classical theatre with its emphasis on three-dimensional space, functional rather than illusionistic props, costumes and sets, the incorporation of the auditorium into the performance space, rhythmic dialogue and plastic movement.

Meyerhold's ideas and innovations were certainly revolutionary in terms of the theatre. But they might have had little significance for the theatre of the revolution had he not linked his new approach to a centuries-old tradition of popular spectacle: mysteries, commedia dell'arte, vaudeville, demonstrative story-telling, music hall and the fairground booth. And the art of the travelling players was based on their skills as mimes, jugglers, conjurers and acrobats. They emphasized movement, improvisation and gestic expressiveness, relating directly to their audiences.

These traditional forms lent themselves to a gestic approach to acting and to the grotesque. They appealed to Meyerhold's own instincts: 'Words in the theatre are only embellishments on the design of movement.'[18] Social attitudes became quotable through the stylization of the gesture or vocal expression, 'bringing out those hidden features'[19] the naturalistic theatre was incapable of grasping in spite of its attempts at completeness. At the same time everyday occurrences could be made to appear 'familiar yet strange'.[20] The similarity to the ideas developed by Brecht some twenty or thirty years later is striking.

In his analytical conception of a drama of stylization Meyerhold had combined the most fundamental elements of the modern revolutionary theatre. He made a detailed critique of the dominant contemporary drama, scoured the entire history of popular dramatic traditions, national and international and selected those with the potential for conveying a message. These he refashioned for the twentieth century and tested in practice in a range of productions between 1902 and 1917, combining them with formal elements of apparently purely aesthetic 'decadent' art forms like symbolism.

But it was not until the political revolution of 1917 that these formal innovations were redefined with overtly political aims in mind. As the labouring classes took power they began the enormous task of abolishing the oppressive conditions which had prevented them from developing their own culture on a large scale. Meyerhold's theatre, with its 'active spectators', its use of forms which were familiar to the people and highly entertaining, its emphasis on making the invisible visible – was uniquely suited to the demands of this cultural revolution.

October in the arts

We have 'only' one thing to do: to make our population so 'civilized' that it will understand all the advantages of participating to the last man in co-operation, and will organize that participation. But for this . . . a whole revolution is necessary, a whole period of cultural development of the entire popular mass.   (Lenin)[21]

In 1897 the Russian literacy census revealed that only 35.8 per cent of men and 12.4 per cent of women were literate. By 1913 the industrial proletariat made up only about 1.41 per cent of the population, the overwhelming majority being peasant. The devastation of World War I was made even worse by the civil war and foreign intervention which followed the revolution. Railways and bridges were blown up, supplies which were not destroyed could not be transported. Epidemics were widespread. On top of all this chaos came one of the worst famines in history.

Against such a background, Narkompros, the People's Commissariat for Education under Lunacharsky, was supposed to carry out the cultural revolution Lenin was talking about. Its difficulties were exacerbated by the widespread hostility to the Bolsheviks from the professional sectors, including the staff and officials of the former Ministry of Education itself. This antagonism expressed itself in non-co-operation, boycotts, even strikes. The All-Russian Teachers' Union, for example, with financial backing from the bankers, threatened a six-months strike if there was any interference with their decision-making powers in matters of education.

As the attempts at creating revolutionary workers' states in Germany, Hungary and other European countries failed, the Bolsheviks' hope that the Russian revolution would be the first in a series began to fade. The possibility of mutual aid was no longer on the cards. The Soviet Union was engaged in a bitter struggle for survival on many fronts. The Red Army had to fight the external enemy, the nations conducting the war of intervention, as well as the White counter-revolutionaries within. But what of those who were simply fearful of communist ideals and a socialist state? New weapons had to be created to win their hearts and minds.

The Party established an agitprop department in its central committee. Draft directives were issued prior to the Seventh Party Congress urging the use of cinema, theatre, concerts and exhibitions to penetrate the country with communist propaganda. Art was to be combined with lectures and meetings to reach both literates and illiterates.

At the same time a number of artists had begun to question fundamentally the relationship between the economic base and superstructure, and with it the role art and culture had to play in a revolutionary process. Particularly active in this process were the Futurists and Proletkultists. They identified with the revolution, partly because the avant-garde had been censored and even persecuted under the Czar. Their only means of expression was through illegal party publications.

This conjuncture of the need for agitprop art and the desire and ability of some artists to contribute to the revolution, explains the rapid quantitative and qualitative growth that took place in almost every cultural sphere. The boundaries of hitherto accepted or even anticipated art forms were broken by a flood of revolutionary fervour, imagination and experimental spirit.

The first and most obvious characteristic of these new forms was that they not only appealed to the masses but were accessible to them. They were displayed or performed in public, not in private galleries or chamber theatres. They became true mass media.

Posters

Lubok on an international theme:
CAPITAL: What's wrong with you?
ENGLAND: England's got some unemployment and then there are all these noises on the side, next to the heart where the colonies are.
CAPITAL: Stick out your tongue, show your glands, don't breathe. Humm, I thought so . . . propaganda.   (Blue Blouse, 1925)[22]

Posters played an enormous part in agitprop. More than 3,000 were produced between 1918 and 1921. The Russian Telegraph Agency's ROSTA posters, spearheaded by Mayakovsky, were primarily designed to inform people of the latest news, but also explained the military, economic and political questions of the day. Their style was reminiscent of the lubok, the old popular broadsheets with an illustrated narrative in strip form, paraphrasing folk themes. (The original luboks were actually peasant paintings on wood.) The agitreklama, advertising posters for everything from books to galoshes, used 'simple lucid ditties, at times cheeky, at times full of wisdom like popular folk proverbs with simple colour and easily remembered imagery and clearly Constructivist composition'.[23]

The poster-makers were also partly inspired by such popular fairground forms as the Petrouchka puppet shows. In turn they soon influenced the theatre. A group called Terevsat (Theatre of Revolutionary Satire) was founded in 1919 by the director of the Vitebsk ROSTA agency, Pustinin. They made use of revue, operetta, vaudeville, and chastushki, traditional limerick-style folk verse, in order to bring to life the ROSTA posters. After Terevsat's arrival in Moscow in 1920 other groups were soon to be seen in the streets, stations and factories. Their sketches dealt with everything from recruitment for the front to preventing disease. The Terevsat groups were almost certainly direct antecedents of the Blue Blouse.

But even if they had not existed the Blue Blouse had much in common with the poster-makers. Both worked in rural as well as urban areas, often for semi-literate audiences. Both frequently received their material from a centre, modifying and developing it to suit local conditions. It is therefore hardly surprising that they took up these highly successful cartoon-like forms, which they converted into living or moving images and collages connected by the rhymes and ditties of narrators.

Cinema

> *Agitki* (agit pieces) come into being, sharp, whip-like, up to the
> minute, directly linked with our everyday life, vivid, bright, easy to
> remember.   (*Blue Blouse*, 1925)[24]

The cinema too was to become a 'real and potent weapon'[25] according
to a resolution passed at a factory committees meeting in September 1917
which was attended by Kalinin and Lunacharsky. The films of Eisenstein
and Pudovkin are well known, but before them came the cine-trains and
boats and agitational shorts, the *agitki*. In February 1919 the cinema
committee of Narkompros released thirteen single-reel *agitki* for showing
to Red Army men, among them *The Last Cartridge*, *We Are Above
Vengeance* and *For the Red Banner*. Neilson, one of the camera men who
filmed at the front, described how

> Certain camera men were transferred from story film cinematography
> to newsreel work and became permanent travelling companions of
> Red Army detachments. . . . Already the cameraman was far from
> the neutral position of the bourgeois newsreel reporter who seeks
> sensational shots. . . . He became an agitator and propagandist,
> frequently changing his camera for a rifle.[26]

The success of the *agitki* can be measured by the fact that when the
Whites recaptured Odessa they staged a public burning of all they could
find.

Sanitation, health, anti-alcoholism, literacy and productivity as well as
the military situation and wider political and economic questions were all
subjects of *agitki*. Their role was to agitate for the progressive approaches
of those regions, factories or collectives which realized party policies in
the most productive way. These were juxtaposed to the old attitudes and
ways which still existed in town and country. As local production of
agitprop material began to increase the story or fictional plot began to
give way to the plot made up of politically significant facts, also often
local.

The new media influenced the old. *Agitki* were soon being used in the
theatre, particularly by the Blue Blouse and later by TRAM, the Theatre
of the Working Youth. They had the advantages of specificity and
flexibility and could be inserted into an 'overview' as the Russians called
the revue. The Blue Blouse's use of montage derived to some extent from
adaptations of the *agitki* used in the early newsreel films and the work of
the ciné-trains from 1919 to 1921.

The mass spectacle

Blue Blouse guest performance in Chemnitz, 1927:
The final scene was devoted to the Red Army. The military exercises
of the infantry, cavalry, and artillery were represented with dance; the
fleet too was represented . . . with the expressive means of the body,
with group formations, and the most deft and baffling acting.

(The Fighter, 1927)[27]

Films and posters were reaching a mass audience and the theatre too
began to come out onto the streets and squares. Again the Soviet artists
were able to link up with a popular tradition, the religious and patriotic
pageant. Theatrical trials were staged with the audience as jury, encouraging them to take sides and make decisions. The accused ranged from
the murderers of Rosa Luxemburg to an effigy of alcoholism. Sometimes
the theatrical innovators themselves were in the dock and artistic controversies would be publicly debated. The participation of official judges,
state solicitors and advocates as well as famous actors was partly responsible for the enormous mass appeal of such trials.

However, in comparison with the mass spectacles which took place
between 1919 and 1923, the 'trials' were minute in scale. Thousands of
participants, tens of thousands of spectators, and a vast 'stage' which
might include the Stock Exchange stairs and square but also nearby
bridges, minesweepers and fortresses – all helped to lend a triumphal
character to these celebrations of the victory of the revolution. The
subjects were equally monumental: *The Play of the Third International*
staged by the Red Army workshop; *The Mystery of Freed Labour*,
which linked the October Revolution to the Spartacist slave revolt in
73 BC and the rebellion led by the Cossack leader Stenka Razin in 1670;
The Blockade of Russia; *In Favour of a World Commune*; *The Storming
of the Winter Palace*; and finally a commemoration by workers,
peasants and soldiers of Ivanovo Voznesensk commemorating the
famous anti-war strike of the city's metal workers in 1915, and the
bloody persecution and mass executions by the czar's troops which
followed.

Kerzhentsev describes the audience reaction to *In Favour of a World
Commune* which ended at 4 a.m. with fireworks, salvos and sirens from
the minesweepers: 'Throughout the long hours the spectators remained
almost motionless and followed the individual scenes with enthusiasm.
The performance also made an extraordinarily deep impression on the
numerous foreign delegates to the Congress.'[28] (The Second Congress of
the Third International.)

The Mystery of Freed Labour had a livelier effect:

Even more gripping was the final scene when the enormous choir of workers started singing 'The Internationale' surrounded by the rays of the rising sun behind the red star. The electrified masses trampled down the fences surrounding the scene of action, stormed the door of the Stock Exchange and joined the actors in the powerful final chorus.[29]

The rehearsals of the mass spectacles had to be organized like a complex military manoeuvre. There were four directors for the three parts of *In Favour of A World Commune* plus one who oversaw the work as a whole. Piotrovsky co-directed the third section. We have supplemented his account as quoted by Frantisek Deak with explanations in brackets from Kerzhentsev.

> Every thousand participants were divided into units of ten with a leader for each unit. The principal rehearsals were held with those leaders who were responsible for their units, instructing them and leading them during the performance. There were also separate leaders for each subject unit (rulers, police, traitors, etc.) as well as for each episode and for each separate part of scenic space. The performance itself was divided into short 'moments' (such as entrances, turns). These 'moments' in numerical order constituted the so-called 'score' of the performance. The number of participants, the beginning and end of each action, props, costumes, sound and light effects were also noted here.
>
> In the staging . . . there were 110 separate moments (episodes). . . . The directorial staff took their places on the captain's bridge. From there they were connected by field phones and light signals with the separate stage areas. . . . By this kind of organization the tempo of separate episodes, the length of pauses, sound and light effects were directly dependent on the wish of the director.[30]

Some observers pointed to similarities between the mass spectacles and the theatrical celebrations of the French Revolution. The physical conditions under which they were performed were certainly similar, as well as the fact that they were both manifestations of the victory of mass movements and therefore had to relate to the masses in both subject matter and treatment.

Other Western European experiences were also utilized. Kerzhentsev's book *The Creative Theatre* published in Russian in 1920 drew on the advice of Romain Rolland and his study of Swiss popular festivals:

1 The writer should choose only well-known historical themes which allow a quick rendering;
2 Everything must be on a grand scale . . .
3 The poetic parts appropriate for a rhythmic singing must be simple and full of feeling; . . .

From this results the energy, speed and variety required by such a
performance. The musician has to compose such a play only in
whole notes . . . there must be no refined details in the
orchestration. . . . Everything must have generous dimensions;
the scenes and images will be viewed from a great distance and
therefore the painter's brush must be more like a broom. . . . Of
course the customary rules of acting and declamation cannot be
applied here. The actor must stand at the end of the stage and
pronounce each word clearly . . . the plot must be simplified as
much as possible, the dialogues must be spaced out, few words
and gestures must be made but their expression heightened. . . .
The crowd is being used in this theatre like the individual in the
old one. . . . Dialogue must be held between groups and double
and triple choirs must be utilized. . . . The place of individual
intrigues will thus be increasingly taken by mass conflicts . . .
strong dramatic contrasts and fantastic light-shadow effects should
exist. The vast dimensions of such performances permit the
simultaneous but separate staging of various episodes.[31]

The creators of the Russian mass spectacles clearly took this advice to
heart. But they were also innovative in their own right, particularly as
far as the imaginative use of home-grown traditions were concerned. On
the one hand there was the clowning and buffoonery of the circus in a
grotesque caricature of political opponents, on the other, the unpolished
realism of the Red Army Theatre representing soldiers, workers and
peasants.

This clash of styles and acting approaches was intentional. It was
another means of exposing the class divisions in society in addition to
symbolic visual techniques like those used in *In Favour of a World
Commune*: the king, courtiers, bankers and industrialists were positioned
on the upper platforms of the Stock Exchange, the grotesque figures
representing the Second International were in the middle of the stairs,
and the square itself was filled with workers. Music too was used to
reinforce these divisions. In Part Three, 'The Russian Commune', the
Strauss waltz representing the joyous ruling class began to halt, became
distorted and faded in response to the rising revolt of their opponents,
slaves, serfs, peasants and workers, whose musical motif gathered strength
accordingly.

Clowning, acrobatics, dance, masks, huge symbolic props were among
the old popular devices and traditions reinvigorated by their use in the
mass spectacles. Less familiar was the frequently changing relationship
between the spectator and the place where the drama was being enacted.
For example in a scene entitled 'The Defence of the Soviet Republic'
from *In Favour of a World Commune* the audience found itself in the

middle of the action. Simple montage principles were evident in light-shadow effects and simultaneous scenes like those used in *The Storming of the Winter Palace*. There was also a new emphasis on the collective, both in production and performance, which provided a model for the work of other revolutionary theatre collectives including the Blue Blouse.

The mass spectacles were affirmative, the concentrated expression of collective and class feelings and aspirations. The Blue Blouse had a much more critical role to play and their resources were puny in comparison with those put at the disposal of the directors of the mass spectacles. Nevertheless, they adopted many of the essential techniques of staging, acting, choral speaking and singing, the imaginative use of visual forms, and the satirical and humourous approach developed in the spectacles.

Meyerhold – breaking through the barriers

> The wheel had come full circle . . . the amateur Komsomol theatre which began with anti-religious propaganda, ended up close to Meyerhold's theatre in its methods . . . the forms of club show productions . . . were later reflected by the left wing professional theatre and were themselves renewed by it . . . the genre of the living newspaper or 'overview' was brilliantly utilized by Meyerhold in *Give Us Europe*. The methods used in this production were frequently applied . . . on the stages of clubs.   (*Blue Blouse*, 1925)[32]

Soon after the revolution the theatrical left took up their cudgels in earnest against the old naturalistic theatre which was seen as a remnant of cultural elitism. Revolutionary writers, directors, and actors such as Mayakovsky and Tretyakov, Meyerhold and Eisenstein and the circus clown Vitaly Lazarenko joined the ranks of the Bolsheviks or at least sympathized openly with the cause of the proletariat. And the new theatre was to be a people's theatre.

> Citizen Meyerhold is very surprised that the soldiers don't come into the theatre and, without a word, liberate it from the audience in the parterre. Enough of the parterre. The intelligentsia will be driven out to where Ostrovsky's imitators flourish . . . and the plays by those authors who were mentioned earlier (Blok, Sologub, Mayakovsky, Remizov – R.S. and K.M.) will be put on for peasants, soldiers and that intelligentsia who will say 'Enough sleeping!' Then the theatre will reach a high point.[33]

These new spectators had to be fully involved but in a way that sharpened their critical faculties. Only in this way could they use their understanding of what lay behind everyday events to revolutionize society. In their search for forms that would make this possible the theatrical left began to examine the history of the theatre and link up with the more 'democratic' popular traditions of the travelling players, circus and fairground booth. The innovations that Meyerhold had pioneered in pre-revolutionary times came into their own, but now with a political purpose.

Mayakovsky's *Mystery-Bouffe*, a wholly unnaturalistic and imaginative allegory of political agitation and propaganda staged to mark the first anniversary of the October Revolution, provided Meyerhold with the ideal vehicle. As in the mass spectacles, the exploiters, seven 'clean' couples who survive the great flood representing world revolution, were portrayed in the knockabout style of travelling players. This was reinforced in the updated version staged at the May Day celebrations of 1921. Edward Braun provides a lively description:

> Amongst the amendments were the inclusion in the ranks of the 'Clean' of Lloyd George and Clemenceau, and the creation of a new central character 'The Conciliator' or Menshevik . . . brilliantly portrayed by the nineteen-year-old Igor Ilinsky in red wig, steel gig-lamps and flapping coat tails, and with an open umbrella to symbolize his readiness for flight. His performance set the key for . . . an hilarious, dynamic, caricaturist rough and tumble, a carnival celebration of victory in the civil war. . . . The 'Unclean' (the international proletariat – R.S. and K.M.) . . . in blue overalls, were of a uniform dullness which not even Mayakovsky's rhetoric could hide. The proscenium was demolished once and for all . . . a broad ramp sloped right down to the first row of the seats, bearing a huge hemisphere over which the cast clambered and which revolved to explose the exit from 'Hell' . . . one of the devils was played by a circus clown, Vitaly Lazarenko, who entered by sliding down a wire and performed acrobatic tricks. In the final act, which depicted the new electrified promised land, the action spilled into the boxes adjacent to the stage, and at the conclusion the audience was invited to mingle with the actors onstage . . .
>
> In this production Meyerhold dispensed finally with the front curtain and flown scenery. The theatre was bursting at the seams, unable to accommodate the kind of popular spectacle which Meyerhold was trying to achieve . . .[34]

In between these two productions of *Mystery-Bouffe* came *The Dawn*, an epic verse drama by the Belgian Symbolist poet Verhaeren. Staged to inaugurate the opening of the Russian Socialist Federal Soviet Republic Theatre No. 1 and timed to coincide with the third anniversary of the October Revolution, the play was adapted by Meyerhold and his assistant Bebutov to make it more relevant to recent political events. Presented in a 'derelict, unheated auditorium with its flaking plaster and broken seats',[35]

The Dawn was like a combination of political meeting and Greek tragedy. The spectators were showered with leaflets, there were placards on the walls, a chorus in the orchestra pit, a claque of actors in the audience, and a herald who would deliver bulletins on the progress of the real civil war going on in the South. According to Braun, 'Meyerhold's highest aspirations were gratified on the night when the Herald announced the decisive break into the Crimea at the Battle of Perekop and the entire audience rose in a triumphant rendering of "The Internationale".'[36]

Although *The Dawn* and the *Mystery-Bouffe* were criticized by the Party and its press for their Symbolist and Futurist obscurity, both were a great success with audiences. In 'the five months up to the end of May 1921, 154 performances of the two plays were watched by roughly 120,000 spectators.'[37]

The stage set and props were reduced to a minimum in Meyerhold's experiments. They had to be strictly functional, direct aids to the actor who was becoming more and more central. This led to an entirely new stage conception based on the principles of Constructivism and also to the demand for a new breed of performer.

Appointed director of the recently established State Higher Theatre Workshop in Moscow in 1921 Meyerhold set about training the students accordingly. He initiated a course in biomechanics, a system of physical exercises which he claimed was the theatrical equivalent of the scientific organization of labour developed by the American Frederick Winslow Taylor. This he contrasted to the 'unscientific' methods of Stanislavsky. (Taylorism and other theories derived from capitalist technology were uncritically accepted as progressive at that time in the Soviet Union, particularly by the Proletkult movement and the Futurists and Constructivists, and also by the Blue Blouse movement.) Exaggerated as these claims were, biomechanics was successful enough to ensure that every Soviet drama school provided systematic physical training for its students. The Blue Blouse were strongly influenced by biomechanics. Whole scenes, usually depicting workers' strength and courage, were made up of the exercises.

Meyerhold's next two productions, Crommelynck's *Magnanimous Cuckold* and Sukhovo-Kobylin's comedy *Tarelkin's Death*, took the satirical and spectacular aspects of knockabout farce and circus in theatre to their highest point yet. However, as they were not directly political, they could more easily be accused of abstractness and aestheticism. Meyerhold's close co-operation with the Constructivists and his hostile attitude to the state theatres led to strained relations with the official cultural and political institutions.

To improve his somewhat tarnished image Meyerhold chose Tretyakov's adaptation of Martinet's *Night* retitled *Earth Rampant*. It was staged as an entirely propagandist play, dedicated to Trotsky and the Red Army, and first performed in February 1923 in celebration of the army's fifth anniversary. The design was strictly utilitarian, no makeup, naturalistic costumes, and 'only' those sets and props required by the action: motorcycles, machine guns, a harvester, a mobile kitchen, an aeroplane! Very much in the tradition of the mass spectacles, the performance for the Fifth Congress of the Comintern in June 1924 had infantry and horse cavalry among the participants and an audience of 25,000. Money was regularly collected after the performances. In 1926 it was put towards the purchase of a military aeroplane which entered the service bearing the name 'Meyerhold'.

Soon after the first production of *Earth Rampant* Meyerhold wrote: 'The Actor-tribune acts not the situation itself, but what is concealed behind it and what it has to reveal for a specifically propagandist purpose.'[38] In the absence of contemporary revolutionary plays with structures which would facilitate this, he resorted to free adaptations of plays such as Ostrovsky's *Forest* and the political revue *Give Us Europe*, staged in 1924. The first was a typical Meyerhold response to Lunacharsky's appeal 'Back to Ostrovsky' (meaning back to realism) and a resumption of his attack on the Academic Theatres. Instead of rounded characterizations of narrow-minded country gentry the audience saw 'social masks' immediately recognizable in terms of their role in the class war. Ostrovsky's original five acts were broken up and re-ordered into thirty-three episodes with

> pantomime interludes for the sake of effective contrasts of mood and tempo . . . in a manner which Meyerhold himself compares on the one hand to Eisenstein's use of 'collision montage' in the cinema, and on the other to the episodic structure employed by Shakespeare and Pushkin. . . . Each episode was announced by the now familiar title projected on to a screen above the stage.[39]

Give Us Europe combined texts from Ehrenburg's novel *The Give Us Europe Trust*, and Kellerman's *The Tunnel* as well as material from Upton Sinclair and Pierre Hamp. The fragmentary plot involved a contest for superiority over a war-torn Europe between millionaires from America and a radio trust from the Soviet Union. Only a few characters appeared twice in the revue's seventeen episodes which meant that ninety-five roles had to be performed by forty-five performers. Among them was the champion quick-change artist Erast Garin. In one fifteen-minute scene he portrayed seven different inventors. The political significance of the events on stage was pointed up by relevant information and quotations from Lenin, Trotsky and Zinoviev projected onto three different screens.

The strength of the Soviet Union was represented by members of the Red Fleet and Komsomol performing marches, dances, acrobatics, biomechanics and even a football match. In contrast the decadence of capitalism was satirized by episodes like 'foxtrotting Europe'. Accompaniment was provided by the first Russian jazz band organized at Meyerhold's request by Sofia Parnok.

This complex montage came close to achieving many of the objectives of Brecht's epic theatre. There was, however, a serious political weakness. Opponents were too often shown as impotent idiots, cowards and libertines, thereby misleading the spectator into thinking they could be dismissed. This tendency was to recur in the Russian and also in the German and British workers' theatre.

The official critics continued to accuse Meyerhold of blind experimentation. In fact he was one of the few, if not the only director who seriously attempted to assess the effects of his productions on the spectator. After he became director of the State Institute of Theatre Art he had teachers and students at his disposal to carry out systematic research. This went far beyond the random collection of subjective responses he himself had gathered since his productions of *Mystery-Bouffe* and *The Dawn*.

Alexander Fevralsky documents this research work which was begun in 1925. A record of the actors' performance, called 'chronometage' was kept which measured and timed their movements, the length of the individual acts and the duration of every episode and scene change within them as well as the number and length of intervals.

Audience reactions were analysed according to a detailed code: a silence; b noise; c loud noise; d collective reading; e singing; f coughing; g knocks or bangs; h scuffling; i exclamations; j weeping; k laughter; l sighs; m action and animation; n applause; o whistling; p catcalls, hisses; q people leaving; r people getting out of their seats; s throwing of objects; t people getting onto stage.[40]

The State Institute of Theatre Art was also used by Meyerhold to supervise and instruct amateur theatre groups in factories, military barracks and student circles. He wanted to forge links between the professional and amateur stages but also to relate his theatre to, and situate it in the working class. This was done without reference to the Proletkult network with which he had become disillusioned, believing it to be a haven for out of work actors. In his view the general level of amateur theatre reflected Proletkult's incompetence and outmoded approach to acting. This attempt to disseminate his own ideas and techniques, although less well known and documented in comparison with his other activities, may well have had its effect on the Blue Blouse. They certainly acknowledge the usefulness of Meyerhold's pioneering experiments and made use of almost all the devices he developed during this period.

Eisenstein and the embryonic montage

> The talented Eisenstein, one of the first, gave an example of
> theatricalized living newspaper with the so-called 'montage of
> attractions' in his agit-buffonade *The Wise Man*. . . . In *The Wise Man*
> we first heard the words of the genuine Soviet variety stage.
>
> (*Blue Blouse*, 1925)[41]

One of Meyerhold's laboratory assistants in *Tarelkin's Death* was Sergei
Eisenstein. The brief period in which he worked in the theatre coincided
with the heyday of the eccentric actor, and the return to the popular arts
of circus and music hall. 'Real' plays were in fact rarely performed. Most
productions were adaptations of novels, scenarios or a conglomerate of a
number of texts, coming close to literary montage. This was an approach
which facilitated the eccentric. *The Soviet Small Encyclopedia of Circus*
defines this term as:

> An artistic device for pointedly comic portrayals of reality, consisting
> of intentional violation of logic, sequentiality and interdependence
> among the events portrayed, and of the alogical (from the point of
> view of generally accepted norms) behaviour of the characters. . . .
> The eccentric performer . . . presents happenings in an unexpected
> light, exposing their hidden truth (for example, the comic portrays
> a man who publicly repents the mistakes that he has made and beats
> himself on the breast; then leaving the platform, the 'orator' pulls
> out from his chest a metal tray with a pillow attached to it, which
> has protected his breast from the blows.[42]

Eisenstein's first production for the Moscow Proletkult Theatre showed
that he was profoundly influenced by these trends but also an original
creator in his own right. Although he was only co-director, his contribution made a deep impression on Moscow theatrical circles. The play
was an adaptation by Arvatov of Jack London's story *The Mexican* and
involved a propaganda-style competition between two rival boxing
promoters in Mexico. The boxing match was staged in the centre of the
audience with frightening realism. The punches, panting and sweat were
completely believable, and the outcome of the fight was never certain
until the end. The rest of the play had an almost surrealist setting, circus
costumes designed by Eisenstein and stylized acting. As Yon Barna put
it,

> By unfolding the action on two planes simultaneously – thereby
> exposing the audience to a dual emotional shock – Eisenstein not
> only disregarded completely the conventional unity of action, but at
> the same time foreshadowed a film-making technique; for the audi-
> ence was, in effect, witnessing a sort of embryonic montage.[43]

After a short stint for Foregger where he continued experimenting with music hall and circus forms in the parodies *Be Kind to Horses* and *The Scarf of Columbine*, and after twelve months' collaboration and study with Meyerhold, Eisenstein returned to the Proletkult Theatre in 1922. There he staged Tretyakov's adaptation of Ostrovsky's comedy *Enough Stupidity in Every Wise Man*. The nineteenth century classic was his response to Lunacharsky's plea 'Back to Ostrovsky'. But like Meyerhold Eisenstein was interested in creating a new kind of theatre, not in a faithful reproduction of an old master, no matter how sharply satirical. The title, the main theme, and the line of action remained roughly the same, everything else was drastically revised.

The stage was in the shape of a circus arena. All the actors, who had less than half a year to train, had to become clowns and acrobats at different points in the play and perform spectacular stunts on top of poles, on high wires, or with parachutes. But these stunts and tricks, like the current popular songs, the jokes and puns, the clowning and novelty acts and other insertions, were there not to divert the audience from the anti-religious theme but to amplify it. Emotions were expressed metaphorically, using the techniques of commedia dell'arte and ancient farce. An actor would not simply start in surprise, he would perform a double somersault.

The production was undoubtedly theatrical. It was also so hard to follow that Tretyakov had to come on stage and summarize the content and plot before the performance. Nevertheless, *The Wise Man* represented a breakthrough in the development of the dramatic montage technique, however rudimentary when compared to Eisenstein's later achievements in film. Among those influenced by it were the Blue Blouse who took this approach to montage as a model for their own work.

For Eisenstein the spectator was central. The means he used were calculated to help his audience understand the ideological content or conclusion of what was being demonstrated. He believed this could be done by subjecting the spectator to a carefully planned series of sensual or psychological stimuli which would produce emotional shocks. In using the term 'psychological' he was not referring to individual psychological problems but to the staging of events or situations which would make an immediate impact and thus have their own reality. For example in the Grand Guignol theatre arms and legs might be amputated or a character take part by long-distance telephone in a terrible event miles away. (The Grand Guignol, with its origins in puppet theatre, is typified by short sensational pieces played successively.) He called these aggressive elements 'attractions'. But he was careful to distinguish between an attraction and a 'stunt' such as an acrobatic trick which is complete in itself.

Eisenstein's notion of attractions depended entirely on a relationship with and reaction from an audience.

In constructing a performance as a whole, he had realized that it was no longer necessary to statically reflect events and logically unfold the related action. Effects which were quite independent of the plot and characters and of each other could be juxtaposed in order to express a theme in a montage of attractions. Representational sections could be woven into the montage in the transition from the imitative theatre but would no longer be self-contained. Consciously chosen with an immediate effect in mind, they would become component parts of the whole. A production would no longer have as its goal the correct interpretation of playwright or period but only a system of attractions in the service of a theme.

The tempest subsides – the new cultural climate

The mass spectacles, the re-discovery of popular forms such as circus and music hall, the experiments of Meyerhold, Eisenstein and other members of the theatrical left, and the influence of the developments in film, poster-making and the other visual arts had all given the Soviet theatre a suppleness and scope unknown in czarist times. But in 1922 the New Economic Policy was introduced. This temporary regression to private enterprise was soon felt in the arts. A number of theatres were returned to private ownership and had to be managed so that they would yield their owners a profit, usually a factor militating against experimentation. Collectives and state-run organizations such as the trade union or Red Army theatres were subject to far more stringent controls than before, and many were forced to close for economic reasons.

Meanwhile the attitude of the relevant state institutions and the Bolshevik leadership to the theatrical left had hardened. Immediately after the revolution it was only the Futurists and Proletkultists who responded to Lunacharsky's appeal to 'stir up the feelings of the masses . . . to agitate . . . to illuminate their consciousness with the ideals of scientific socialism . . . to propagandize.'[44] Faced with the cold shoulder from other artists the Bolsheviks had accepted the co-operation of the leftists but they were by no means overwhelmed by their artistic achievements.

Meyerhold and the avant-garde

Meyerhold's tenure as head of the Theatrical Department for the entire Soviet Republic in 1920 was stormy and short-lived. Through the editorial

columns of the Department's publication *The Theatre Herald* he launched
an aggressive attack on Moscow's Academic Theatres. (They were given
this name in honour of their role as treasure houses and teachers of
theatrical art.) Accusing them of outdated styles and repertoire, he
demanded that their considerable resources be redistributed to the
amateur, provincial and Red Army theatres. He liquidated the State
Model Theatre and gave its premises to Proletkult. He argued for the full
nationalization of all theatres and the abolition of the autonomous or semi-
autonomous status accorded to the established theatres. He wanted to
introduce revolutionary plays according to the directives of a general
repertory plan. He supported the struggle against false ideology in the
theatre, the abandonment of literature, psychology and representational
realism, and the use instead of the techniques of Cubism, Futurism and
Constructivism.

Lunacharsky had appointed Meyerhold but his response to his protégé's
proclamation of the October Revolution in the theatre was unequivocal
and not without sarcasm:

> Now that the tiny theatrical October is arriving, it would, of course,
> be ridiculous to give it the valuables which were preserved not
> without great labour at the time of the gigantic tempest in the real
> October . . . I can entrust Comrade Meyerhold with the destruction
> of what is old and bad and with the creation of what is new and
> good, but I cannot entrust him with preserving whatever is old and
> good.[45]

All Academic Theatres in Moscow and Petrograd which included the
Bolshoi, the Moscow Art Theatre and its studios, and the Moscow Children's Theatre, were brought under the umbrella of the Commissariat
for Education. Meyerhold's wings had been clipped; he resigned on 26
February, 1921. His defeat marked the beginning of the state's policy of
supporting the traditional arts at the expense of the 'revolutionary' ones.

There was undoubtedly some truth in Lunacharsky's barbed statement
and in the criticism by Lenin and others that the leftists who had had
the benefit of assimilating the cultural heritage wanted to destroy it before
the masses had even learned to read. But it is also true that most of the
party's leaders favoured a conception of art that merely reflected reality
rather than one that acted as a dynamo. The supporters of the second
approach were not content with producing art for quiet consumers. They
argued that a critical, actively engaged public could not be built without
forms capable of dealing with the themes thrown up by the revolution.
New wine could not be forced into old bottles.

At this time there were three main cultural tendencies in the arts.
The avant-garde, persecuted before the revolution, considered themselves
revolutionary because they had broken with the old formal traditions.

They were the Modernists, Formalists, Cubists, Futurists and Constructivists. They used the materials and working methods of the newly arrived industrial age – steel, concrete, cubes and constructions – in painting, sculpture and architecture. In writing and the theatre they applied the constructivist method by making montages of different types of literary or dramatic elements. Politically they embraced a wide spectrum ranging from abstract artists of vaguely progressive persuasion to those using their artistic 'constructions' in an overt and conscious revolutionary way.

Foremost among the latter were the group of left artists around Mayakovsky which included Tretyakov, Brik, Shklovsky, Rodchenko, Stepanova, Vertov and Eisenstein. Their journal *LEF* (Left Front of the Arts) was edited by Mayakovsky from 1923 to 1925 and re-appeared from 1927 to 1928 under the title *New LEF*. Theoretically they supported a dynamic conception of the arts. In Meyerhold, Eisenstein, Mayakovsky and Tretyakov they had their most exemplary practitioners.

Proletkult

Another important cultural current was the Proletkult movement which grew out of the Party school in Capri in 1908 dominated by the group which later broke with the Bolsheviks. Centred around the *Vpered* journal, they at that time included Bogdanov, Gorky and Lunacharsky. They saw the development of proletarian culture as a means of heightening the class awareness of the proletariat and of promoting a spirit of militant enthusiasm for the achievement of working class aims, uninhibited by bourgeois ideology foreign and hostile to the working class. For this reason, they emphasized the independent cultural activity of the working class. Little stress was put on assimilating the cultural heritage or co-operating with the cultural intelligentsia.

The main task of Proletkult was seen as the development of a 'pure or undiluted' proletarian ideology and artistic activity. Put crudely, they held that proletarian culture can be created only by artists who had personally experienced the emotions and thoughts of the working class in order to create works of art which are their genuine expression. In other words these artists had to emanate from the proletariat. Bogdanov incorporated concepts of proletarian culture and the organization of proletarian consciousness into the framework of a general 'organizational science'. He believed that the sphere of proletarian cultural organization must be independent of the political sphere.

Beyond these basic ideas Proletkult had no aesthetic theories of its own although it had in Bogdanov, F. I. Kalinin and Kerzhentsev outstanding theoreticians. Meyerhold and Eisenstein worked with and supported

Proletkult theatres but never became members. In fact Proletkult could claim only a few outstanding writers, among them Biedny, Gastev, Kirillov and Gerasimov. In the other arts its adherents achieved very little.

By 1918 however Proletkult had grown into a formidable organization. The largest centres in big industrial towns and capitals had an administrative apparatus divided into different departments: publishing, theatre, music, art, finance and the clubs. The Proletkult structure was almost identical with the *Narkompros* departments and it rivalled it in its extramural activities. By 1919 there was a Proletkult cell in every big factory of the industrial town Ivanovo Voznesensk, an indication of its success in attracting workers. Here the rivalry was probably more with the unions or local Party committees. Then there were the studios or clubs where workers learned and practised the arts. From 1918 onward the journal *Proletarian Culture* was published. It was succeeded by *On Guard* edited by Lelevič.

At the First All-Russia Congress held in Moscow October 5 to 12, 1920 a resolution was put forward that the Proletkult should be the autonomous cultural organization of the proletariat. Equal to the trade unions and the Party it should therefore be separate from *Narkompros*, but receive state subsidy. Lenin personally intervened with a five point counter-resolution which was accepted. As a result the Proletkult movement was incorporated into the framework of the Ministry of Education.

The 'Fellow Travellers'

The third tendency in the arts, actually only a group of writers, was dubbed by Trotsky the 'Fellow Travellers'. They revolved around the independent group 'Mountain Pass' whose journal *Red Virgin Land* was edited by A. Voronsky. Although they produced no new theories or works of art that pointed a way forward towards new literary techniques they were the most widely read writers of their day. They used traditional realistic forms and were therefore more comprehensible to the broad masses. Closer to the peasantry than to any other class, they saw the revolution as a Russian phenomenon, a 'natural' upheaval like an earthquake. Among their leading writers were Pilnyak, Ivanov, Tikhonov, Yessenin and Blok.

Arvatov's programme

In 1921 the Ministry of Education was reorganized and a whole number of leftists in the arts were removed from influential positions. The Futurists and Proletkult had competed with each other for official recognition by the Bolshevks as *the* communist tendency in the arts, the one group on the basis of its revolutionary approach to artistic forms, the other on the grounds of its class origins and authentic portrayal of revolutionary feelings and attitudes. Both failed to achieve this acceptance, probably because their programmes tended to be maximalist. They required a rapid transition from capitalism to communism, and with it the speedy overcoming of the separation between toil and leisure, life and art.

For the Futurists and Constructivists the technological backwardness of the country was a serious obstacle to the development and realization of their ideas. For Proletkult the cultural backwardness of the people meant that the development of worker and peasant artists was a slow and painful process. NEP appeared to the leaders of both camps as a further setback or even betrayal – at least on a cultural level.

It was in this extremely difficult situation that the Marxist factions of these two movements combined. One of them, the production artist Arvatov, a representative of the predominantly Futurist Front of Left Artists and one of the most prolific members of the Moscow Proletkult, projected a revolutionary programme for the theatre in this transitional period:

Reflect, Copy or Transform? (1922)
In good Marxist company it is a matter of etiquette to view theatre as a reflection of life. And as proletarian theatre is the theatre of a class that thinks in a Marxist way and as Marxism reveals the real essence of life, the proletarian theatre has to be the truthful, correct and precise reflection of reality . . . Therefore Realism. Realism in the theatre means – everyday life. But what for? What is its social significance? The comrade ideologues lecture us: 'It is in the cognitive function of art to let the proletariat get to know concrete reality.'. . . But in our time any organized process of cognition makes sense only if it is precise, objective and strictly scientific. . . . But theatre is incapable of objective portrayal by the very nature of its being based on fiction and convention. . . .

They come back and say: 'But what about the creation of symbols, types, generalizations?' Realism never had a sole patent on such creative activity, which became rather imprisoned by the realistic theatre's demand for 'true-to-life' portrayal killing all fantasy and rendering the active and free shaper impotent.

As long as plays and theatre exist, Arvatov, continues, one must use them openly and tendentiously for the class struggle. And within the theatre apparatus all means must be utilized to achieve real agitational force.

The purpose is not to entertain the spectator with little pictures of life, . . . or delectate him with spectacles, but to prove, convince, and propagate, actively, purposefully and consciously. . . .

Art, as the creation of forms which have an immediate effect, is defined by four factors: the material, the condition of its reception, the organizational task, the process of production, of shaping. (The word 'material' is used by Arvatov in a double sense. It refers to the literary material used as well as the entire arsenal of dramatic techniques, and it also means people and their behaviour and attitudes which are the focal point of theatre – R.S. and K.M.) All these factors function wholly and immediately as social phenomena – every form as such is a social form – and are therefore in our living conditions class phenomena. Form as ideology can only be defined in the context of its material existence.

Accordingly, theatre is for Arvatov the organizing, consciously or unconsciously, of actions. In a proletarian theatre they must correspond to the many, changing tasks of the proletariat, the social function of such a theatre must be developed consciously. Therefore,

– One cannot start with ready-made forms but with tasks posed consciously, for each of which a new and independent form must be constructed;

– a break with alienation from life, with isolated aestheticism however many revolutionary masks it may hide behind;

– the proletarian theatre must become a tool for the transformation of life; therefore the forms of action of this theatre must necessarily derive from the requirements of material construction, because the non-constructive is not alive;

– one can construct only if one knows the material and takes it as the starting point.

Arvatov concludes:

1 As long as the realistic-descriptive theatre (the Maly, the Moscow Art Theatre and others) repeats, aestheticizes and sanctions the status quo, as long as the form of its plot is defined by the similarity to life – this theatre will be thrown by the proletariat into the dustbin of history.

2 As long as the stylistic theatre (e.g. the Chamber Theatre) starts with ready-made aesthetic laws, it will be rejected – even when it tries to deal with present day problems in its content.

3 The destruction of the literary chains that fetter theatrical material and limit its effectiveness is unavoidable for the constructive theatre. Therefore our demand: down with the traditional repertoire of 'plays'.

4 The autonomy of the material, the 'amnesty' for human beings and

things, the liberation of the plot demand the death of the self-
contained 'sujet', the jailer of theatrical freedom. (With the term
'sujet' Arvatov is referring to the fictional plot or story line which
usually determined a play's structure and mode of expression –
R.S. and K.M.)

Freed from clichés and the restrictions of outmoded notions of what is
acceptable, the proletarian theatre will become a laboratory in which
forms will be determined by knowledge of the material and in which the
material itself, 'the human being acting in the material environment' will
be analysed 'as an aesthetic phenomenon', accepting the material

in its real, practical function; the human being will not be an actor
but a qualified person, a board will not be decoration but shaped
wood, light will not be a scenic effect but illumination.

8 What will happen to the descriptive 'sujet' theatre? Can one do
without it? Of course not. But this is a question of revolutionizing
the 'sujet' . . . one fundamental point must be kept in mind: as
long as we have no scientific organization of the theatre the subjugation under the old forms of the stage will continue – even when
proletarian heels pound its boards.

As the completion of the revolution both in life and the theatre could
not be expected overnight, the 'sujet' would gradually disappear, subordi-
nated to different theatrical tasks, dissolved into theatrical action. The
revue and circus would be introduced into the theatre, a transition from
the 'sujet' theatre to the theatre as work on pure material would take
place with the evolution of aesthetic methods and forms connected with
real life.

The theatrical left had probably achieved some of these 'transitional'
forms and had prepared the ground for their further development. It did
this, however, in the more congenial atmosphere of the immediate post-
revolutionary period, mainly in the political and cultural centres of the
Soviet Union, and therefore to a somewhat prepared audience, itself in
the mainstream of the Revolution.

But by 1923, after the defeat of 'October' in the theatre and the harsh
reality of NEP with a cultural reaction in its trail, it was more difficult
to pursue the complex path laid out by Arvatov. This was particularly
true in the areas of the Soviet Union where the Revolution was still in its
infancy and where the people were much less sophisticated. However,
this was the task the Blue Blouse movement set itself.

3 · Born of the press

An evening with the Blue Blouse

The typical Blue Blouse programme followed a living newspaper format with headlines, news items, editorials, cartoons and official decrees. However,

> The Living Newspaper does not want to and cannot replace the printed newspaper. Their paths lie alongside one another. The Living Newspaper takes its main themes from the printed one . . . and it reconstructs them into lively action, filled with images. The Living Newspaper . . . does not give an exhaustive treatment of its themes, it only puts them on the agenda, it agitates, it helps to make these themes penetrate the masses more deeply. Very often it presupposes that the content of the questions dealt with is already known to the viewer, it tries only to get an understanding, an interpretation of the given theme into his consciousness.[1]

The stage was normally bare, except for a piano, perhaps the bough of a tree, a few things necessary for demonstration: 'We are against bright beauty and realistic sets and decoration (no little birch trees and rivers), no clumsy props and set.'[2]

The evening always began with a *parade entrée*, the headlines. The parade introduced the troupe to the audience and helped establish a close relationship between performers and spectators. It also made the printing of a programme unnecessary. The entire collective would enter singing. Twelve to twenty in number, with two to three times as many men as women, they all wore blue blouses and black trousers or skirts, black stockings and shoes: 'Down with naturalistic costumes, peasant shoes, blankets and birch (footwear – R.S. and K.M.) – folksy stuff, wigs, down with them.'[3]

> I've come to tell you, tell you, tell you
> About private speculation
> Trusts and co-operation . . .
> We've come to tell you, tell you, tell you
> What you all must know, must know, must know . . .[4]

The first four lines were sung in unison, then sixteen lines would be recited, two by each individual performer, then five lines again in unison, and two by individuals. The repetitive verse was in the form of folk poetry, the subjects introduced might include the international situation, the workers' movement, the new life, the factories, schools, red power, electrification, and NEP. All would then exit to a march.

The next item was often an *oratorio*, an old form of choral music or mass speaking modified by the Blue Blouse into a report. The subject matter was usually serious and of historical significance: 'The Decembrists Pugachov and Razin – Steps leading to October', 'Let us not forget the general rehearsal – 1905', 'To the memory of leaders'. There were exceptions: the oratorio entitled 'On May Day it's expected that some will be celebrating and some will be wearing themselves out' probably dealt satirically with all too contemporary oppression of women. Solo and choral singing and speaking alternated, usually accompanied by music.

Groups were advised to start each program with serious articles providing a deeper, more profound working through of a theme, possibly including diagrams and posters. Gradually they progressed to more humourous and entertaining items which might depart from the main theme or merely accompany it, with considerable freedom of interpretation and treatment. The oratorio was therefore usually followed by an *international survey* such as 'The hitch in Europe – Stabilisation in brackets'. The setting was a spa, the characters included the chief doctor, Capital, his lackey, the Second International, and his patients England and France. Leggings, stripes, cuffs and collars, belts, bibs and hats would be attached to the basic costume to differentiate the characters. A striking feature of this sketch not obvious in translation is the almost continuous use of verse and punning, both used a lot by Mayakovsky. The following excerpts are taken from an analysis in the *Blue Blouse*, the approving comments are from the editorial board.

SECOND INTERNATIONAL: Man here, man there, at your service, gentlemen.

CAPITAL: Hey, who are you there? You come from number 2½.

This section is coarse and accurate as is the following dialogue:

ENGLAND: Oh, Madame, are you here? How strange.

FRANCE: I thought you were ill as well.

ENGLAND: Oh well, I just find the air better here, I had a slight attack of the English illness.

FRANCE: What do you say? Well, well. (*In a whisper.*) Have I got the French illness?

ENGLAND: We should broadcast all over the world that she is in the tertiary stage.

Further on the following idea is successful, taking the form of the Agit-Guignol:

ENGLAND: Man!

SECOND INTERNATIONAL: What do you wish to order?

ENGLAND: Where is my beefsteak?

SECOND INTERNATIONAL: It'll be ready in a moment. (*A gun shot behind curtain.*)

ENGLAND: Tat, tat, tat, tat.

FRANCE: Ah, what is that, is that the Sofia Cathedral going up again?

ENGLAND: Oh, no, no, that's my English beefsteak. To make it to my taste, you have to take one raw Indian, tie him to a cannon, you shoot and the beefsteak is ready simply and quickly.

This explanation, in the spirit of English cannibal colonial coldbloodedness is typically authentic.[5]

From an international subject, the focus would then switch to a more domestic theme dealt with in a *feuilleton* which might be in the form of vaudeville (the rural or village *feuilleton*) or a sketch (the urban or town *feuilleton*). We have included examples of both.

On Komsomol morality and its distortion (town type)

Characters: Komsomolzi, male members – Semyon, Peter; Komsomolki, female members – Irina, Marusya

SEMYON: Hi, Petka.

PETER: Hi, Senka.

SEMYON: Well, let's have a little chat.

PETER: I have no time, I'm off to a meeting, we've got an extraordinary session on today on the question of Komsomol morality. Come along . . .

SEMYON: I can't. I'm waiting for someone here. You just use your tongue, whereas I'm practising morality.

PETER: How do you do that?

SEMYON: Oh, I take Katya or Natalia, I suggest a rendezvous on the boulevard, I take her by the waist straight away, and squeeze out her petit-bourgeois self-consciousness.

PETER: But what if her waist gets fatter after that?

SEMYON: Well, she'll have to cope with that as well as she can. She can give birth or abort, 'liquidate', my job is only to agitate. I have a really original system. (*He sings*)

> I must show young ladies,
> That in the USSR – love is free,
> She only needs to give birth twice a year,
> And as soon as the baby appears in the world,
> I shall certainly disappear.
> It is original – no doubt,

But it is – agitational.
Yesterday, look, I made fun of some priests,
And made a noise in the church;
In place of the icons of Sabaoth
I hung up a portrait of Kalinin.
And there you are, the old women
Started crossing themselves in front of this portrait
As if it was an icon.
That is original – no doubt,
But it's also – agitational.
In the villas there goes the NEP man,
Enjoying himself, but I use my good sense,
I climb up on the roofs of one of his villas,
And empty my belly on it.
And I hang up a notice – 'Greetings
From the Komsomol Semyon.'
That's original – there's no doubt about it,
But it's also agitational.
– So what do you think of that?

PETER: I think that's horrible and disgusting. You can't fight with means like those. A Komsomol won't achieve anything like that, apart from social contempt from all sides. And you, brother, are a scoundrel, not just a fool.

SEMYON: Oh, go off like a sausage. Give yourself airs like some blasted creature. However, why hasn't my jade turned up, I have been standing here like a fool for a whole hour.

(*Peter exits, Marusya enters*)

MARUSYA: I'm sorry that I kept you waiting. I would have come punctually, I would even have turned up early, but we had a report today about the position of women in the East.

SEMYON: Let me tell you openly that your attempts are quite in vain, the women's question cannot be decided while you remain a virgin, and your virginity is totally unnatural. And in any case, one needs so little to destroy your backwardness.

MARUSYA: Semyon, I don't like that, Semyon, I'm afraid . . .

SEMYON: Comrade Marrrrusya . . .

MARUSYA: But I don't believe that you'll make me happy . . .

SEMYON: Ha, petty individual motivations, typical intellectual pessimism, you are deviating into Menshevism, I shall tell everybody about this deviation, and in no time you'll be out of the Komsomol.

MARUSYA: (*sings*) I don't want to leave the Komsomol, Tell me, what is my crime, Semyon?

SEMYON: You must solve the problem of sex.

MARUSYA: Semyon, it's too early, I'm only sixteen . . .

SEMYON: I see, that means that you are in favour of Millerand, of the Fascists – or not? (Alexandre Millerand was president of France from 1920–1924 – R.S. and K.M.)

MARUSYA: I don't understand, it's rubbish and nonsense.

SEMYON: Listen to my command and sit down here.

MARUSYA: But what if there are children?

SEMYON: That's a vain fear, in the Komsomol cadre card there is no mention of children.

MARUSYA: Semyon, I'm frightened, I'm not used to it, where will I put them, what will I do with them?

SEMYON: You can teach them to sell matches on the Moscow pavements.

MARUSYA: I can't do it just like that, I feel that I will be in trouble.

SEMYON: Listen to my command and sit down here.

MARUSYA: Oh, I suppose I have to listen to your command, I'm burning with shame.

(*Enter Irina and Peter*)

IRINA: A delightful picture.

SEMYON: Ah, hello, Comrade Irina.

PETER: Comrade Marusya, hello.

SEMYON: Comrade Irina – just two words, you see me here at work. I was trying to agitate an unconscious element, but she won't listen to propaganda. My heart beats only for you now, I honestly offer you cohabitation, in the order of shock, party and construction, with the object of giving birth to a future Red Army soldier, and I hope that you have no objections.

IRINA: Excuse me, comrade, that I cannot do, I will only marry a Komsomol.

SEMYON: But I am a Komsomol – here is my card.

IRINA: (*Tearing it up.*) That was your card, but it's not now. Here is a note from the Central Committee of the Komsomol's Protocol of the Revolution.

PETER: And in our ranks there is no place for you.

SEMYON: I spit on that. I've got a NEP-man's daughter as my bride, who has promised to marry me in church and will provide a lot of money too.

PETER: Well, well, then go ahead, but we shall not allow any mendacity to pervert Komsomol morality.

IRINA: And we are sick of keeping such scoundrels who spurn our great cause. And you, Marusya, don't be such a fool, you nearly paid for it with your skin. Without true love, comrade to comrade, you'll never cook up true communist porridge.

PETER: Passion, in any case, is not enough, we have to have common ideals, so that on the difficult great Leninist path we go hand in hand with one another, so that we do not slip up as he does – understand?

MARUSYA: Thank you, comrade, I do understand.

MARUSYA and PETER: In the Komsomol

> Everybody has sufficient freedom,
> Choose your lives, companions,
> Seriously and not for the moment,
> That means, brothers, don't play in vain with emotions,
> Forward Komsomol,
> The working hour has struck,
> Boldly resist and throw aside
> Loafers and good-for-nothings.
> In the Komsomol we don't want
> And can't stand such riff-raff anymore,
> Our order is friendly,
> We don't need lewdness.
> We shall be able to build our new morality
> Without it.
> Forward Komsomol
> The working hour has struck,
> You must now build a new morality.[6]

The Speculator in the Country-side (village type *feuilleton*)

COUNTRY-SIDE: (*Sings to well-known folk tune 'Monotonously Tolls the Little Bell'*)

> Under the red Soviet star,
> Song flows quietly in the fields.

THE MERCHANT OBIRALOV: (The verb *obirat* means to fleece, swindle, rip off – R.S. and K.M.) (*Off-stage, sings to jaunty popular air*)

> The proletarians took my trade from me,
> So I indulge in various speculations.
> I flog illicit liquor, sugar, salt, soap,
> I flog cloth,
> I'll rip you off, Countryside.

COUNTRY-SIDE: (*sings*)

> The birdie sang too soon,
> The cat came and got it.
> The bourgeois hold is strong,
> Stronger still is the hold of the proletariat.

OBIRALOV:
> Join me, don't fear me, my dear,
> It'll be heaven.

THE CO-OPERATIVE: (*enters singing to folk tune*)
> Greetings, Country-side,
> I've been sent by the Soviet from the town
> To fulfil Lenin's edict
> To fight to the death against the speculator.

COUNTRY-SIDE: (*sings to folk song 'The Moon Has Hidden Behind the Clouds'*)
> I've waited for you day and night,
> I've been ripped off by the merchants.

CO-OPERATIVE: We shall squeeze the merchant. (*Co-op sings in chastushki rhythm, the Country-side joins in the last two lines of each verse.*)
> The light burns bright,
> To the devil with machination.
> The Commissar's Council has issued a decree
> On co-operation.

COUNTRY-SIDE AND CO-OPERATIVE:
> I've waited for you, dearest Co-op,
> I've come to you with greetings from the factory hooter,
> Hammer and sickle, friends together, united in labour.

CO-OPERATIVE:
> Let the Speculator
> Sing a song of sorrow.
> Workers, strengthen your co-operative![7]

This was followed on by the sketch 'If You Want to Reach Communism – Join a Co-operative'.

A *lubok* scene or 'living poster' was usually next on the programme. Three or four performers would act through painted cut-outs with holes for heads, arms, legs, or create a series of images by arranging them in relation to each other. Although they were very popular we could only find one *lubok* as such listed in the Blue Blouse Repertoire Index (1924–1926).[8] It was fetchingly entitled 'Let Monsieur and Sir Know the Meaning of Loans in the USSR'.

The *dialogue-duets* which usually followed the *lubok* were also in short supply in the index. In the section covering international politics was a dialogue with the somewhat opaque title 'Proverbs Played in Person'. A second, 'Young People about Theatre', was listed in the section 'Education and Liquidating Illiteracy'.

The program continued with a *rayok*, a quick-fire speech, tongue twister or story, mostly rhymed and full of puns. The language was very colloquial, with turns of phrase and idioms taken from folk chants. This example is an abbreviated version of a *rayok* called 'Beggars' Moscow' by Yuzhanin, the 'father' of the Blue Blouse.

'Well, mates, it's yer old Uncle All-Wise again, let me tell you a story . . .'

He has been walking through Moscow just having got his wages when he meets a boy beggar, and gives him some money; then he meets another who hasn't eaten for three days, and he puts some money into his hat. He meets a third – and begins to have doubts. Next he meets a man with a stick and a woman with six kids – all with different coloured hair and complexions – and gives them money. Then comes a plump young man, well dressed, who says, 'Guv, I haven't eaten for weeks.' He too receives money. He gives a blind man a 5,000 rouble note. 'Hoy,' says the blind man, 'this is a forgery.' 'You're not blind,' says Uncle All-Wise. 'No, I'm replacing the real blind man for a bit – he's gone to the pictures to see a film.'

'So, comrades,' says Uncle All-Wise, 'It's all a left-over from capitalism. I had only a few roubles left from my wages. Then I saw a great big tall geezer dragging along a cart with a cripple. "Is it hard dragging him?" I asked. "We take turns – he pulls me tomorrow," says the one pulling.'

'Akh,' says Uncle All-Wise, 'My head's spinning, I waved my hand in disgust and went home.'[9]

Chastushki, traditional limerick-style folk verse, were always included. They were topical, humorous, satirical, and sung in a lively manner, if possible to the accompaniment of harmonica and balalaika. Each verse had four lines and there was a chorus in ABAB rhyme. This one is called 'Women Party Members'.

> We'll create the USSR
> With no help from God or Czar.
> The first example of this was given by working women.
> The progressive avant-garde were Soviet women.

> Come on, Sister, come on, Auntie,
> From old to young,
> Everybody get together,
> Let's all join the Communists.[10]

Towards the end of the evening a *local theme* was normally included. Written by a local Blue Blouse member these items were not published in the journal. It is likely however that the authors drew upon the material in the 'Trade Union' and 'Everyday Life' sections in the Blue Blouse Repertoire Index. Items such as 'You Will Raise Your Wages By One

Means – Productivity of Labour', *chastushki* for print, wood and other workers, 'Get the Nucleus of Active People into the Works Committee', an oratorio which explained the Blue Blouse code of labour safety, and a rhyme which advised the spectator to 'Find Your Ally Not in Vodka and Beer But in the Club and in the Co-operative' must certainly have been easy to adapt for local factories. There was a strong emphasis in the 'Everyday Life' numbers on women and family relationships as indicated by the following titles: 'About the Slavery of the Kitchen' (*rayok*), 'Alimony' (A scene from the law court), 'Marriage, the Family, the Sex Question', 'Husband Investigation Department', 'The Deserted Children', 'About Comrade Kollontai, the New Law, Marriage, and the Formidable Wife, or, The Wife Who Lays About Her.' These too were sure to have inspired local versions.

The evening would end with a *Finale-March*:

ALL: We have demonstrated before you the Living Newspaper. In it you've found poetical newspaper sketches, humorous rhymes

For everybody!

INDIVIDUALS:
1 For the railway workers.
2 For the seamstress and cobbler.
3 Textile and foodworkers.
4 Non-party members and Bolsheviks.
5 Print and metal workers.
6 Sympathizers and Communists.

1 For peasants and workers.
2 Always to know the truth.
3 In your evening spare time.
4 Don't just seek out each other.
5 Everything in it is new, interesting.
6 There's something in it on local life.

(The last six lines are in rhyme – R.S. and K.M.)

ALL: *In it –*
1 Each word is the roar of a dynamo.
2 Every line is the drone of a motor.
3 Every letter is the hum of electric current.
4 Every column is collective labour.
  (*All sing to well known song*)
We've come to tell you, comrades, how the workers are winning,
How capitalism's falling apart at the seams,
Embraced by the fire of revolution.

We can proudly, boldly say to you
That we are creating a living work.

We stand like a mountain for the proletariat,
And for unity with the peasants.
So listen to us, everybody,
We carry the light of culture through our paper
To the working masses.
Let's continue to fight for the union of peasant and worker.
To shine everywhere and always
That is our motto and the motto of the sun.[11]
The entire evening lasted from one-and-a-half to two hours.

From the clubs to the pubs

The Blue Blouse had sprung up within the Institute of Journalism, but soon had a much wider public. Initially they served the tea shops of the Moscow Trade Union Organization and then workers' clubs. According to the *Blue Blouse* their success was spectacular:

In its first two months of existence Blue Blouse performed to 80,000 people. During April and May 104 shows were put on . . . 153 clubs in Moscow, which up until that time had been concerned with putting on productions of bourgeois and petit bourgeois plays, created their own Living Newspapers. The correctness of the line of the Blue Blouse as production agitators and collective propagandists was recognized.[12]

Usually attached to a factory or agricultural co-operative, the clubs were supposed to satisfy both the mental and physical needs of individual workers and to strengthen the ideology of the proletarian movement.

ALL: Oy, comrade, so that you don't get confused (in Russian, *konfooza*) Remember the songs of the Blue Blouse. (*blooza* – R.S. and K.M.)

1 The one word – club.
2 This is intellectual relaxation.
3 The club is development of mind and body.
4 The club is the school of Leninism.
5 The club is a place for coming together in friendship.
6 The club is a workshop of culture; the club is our fiery victory.[13]

(End of the sketch 'The Church, the Pub and the Club'.)

Ideally each club had informational facilities run by the Party committee as well as a room for trade union business. It should have mounted exhibits about the nature and organization of the work carried out in the establishment to which the club was attached as well as details of wages and conditions. Also considered essential was a reading room and a small library, exhibiting model programmes for short courses, as well as a reading or lecture hall where literature could be read and discussed. An orchestra, choir and music studio were required as well as a theatre studio, a school for social sciences, and a canteen or at least a tea room.

Early in 1924 the Moscow Council of Trade Unions began to sponsor the Blue Blouse, which now had fourteen working groups. To be made an official cultural representative of the trade unions was undoubtedly an important step forward. Gradually, they began to build up contacts outside the large cities. Their audiences numbered from 3,000 to 30,000, ranging from a club of porters to the Congress of the Trade Union International. The reception was almost always positive; as the workers' correspondent from the 'Dynamo' factory wrote in *Pravda* February 22, 1924:

> With its lively and healthy humour and the sharpness of its satire, the newspaper has won popularity among the workers. . . . It makes excellent listening. . . . Here is something with which they have succeeded in approaching the workers effectively.[14]

Popularity brought practical problems however:

> Our difficulty, which is shared by all variety people, is the uneven work load. . . . Usually, it's one or two performances a day. But on November 7, March 8 and so on, every group will have four or five journeys to make. (This presumably related to the professional groups. R.S. and K.M.) If we don't accept a request from an organization, they threaten to send in a complaint. And if you accept too many invitations then sooner or later you are inevitably going to be late for some.
>
> This is characteristic in a place where the main speaker has not finished his report yet, where maybe they haven't even started the meeting yet. . . . They may keep you waiting for one or two hours before you can go on stage, and in the next place, though the Blue Blouse had flown head-long in a taxi, everyone is dissatisfied, we are late. And of course the giver of the main report this time turned out not to be talkative, he finished quickly and the audience are a highly conscious lot who arrived on time. The net result, of course, is that it is all our fault.
>
> And every club considers itself honour bound when they ask for us to add the proviso: 'Of course, you'll put on your latest thing for us, won't you?'. . . If somebody had heard of Comrade Rykov yesterday, today we must have something about this. 'Of course,' we answer, 'we work over everything, we definitely will put this on, we won't do it just anyhow, so today we can't produce what you ask but a week later we certainly can.' But we can note important current

events almost the same day by using our chastushki. Local themes are dealt with in the same way.[15]

But the relentless demand for topical material was not the only pressure put on by the clubs. 'After two years of work life is pushing us to make the range of Living Newspaper work deeper and wider.'[16] The following analysis from 'On the Blue Blouse Front' published in the journal in 1925, shows how seriously the Blue Blouse took their relationship with their audience, and how the forms they used were a response to the needs of that audience.

As a means of organizing leisure, Blue Blouse stands on a par with the cinema. The importance of the rational organization of rational leisure for the working man is still insufficiently understood and this to a large extent explains the phenomenon, which we can now observe, of the adult working masses turning away from the club. When he is tired out at the end of the day, especially from doing monotonous work, the working man looks to his club, not for a school, but for entertainment as well. The thirst for political development and self-education among the masses is enormous, and the demands grow year by year. But it is very important, when we are seeking to give the masses the greatest amount of theoretical material, to be conscious of and to feel out the limits within which this material can be taken in, to establish the attention span of the audience . . .

The opinion is widespread that replacing physical labour with mental labour already gives you leisure. This is a profound mistake. Only very light mental work can give a certain and then only relative degree of rest or recreation. To read a book, to see a play, even to play chess is considerable labour. Club evenings with long monotonous lectures, one man speaking in the same tone of voice for a long time, plays, equally long, and very often very badly organized, with immensely long intervals, often tend to over-fatigue the masses. And over-fatigue when it becomes chronic, as we are observing with our young people, leads to physical weakness and to the creation of exceptionally favourable conditions for the development of infectious diseases. . . . Stage productions . . . create positive emotions, they 'infect' the viewer with energy, activity, they help remove disintegrating tissues, they cleanse the blood . . . *it is the business of a stage presentation to give a very bright succession of brief, juicy, colourful artistic compositions which sharpen the viewer's awareness on themes which are close to him in his social and productive life, and this is what Blue Blouse is doing.*[17]

But the club, Party and trade union venues were no longer enough for the rapidly growing Blue Blouse movement. They sought an even greater challenge: the pubs, canteens and tea houses whose customers had nothing to do with clubs themselves. The Living Newspapers of MOSSELPROM (the Moscow-Rural-Industries, a department store) were created. Ossip Brik wrote about their initial impact in 1927 in 'The Stage in Front of Little Tables'.

The first performances of the Blue Blouse caused bewilderment but also interest. It was very unexpected for people in blue blouses to appear amongst the beer, the lobsters and peas, sing scurrilous couplets, ambiguous songs and . . . speak on current . . . political themes. . . . The scenic organization . . . was extremely simple and caricatured. A woman would come on stage . . . with a placard saying 'Soviet Russia', then several men . . . would appear, wearing bowlers or top hats . . . carrying the inscription 'Italy', 'France', 'England' and 'Japan'. The men would sing couplets about how they could not avoid recognizing Soviet Russia, and would make . . . postures around her while the woman would accept their recognition mockingly and sing to the applicants all sorts of malicious remarks agreeing to her recognition. (In Russian the word 'recognition' can also be a declaration of love. When Russia 'agrees to be recognized' she could also be accepting the men's attentions – R.S. and K.M.) But despite this primitiveness, despite the fact that the couplets were badly rhymed, the theme itself was so alive and topical that the pub audiences listened very attentively. . . . In some pubs the success was so great that the clients came long before the beginning of the program, with wife and kids, as in a theatre. No less success was enjoyed by the items on anti-religious and everyday themes. . . . The public divided into two camps and 'serious' discussions took place on the subject 'Are the priests villains or not?' and 'What's better – private trade or co-operation?'[18]

It soon became clear however that the repertoire developed from club activities was not really suitable for the new venues. Ossip Brik again, in 1928:

the initial success swiftly dried up. . . . In their original poster-like appearance the Blue Blouse quickly became boring and the public began to want something else. Unlike the previous music, customers had to pay attention to what the Blue Blouse were saying – they were not just background noise. The pub managers started complaining that the Blue Blouse were turning pubs into propaganda places. . . . In a club people know they are going there for propaganda, but the same people go to a pub precisely to get away from topical politics. The intrusion of politics into pubs was seen as an infringement of the age-old right of 'pub freedom'.

The problem was to devise the sort of variety performance, which, while not losing its political significance, would resemble the normal amusing type of variety performance. It was necessary to combine the Blue Blouse with age-old variety effects. The task was extremely complex and . . . is extremely slowly being realized.[19]

The *Blue Blouse* refers fleetingly to the use of new varieties of living newspaper developed for the beer houses, the 'polit-petrushka' or political Punch and Judy, and the 'polit-tricks', meaning political conjuring.[20] The adoption of a Master of Ceremonies or narrator who would explain content and sequence if necessary in a few crisp phrases must have also proved helpful in attracting and holding the audience's attention.

Propaganda in production

The Blue Blouse, although guided and inspired by professionals, were predominantly amateurs. They knew their audience intimately because they came from among its ranks. And they had set themselves the task of raising the consciousness of that audience in a much more practical, immediate and specific way than such theatrical innovators as Meyerhold and Eisenstein whose formal influence they certainly acknowledged.

> The declaration of the Blue Blouse is being worked out. Its task has become propaganda in production. (This was in accordance with the principles of the production artists: to integrate art or rather make it part of the construction of a new life and of production. R.S. and K.M.) The very name Blue Blouse refers to the work clothes of the industrial worker. Starting from the fact that the milieu, the environment, determines our consciousness, and that even with workers who have a revolutionary consciousness, the degree of their enlightenment still varies, Blue Blouse decides to carry on communist production propaganda in order to:
>
> 1 help the worker to become fully conscious of his own position, his aims and the tasks of his class;
> 2 to fill him with proletarian solidarity and comradeship;
> 3 to draw him into social struggle for the interests of the working class.   (From 'Two Years of Living Newspaper of the Blue Blouse', 1925)[21]

'Born of the press', there were two distinct concepts of the living newspaper among the Blue Blouse. Some troupes took as their starting point 'the oral newspapers of war time, which during the years of blockade filled the gap left by the lack of printed newspapers'. Others preferred, via the theatricalization of texts, 'to take Living Newspaper through the forms of polit-cabaret and variety to a contemporary theatre of review.'[22]

Both tendencies had the unenviable task of translating 'into a language of striking artistic images within the understanding of the broad masses, the dry formulae of newspaper articles, resolutions and directives from the leading organs of the Party and trade unions.'[23] But they were not only agitators and propagandists on behalf of Soviet power. They were also concerned to 'show the negative sides of life which hinder our constructive work'.[24] They 'fought against cultural backwardness, against survivals and superstitions'.[25] This too was no small order under the conditions which existed at the time in the USSR, and must have become increasingly difficult the more the Blue Blouse extended its network into the countryside and away from the supportive climate of the clubs. (Political theatre groups today, however, are rarely able to incorporate positive concepts or policies in their work. In the main their plays are limited to criticisms of the current state of affairs and defensive agitation against further attacks by the ruling class. In this sense these two major aims of the Blue Blouse were complementary: it is much easier to criticize if you can offer a concrete alternative.)

On the one hand, the spectators had to be 'charged with energy', 'roused to the struggle for the socialist reconstruction of society', 'educated in the habits of a class fighter and builder', and imbued with 'confidence in the final victory'.[26] On the other, they must be helped to critically apply themselves to the mundane everyday problems which made this reconstruction so difficult and must on no account be alienated when the critical spotlight was turned on them, their families, their co-workers. This helps explain the Blue Blouse emphasis on entertainment, their use of popular forms, of humour, music and strong visual images, as well as the attention to specifics, the stress put on facts and the tasks of the day. Tretyakov sums up this approach very well:

It can bring out the heroism and underline in red the minutest instance of our construction. It can be the megaphone of social praise or reproach of every production collective, of each two-legged molecule of this collective. The serious variety show will live and develop – grown as it is out of the production collective – if it does not distance itself from everyday life; it will observe attentively the smallest manifestations of our cultural growth and will give its performance the utmost topicality . . . this means: focussing on facts, local themes, local achievements and offences, stating first and second names, dates, addresses, prodding people's memories and linking all this to our construction.[27]

The importance of the notions of 'reconstruction' and 'organizing society' which appear so often in the *Blue Blouse* cannot be underestimated. For it was this more than anything else which led them to try to solve the artistic problem of finding new forms for the new content. 'But while the content was dictated by life itself, finding a new form was more difficult.'[28]

Sparks in the streets – the small forms

The Blue Blouse advocated the critical absorption and reconstruction of pre-revolutionary forms, and the use of technical resources accumulated from the best epochs of theatre. But although not as antagonistic as many of their contemporaries they found little to inspire them in the old theatre 'still ailing away in its neutrality.'[29]

> The professional theatre, the greater part of it, did not pass the test. Separated from real life, it stagnated under the ancient shift of tradition and kept up its existence with the help of food rations (especially for art workers). The influence of the old culture was too strong, it made the new content subordinate to itself, swallowed it without a trace. *The new forms were born in mass work.*[30]

The framework of everyday life had been broken up by the revolution. Meetings, demonstrations, mass actions, or spectacles and carnival processions were all a part of the new collective experience of ordinary people. Professional art workers helping to organize these events found 'the sparks of an active art which could suggest a way forward'[31] in the streets far from the old theatre of dead 'big' forms.

> Theatre in the open square, under the open sky, on lorries, and wagons, on temporary platforms and on carts brought back to life the long forgotten forms of the fairground booth (*balagan*). 'Small' forms which came from below, the chastushka, the song, the folk dance, were accepted on equal terms within the arts. The arguments from the time of the commedia dell'arte arose again between the improvised popular and 'literary' theatre.[32]

The big forms were archaic, out of step with the tempo, rhythm and pulse of an industrial age, unable to communicate to the social conscious-ness of the new class which had come to power. The Blue Blouse, although critical of stereotyped 'utilitarian' mass production in the arts, 'accepted constructivism as an artistic method of laying bare, drawing away the artistic clothing of the past, as a method of showing life realistically.'[33] Their models were Meyerhold's *Give Us Europe*, and Eisenstein's *The Wise Man*, the one utilizing living newspaper, the other variety.

Speech construction and lit-montage

The Blue Blouse living newspaper texts were roughly divided into three categories: pathos, humour and slogan. 'We did have specialists and literary workers to do this, really expert ones, but they soon took off.'[34] The movement was forced to rely on its own resources. And there were those like the founder of the Blue Blouse Yuzhanin who refused to use the work of professional writers.

> He tried to create new pieces for the Blue Blouse, he had had enough of the old stuff. In his journal in 1923 he wrote: 'I am writing the texts almost alone, compile everything useful from magazines and papers, and I get pieces which are interesting in their simplicity. We are getting somewhere.'[35]

In 1924 Yuzhanin became the editor-in-chief of the new bi-weekly magazine *Blue Blouse*. An editorial team of four journalists worked with him. They were responsible for supplying the regional and provincial club nuclei of the Blue Blouse with exemplary literary material. Not only did they publish texts but complete production notes and photographs of the original. Local groups could virtually reproduce the staging, set and costume design as evolved by the centre.

> The periodicals are well-bound with sixty or seventy pages of thick paper; on the cover there is a photomontage of examples of practical work of Blue Blouse participants . . . in form the issues try to be of one type, keeping the appearance of a theatricalized living newspaper. First of all there are special leading articles on the substance, form and methods of Blue Blouse work, then there are six types of living newspaper texts.[36]

Besides those described earlier these included 'scenarios', otherwise known as 'carcasses' or 'frameworks', which were plays with constant characters but a text which was periodically renewed. There were also the chronicle and post box sections which were used to inform the individual groups about each other's activities and experiences.

The journal had a circulation of 7,000 and was obviously of enormous theoretical and practical importance:

> The leaders of Blue Blouse have made it their objective to create a new form of art and to educate a new type of actor. The editorial board, the central staff, the laboratory of the Blue Blouse people, is the meeting place for authors, producers, composers, artists and actors.[37]

Poets of the calibre of Tretyakov, Aseev and Mayakovsky were soon contributing work to the Blue Blouse and were in turn imitated by the aspiring authors of the movement. Nevertheless, there was always a shortage of good new scripts, and the Blue Blouse welcomed the many young writers who showed interest in variety but had been put off by the clichés of 'the old pub-type variety stage which was conservative, vulgar and backward.'[38]

By 1925 the Blue Blouse had become aware that although they had developed a number of new forms their work was by and large superficial: they relied too often on the primitive poster-like *lubok* and the schematic *agitki*:

> Meanwhile, the working audience has grown up a lot and already makes very serious demands on the shows it sees. . . . *It is impossible just to make a figure of fun of the capitalist.* To do so means to weaken the accent on class struggle. What you get is an under-estimation of the enemy. It is essential to find ways of showing the capitalist which don't just poke fun at him but stress what is dangerous in him and still calls for prolonged struggle. It is not enough to show the negative type of Komsomol member . . . we must know how to lay bare the roots of these phenomena, reveal their social causes and show means of struggling with them. . . . Both the Blue Blouse writer and the Blue Blouse producer and actor are still far from living up to these requirements. A task on the agenda of the day is to heighten the ideological qualifications of the workers in Blue Blouse.[39]

An All-Union (national) Conference was organized, and an entire double issue, Nos. 23–24, of the journal devoted to an in-depth analysis of the history, theory and practice of Blue Blouse work. The first resolution of the 1925 conference called for an end to 'the cliché-like . . . well-worn happy endings . . . to *chastushki* in the spirit of the Ukrainian song and dance plays, showing strong enemies . . . falling apart at one puff from the proletariat.'[40]

The way forward was increasingly defined as the revue form: 'A contemporary vaudeville with song which is far removed from salon operetta and which is also a satirical topical review, sometimes a musical mosaic.' In future individual items would be 'linked, by a single skeleton of action, and the place of a lecturer will be taken by a reviewer as the link element.'[41] Already in the transition phase skeletal sketches were growing 'plot-tissue' and the 'framework mask' was giving way 'to the typical person, the character'.[42]

Their theoretical articles were sometimes pretentious due to mechanical attempts to apply pseudo-scientific methods used in industry. Nevertheless, the Blue Blouse did seriously try to work out a theory which would enable its members to make conscious decisions about the forms they used.

In contrast to the young Meyerhold, and perhaps as a reflection of their journalistic origins, they emphasized words as the 'basic principal material'.

In order for Blue Blouse transmission to be well-received we need
to have a verbal literary product which is well prepared, thoroughly
worked out, fresh, topical; so that when you see and hear it your
emotional and sensual saliva begin to flow.[43]

The word in its organic physiological nature was first of all gesture,
mimicry, movement, then it took on sound, sound-signs, speech,
and only later did it turn into a visual form – and signs, letters,
manuscripts, print. These basic natural, physiological properties
should be taken into consideration in all artistic work with words.[44]

The use of mime, movement, sound and illustrative signs were seen as
externalizations of the word, 'amplifying agents of agitational impact' to
be organized

on the basis of an exact calculation of how they can help one another
so that the significance of the word is not overwhelmed. This happens
when an uncalculated energy of music and sound pushes out and
overwhelms the speech sound or the play of movement and therefore
breaks up the play of movement and destroys the unity and logic of
the verbal or word-speech movement.[45]

Maximum agitational effectiveness would be achieved through a
complex montage of speech-gesture-sound. The specialist 'speech
constructor', bearing in mind that the 'material basis of the word in
speech will be sound and the instrument of transmission the voice', must
try to 'create the greatest number of opportunities for the orator or reader
to make use of the meaning of the word and not its aesthetic quality.'[46]
The model form for the Blue Blouse was 'lit-montage'

put together like a technical mechanism, from parts taken from
literary productions, living newspaper material, historical and
contemporary documents, particularly from the living fund of the
literature of worker correspondents . . . the collecting centre of all
elements that are life-building and new in purpose . . . this device
is authentically dialectical, supple in its work because it facilitates
combinations . . . which is incompatible with the old individualist
authorship.[47]

The effect of the individual pieces was calculated and they were distributed so that the montage held together firmly. Model bits from
outstanding contemporary 'word organizers' like Mayakovsky were
provided in the journal, as well as selections from folk ballads and speech.

In an attempt to explain these theories in concrete terms and give
practical examples as to what constituted good and bad literary pieces,
the board reviewed the texts in sixteen issues of the journal. This analysis
of the oratorio 'In Memory of Lenin' was fairly typical:

The shock exclamations of the collective readings are successfully
distributed, with the exception of the exclamation 'and in the field'

which for some incomprehensible reason is separated out in the collective reading and split off from 'in the factories, at the docks' and read individually. (The unity of peasants and workers was emphasized by the Party at this time. It was therefore considered incorrect to divide town and country even in a reading – R.S. and K.M.) The combination of word and placard is under-used. The text is generally overloaded by verse, which is weak in its arrangement. The images 'shouted like steel' and 'eyes of burning steel' are in the first case inaccurate, in the second case hackneyed because steel does not 'cry' and 'burning' is doubtful for defining the quality of a leader's look. We think that melo-declamation (reading to musical accompaniment – R.S. and K.M.) is used wrongly, it does not really fit in here, it tends to introduce sentimental vagueness in the sounds of the words. The end, which uses the verse device of Tretyakov, is good.[48]

The political review 'Seven Octobers' was slated for overblown, incomprehensible symbolism in an unsuccessful attempt to imitate Mayakovsky. 'Evening Devoted to Liquidation of Illiteracy', a report combining megaphone exclamations, ballads, and *rayok* verses, as well as ordinary verbal exclamations, received praise, particularly

the speech of the third participant, a woman worker, in which simplicity and naturalness combined with a new everyday pathos which is neither shrieked nor shouted but soft and convincing. In the finale the paraphrase of Mayakovsky's 'to shine everywhere, to shine always' is very well mounted in the text.[49]

The board supported the attempt to explain the economy of the USSR by using words and figures on posters and diagrams in 'Our Economy', but complained that it was too static. They were impressed however with the montage of the 'modern' language of 1925 and the phraseology of the period of war communism a few years earlier.

Individual groups and authors could also write to the editors for specific advice. Perhaps of necessity the guidance they received was much more blunt and down to earth:

To Comrade Kranovsky from Gubernia Barnau:
. . . the material submitted is weak . . . and cannot be published in its present form. Read the classics and contemporary revolutionary poets and writers, get in touch with the local organs of proletarian writers. . . .

To a GPU member in Pskov (The GPU was the State Political Administration which replaced the Cheka, the secret police, in 1922 – R.S. and K.M.): . . . If you have no experienced authors yet, just write on local themes, using *rayok* and *chastushki*.

To a miners' club in Kazan:

. . .'Hands off China' which your club has sent is old in its theme and weak in literary quality. The amateur theatre performances finish not only with a theme on a world scale but also by incorporating that theme in the dramatization of local day to day, domestic themes. The more of your own material that you write and present, the more you will approach the true character of the living paper. Endeavour to write without such high-powered words as in 'Hands Off China', write in the language used by the people around you.[50]

By 1928 Blue Blouse literature had become more polished. The rough verbal agitation of the early years had given way to a more careful kind of visual or scenic agitating, and the potential for the audience to learn was increasing. In addition they no longer limited themselves to a single theme

dictated by the Soviet calendar or by some particular campaign . . . we have started to paint big canvases, a whole montage of several contemporary themes today. . . . The sub-titles have been given up, instead of these we have a universality which demands still greater precision, greater artistry.[51]

Down with musical home-brew!

The gradual improvement of living newspaper texts made the weakness of the music used by the Blue Blouse even more obvious. The movement had no composers of its own, the majority at the time tended to be academic and deeply conservative. Musicians too were generally scornful of the vaudeville genre.

During the revolution and civil war, the seriousness of the economic and military situation tended to inspire heroic songs in place of the romantic music of czarist times. (Even then the words of 'Power to the Soviets' were set to the tune of 'White Acacia' a 'gypsy' melody.) But with the restoration of the economy and development of industry, heroic wartime melodies were insufficient or inappropriate. The Blue Blouse musicians turned to the sentimental ballads and operettas, wrongly termed 'popular', which had been so widespread in the past. In the beginning they excused themselves with the argument that the words of new *chastu-shki* were easier to remember with the old music. But it wasn't long before their audiences had discarded the new revolutionary texts of the Blue Blouse and were happily singing 'The Dashing Merchants' or 'One Evening Late in the Wood' with the original words once again.

Such tunes did not work too badly as parodies as a woman member of Blue Blouse explained:

In time each group of characters gathered its own motif. The sharks of imperialism and the bourgeois ministers put forward their ultimata accompanied by 'Kamarinska' or 'Razluka', a song about parting. The priests, specialists and NEP men were exposed to the sounds of operettas and gypsy romances.[52]

But as Osip Brik pointed out, 'They were no use at all when a more resounding effect was needed. It sounded stupid when an actress representing the Soviet Union or an actor representing the world proletariat sang his words to banal popular songs.'[53]

A. Lubimov, in a major polemic in the *Blue Blouse* in 1925 entitled 'Musical Arrangements of the Blue Blouse Texts' accused the journal itself of offering 'musical home-brew':[54]

The masses quickly recalled the effect of this poison which they used to take during their life under czarism, and wandering once again from pub to pub they began to get used to the old bourgeois agitation which appeared to have died out.

The music played by the Moscow collectives was certainly better than that recommended by the journal. But, complained Lubimov,

despite the presence of quite talented and creative pianists . . . in a majority of cases there is an extraordinary medley and confusion of styles and lack of an ability to capture the moment being described or the characters. This happens in oratorios and in items on everyday life – there is a complete absence of musical planning. . . . The text goes to the director of the collective, who then seats his pianist at the piano and asks him to work out some music for it. . . . Who can ensure that this music is good music, the more so as the director has sometimes composed it himself.

Lubimov quoted Bukharin's *Theory of Historical Materialism* in support of his argument that music is a product of social conditions and material labour. The difference in form, rhythm and style between music produced by the peasantry and that of the elite reflects the differing opportunities for artistic development of these classes (education, leisure time, etc.) as well as the increasing complexity of upper-class life. The ruling class, which 'defines the needs, determines the views, educates the feelings and creates the moods', will try to dominate all other classes in the arts as in production. Because the style and content of the musical techniques and discoveries of the past are so totally related to bourgeois production they must be rejected.

Opera theatres and houses, concerts, symphonic and chamber music were designed only for a special circle of people who understand this kind of art. What can an untrained worker take from the Bolshoi Theatre? A chorus of orchestral sound can't be assimilated by the untrained ear, and for the worker it remains an illegible document.

What can a worker or peasant learn from an opera? This would
be like asking a person who only knows the first four stages of
arithmetic to solve problems of integral or differential calculus. A
long and systematic educational process is needed via proletarian
musical organizations which would lead the worker to an understanding of musical art.

This rejection of the classics was not as sweeping as it appears at first
glance. (Elsewhere in the journal it was stated quite firmly that 'Musicians
must definitely be familiar with classical music, be able to read scores
and have good technique.'[55]) Lubimov went on to suggest Beethoven,
Glinka and Mussorgsky as three great composers whose experience and
technique should be studied, the first two because they created entire
musical schools, the latter because he 'first raised musical questions which
led the way to new shores'.

As for contemporary composers he devoted considerable space to a
virulent attack on 'the last of the Mohicans, Scriabin, an aristocratic
degenerate . . . he expressed the essence of his class's final disintegration.'
However, his 'unorganized' music (a major defect in the eyes of the Blue
Blouse) as well as that of Stravinsky, Smetana and Prokofiev could be
used for characterizing disintegrating types' or to accompany texts about
bourgeois countries and their ideology or portrayals of emigré life. Their
melodies would be alien to the spectator who would hear these distorted
forms as parodies or representations of the upper classes. After all, it was
only important for the spectator to remember 'matters from the spectacle
which are important to him from the class point of view'. But in most
other situations Lubimov recommended the

indisputable composer who is near to us . . . the people of the past,
the worker and the peasant, who created the most brilliant of forms,
the popular . . . folk song, majestic in its simplicity, force and
content. These songs may be divided into a) everyday themes, b)
heroic, c) labour processes, d) revolutionary. All four aspects can be
used by us.

He advocated simple new music reflecting the character of the poem it was
supposed to be illustrating and based on popular work songs, peasant rebel
songs, robber songs and the revolutionary songs of pre- and post-October.

The Russian folk song has an unusually rich melody and elements
of everyday life and all it requires is a special harmony which would
reflect the labour processes. Since we know that the working masses
are in essence linked to the peasantry, since the majority of working
families lead peasant lives in the villages, the Russian song . . . will
also answer the needs of the working masses. This task was resolved
well by Lazarev in his 'Cradle Song' published by the Musical Sector.
In the second part there is a melody recalling a particular tune which

has its own harmony and speaks in a clear bass construction of victorious labour. Korchmarev, in his 'Song of the Sowing Machines' also produced a song which reflected popular life, and in its accompaniment reflected the work of the sowing machine.

We see the same thing in A. Sergeev's 'Workshop' where a wood-cutter cuts down a tree in successive grace notes. . . . In the musical literature which is being written there should be productive moments reflecting the mechanization of work processes, the rhythm, mechanical metre, the humming of a tractor, the screeching of wheels, the chugging of trains, the whistles of factories and steamers. . . . There are a lot of noise instruments . . . capable of producing these effects.

Oratorios which focus on the major dynamic events of Soviet life 'oblige us musicians to produce music that corresponds to the event itself':

We must construct our music on the basis of heroic melodies which at the same time are close to the masses. For example, 'The Internationale' is always so strong that the inspired masses pick up the tune and sing it with heightened feeling. In this melody there is boldness, strength, toughness of harmony, a structure based on fourths and fifths, unison, a strong two-voice structure with interweaving sub-parts, a melody which can be quickly got hold of and can be sung without accompaniment. The oratorios should be constructed along these lines so that they are performable without a piano and without losing their sound texture.

This necessitates the members of the collective having musical lessons, linked with the study of the score of the oratorio. The . . . score should be constructed in such a way that the music underlines and characterizes the text and doesn't destroy it by disconnectedness and stereotyped harmonies.

The circle leader, urged Lubimov, must take care that his arrangements do not depart from the text. The metre and accent of the music must coincide with the logical rhythm and emphasis of the text. All rhythmical movements must be based on physical culture, not dance, the waltz, but marches such as those from the opera *Carmen* or Pototsky's 'Pulinovsky' or 'Young Communist Sailor March', the *carmagnole* (popular song and dance of the time of the French Revolution), 'We Are the Komsomol' by Alekseev, etc. Two-, three-, and four-part music should be used by the professional collectives. Personal idiosyncrasies such as ornamental modulations, improvised harmonies or musical fragments from the past were to be avoided. The Blue Blouse collective must learn to appear and act on cue to musical accompaniment, to prevent the musicians resorting to 'barbaric distortions' of the piano part by having to repeat two or three chords. If all his advice was followed, claimed Lubimov, the Blue Blouse would 'help lay the foundations of a burgeoning proletarian musical art.'

The extent to which Lubimov's ideas were realized in practice is difficult to gauge. Brik, writing in 1927, says 'This musical famine still exists, and variety theatre music is still a compilation of old tunes.'[56] Attempts were certainly made to improve Blue Blouse music and to educate or at least develop the taste of the masses. An important step in this direction was the organization of a college of proletarian musicians attached to the Blue Blouse with the task of carefully selecting good music.

The producer

The poor quality of so much Blue Blouse raw material posed a considerable challenge to the producers who had to develop methods of disguising or injecting life into texts that were often crudely written or bone-dry. A revealing reply to the questionnaire sent out to Blue Blouse producers came from a Comrade Tomis.

> If people . . . want to know how I work, the answer can be given in four words – I take, I correct, I note and I put on. I take material, both literary and the live material of the actors, and according to this I note the layout, the blocking, the structure, I correct because the plans of producer and author are almost always different. The author puts forward his hero, writes thundering monologues for him, but I, the producer, fancy the unnoticeable but true-to-life type sketched in with a couple of lines, and I, brazenly and improbably, make the culminating point of the sketch a scene with this Mr X, not the place where according to the author's written notes the audience should be laughing or weeping. . . . For example, in the Blue Blouse production 'The Red Army' we have as culminating point the march of the soldiers, the physical culture bit. That is a scene which was not noted by the author, but which cut its way into the production thanks to a free association. . . . When I amblocking I take the best from the left producers, I digest it, add a lot, I take a lot from the cinema.[57]

(There are other references in the *Blue Blouse* to experiments based on productions in the left wing Moscow theatres. Vakhtangov's *Princess Turandot* for example, inspired the article 'The Turkish Miracle'. The characters were introduced in a specially written entrée, during which the actors put on their costumes in full view of the audience. In the finale makeup and costumes were removed and the article ended with a song.)

The good director had to be inventive but avoid abstract aestheticism and over-elaboration. He had to know the difference between engaging and convincing his audience, and buttonholing them. It was he more than anyone who was responsible for the organic synthesis of forms which characterized variety, forms which had to be 'strictly defined, cleanly minted',[58] based on externally expressive means. 'When you have a five- to ten-minute variety or living newspaper number, everything is important down to the last comma, everything must stand out in relief.'[59] The ability to use contrasting means of affecting the audience without piling them on too thickly, was essential.

The ideal producer was an all-rounder:

Even if the producer himself can't sing or dance or do somersaults, he must still know how necessary it is to do all this and must be able to explain it.[60]

If a drama producer is a specialist in everyday life scenes . . . the oratorios will be without interest for him and difficult. And his chastushki will always have to have accordion accompaniment with the man sitting down or standing, and an international review will always have to be done in the lubok form.

If a producer is only a physical culture man then he can't depict types without cliché, he can't give texts sharpness, and most of all he is immoderate in giving movements, he wears out the viewer and obscures the sense of the article.[61]

He must help the performers avoid stereotypes within the limits of their 'masks' or roles: 'He must not make the actor who is playing an American tap dance too often.'[62]

But in the Blue Blouse one of the producer's most important attributes was undoubtedly speed. Some churned out more than a hundred new articles a year. The necessity of remaining topical and of living up to their audience's demands for something new dictated a horrendous work pace.

Here is the timing and the stages of the producer's work. During the day he receives his material, in the evening he blocks it through and works it over, a second copy is immediately given to the musician. At the rehearsal the musical numbers are checked through and changed according to the production plan, the roles are assigned and the singing is practised by the actors at the piano. Only when the music has been learned does the blocking go forward. Two days for cleaning up and the last, fourth, day for viewing of the article in costume and with props.[63]

(Makeup was considered unnecessary or even a distraction by the Blue Blouse 'with the exception of portrait makeup and the ultra-comic'.[64] The actors would adopt a characteristic facial expression which was stressed by a few lines. They shied away from real frock coats or sailor's uniforms, preferring constructivist costumes, additions in appliqué or even posters through which head and limbs could be thrust and moved. These had more meaning and were better for quick changes. Props were all bright, colourful, large, portable and functional – R.S. and K.M.)

Better that than to mess about for a week, have three viewings and to rehearse the number to the point where it makes the actor, pianist, producer and everyone sick. Up to now this is the method that has been followed in Blue Blouse and it has always given excellent results. The point at which it is possible to put an article onto the boards can only be established by the feel the producer has. Movements must be sharp or precisely defined, no superfluous gestures, words heard clearly and mass scenes cleanly performed. The work can be finally polished in public, in front of the audience, in performance. One cannot attain perfect acting in laboratory work, it only leads to a dry, over-learned performance on stage. One thing is without doubt – the producer must come to the rehearsal with a plan for the production and with a precisely worked out finale, for however good a piece may be if it ends feebly it will only confuse the viewer and no agitation is possible. One must dot the i's. The . . . outcome, the moral, the lesson given, the triumph of virtue, the final slogan, . . . the summation of the content, must be interesting, lively, with a trick, it must involve a whole group, it must provide some spectacle and without fail something new. One cannot limit oneself to letting the characters go off into the wings with upraised hands but indifferent faces.[65]

Just as creative writers and musicians were in short supply, there were undoubtedly many groups which lacked this 'organizing centre of the collective . . . the theatrical master . . . of physical culture, mechanized movement . . . clear gestures and control of body and language'.[66] The board had to remind them of the most basic principles:

From most of the material sent from the localities we can see that they have used mostly material from issues 1 and 2. As a result they are only using the happy feuilletons in the Blue Blouse repertoire; by no means should they shun such articles as 'The Economy of the USSR', 'The Budget of the USSR' and others.

News is coming from the towns of the Povolzhiye, Siberia and Ukraine that they are performing our 'Confession' and 'The Kalifat' and call it a newspaper. Apart from that our comrades still have not learned that the application of commonplace opera motifs, and deviations in the presentation of foxtrotting, decadent Europe only gives the living newspaper a bad name. . . . We repeat that the plan of the newspaper must be sustained from the beginning to the end. . . .

To Comrade Rasin, Samara:
. . . we recommend that you not chase after everything, but work

through each production in detail. Play without a prompter. If possible simplify things, but definitely carry through the programme in the form or character of the newspaper. Begin with the serious and gradually go over to the humorous. Local material should take up half the performance.[67]

Long live the new actor, the virtuoso of variety!

Although the Blue Blouse considered words so important, they were stronger in physical rather than verbal expression. There are several reasons for this. The monotony or roughness of many living newspaper texts may have pushed them to develop a highly visual style to compensate for these deficiencies. Their interest in popular forms such as commedia dell'arte and circus was undoubtedly a contributing factor as well as the influence of the mass spectacles, the left theatres and film makers for whom plastic movement and a rapid succession of images was so important. The actual physical conditions under which they worked should not be overlooked: in a normal theatre setting the hall is darkened and quiet, the rows of seats are arranged so that the focus is on the stage cut into one end. On the back of a lorry or in a reading room in a rural hut, in a tea shop or pub there are many more distractions all around, the performers cannot hope to maintain the attention of the audience unless they give them something striking to look at.

Besides, the Blue Blouse were 'aiming at the tempo of today, the tempo of machine technology' in order to 'achieve the effect of an electrical current, so that the viewer gets a shaking up of a psychic and physical character, and is charged with energy'.[68] In this they were influenced by Foregger's music hall:

Foregger's theatre, which as far as ideology is concerned, limped on all four feet, left behind many purely formal achievements. The chief ones are: the *physical training of the actor* and the truly *American rhythm of his technique.*

They (the Blue Blouse – R.S. and K.M.) took from the followers of Foregger the dynamism, the precisely mechanized gestures, which often had no subject, and were not illustrative, as well as their 'industrial' movements, imitations of mechanical work by a group of human bodies.[69]

The concept of a contemporary theatre of masks also came from Foregger. The Blue Blouse defined them as skeletal or framework characters: the Conformist, the Fascist, the Home-distiller Woman, the Specialist, the Prime Minister, the Kulak, etc. Here were the seeds of the modern commedia dell'arte. As Blue Blouse work became more sophisticated the old 'masks' were replaced by new stock characters which required a higher level of social and political consciousness from the actors who had to present them.

In order to agitate you have to know what you are agitating for. Meyerhold, the most consistent advocate of portraying theatrical characters according to their class said: 'The contemporary actor must be the advocate, and the prosecutor of his own part.' Meyerhold was also the first to put forward in concrete terms the question of the 'Actor-Tribune'.[70]

There was no school to which Blue Blouse actors could go to develop their consciousness. They were expected to become more aware through their practice.

Daily rehearsals, constant contact with political questions of the day, and the actor is educated without noticing, and soaked through with the Soviet spirit. Equal payment of all workers, when there is a comparatively uniform level of qualification and work load, means that there is no cause for squabbles and intrigues to arise – those essential 'attachments' to the home life of all theatres. Old actors who have tried to bring in from backstage in their own theatrical undertakings a little taste of the intriguing spirit have either been removed by a succession of efforts or left the Blue Blouse of their own accord. Working for a workers' audience and the very orientation or set of the Blue Blouse poses to the actor the necessity of reconciling himself to the demands of Blue Blouse etiquette. 'Our rules are strict – no rings or ear-rings, our ethics – no cosmetics.'[71]

This sounds terribly prim and proper, but although 'excess' emotionalism was frowned on, the Blue Blouse actors were far from colourless.

We get a concrete picture of this variety artist: a young deft man, trained in physical culture, trained in the striking word, in the cheerful, bold and hard-hitting song and couplet, in the contemporary rhythm of the grotesque and the eccentric. . . . Young people are flexible and can take in all that's new, don't even object when they have to sing standing on their heads, are able to move and carry along an audience. These are the people who can be real Blue Blouse actors. Essential things are precise diction, mimicry, mime and simple gesture, and a musical ear.[72]

Youthful energy and revolutionary fervor were plentiful in the USSR and the Blue Blouse often achieved a very high standard of performance. In fact the skill of their actors was probably the single most important reason for their appeal.

. . . (The Blue Blouse – R.S. and K.M.) gives one of the freshest and liveliest comic performances to be seen anywhere in the city. . . . They sing, dance, play the accordion, act and change costumes on

the stage with sleight-of-hand rapidity. If they are still inferior to the
Chauve-Souris (Literally, 'bats'. A Parisian cabaret troupe – R.S.
and K.M.) in finesse they possess more agility. Their handsprings,
somersaults and balancing feats are not the least striking feature of
their production.

One of their most effective skits is entitled 'Industrialization'. One
after the other the actors come out in fantastic costumes, adorned
with symbols indicating factory buildings, installations of electrical
stations or other items in the programme of industrialization. Finally,
chanting in chorus lively verses, they scramble on each other's backs
and shoulders, forming a structure which is supposed to represent
the finished industrial system. The theme of one of their satirical
pieces is the unfortunate plight of a poor Soviet citizen whose existence the bureaucrats in various institutions refuse to recognize,
because he has somewhere mislaid his indispensable 'document' or
passport. The familiar types in state institutions with preoccupied
faces and the inevitably bulging portfolios are hit off neatly, while a
huge red pencil in the hand of the 'bureaucrat' adds a further element
of the grotesque and the ludicrous.*

* A piano furnishes brisk accompaniment, usually jazz, to most of the
performances, and snatches of Russian songs and melodies, played on
the accordion, are interspersed.

(*The Christian Science Monitor* (Moscow correspondent, 1928)[73]

The decline of the Blue Blouse: 'So why Comrades, don't they love us?'

In 1927 at an All-Union Production Conference of Blue Blouse workers
marking the fourth anniversary of the movement the leadership began to
work towards the incorporation of the Blue Blouse in the trade unions.
A meeting was held in the agitprop department of the Central Committee
of the Bolshevik Party in the presence of representatives of GPP and the
All-Union Central Council of Trade Unions. The Central Council, it was
decided, should take over the ideological leadership of the Blue Blouse.

This momentous decision led to what Yuzhanin described in the journal
as 'an extended committee period in the history of the Blue Blouse'.[74] He
complained that attendance at the couple of dozen meetings which took
place in the first half of 1927 changed constantly. Propositions agreed at
one meeting would be rejected at the next and new proposals put forward
in their place. But although the personnel may have changed, the general
direction did not, the Blue Blouse representatives found themselves

constantly in the minority in their defence of small forms. The professional theatre workers invited to participate supported the 'big play', the trade union workers followed their lead. According to Yuzhanin, 'Very often those who were talking about Blue Blouse had not even seen it at work and were judging it superficially on what they had heard.'[75]

But by June 1927 agreement was reached on a new journal. It was to be an organ of the Central Council and the MGSPS, the Moscow Council of Trade Unions. Retitled *The Club Stage* there were to be two sections, the first devoted to theoretical articles and practical discussions relevant to club theatre. The second half was reserved for the Blue Blouse. But this format was never realized. At a subsequent meeting there were objections from the supporters of the big forms to the Blue Blouse repertoire, which had been previously approved and was already in galley form. Yuzhanin, arguing that the repertoire needed had not yet been found, proposed the postponement of publication until the right material could be gathered. In the meantime, 'although we have said goodbye to all the Blue Blouse workers',[76] the old journal was to continue. This was agreed and *The Club Stage* was published shortly afterwards without the Blue Blouse section.

These squabbles over the journal are indicative of the growing difficulties the movement was experiencing. 'The masses have accepted and recognized Blue Blouse. But it is still a long way from official recognition.'[77] Opponents agreed that while the Blue Blouse had made a valid contribution to the cultural enrichment of the proletariat, it had outlived itself. There was criticism of the vulgarity of Blue Blouse performances:

In Moscow we have been able to see plays, even in the Theatre of the Revolution and the Theatre of the Moscow Trade Unions, with very vulgar bits, including lavatories, chamber pots, etc. (*Style* by Belotserkovsky). This gets by, but in the living newspaper movement a *chastushka* about alimony is slipped in and the performance evokes a storm of attack.

At the beginning of 1927 *Izvestiya* carried a *feuilleton* in which attention was drawn to a phrase in the Melitopo Blue Blouse production of the atheistic duet 'Sashka and Mashka': 'Then, bang, Christ is born.' Or in *Pravda*, 25.9.1927 there is something about one of the Moscow living newspaper groups (which is also referred to as Blue Blouse) where they were singing, 'It's not any worse than playing on one's belly.' Our Moscow groups do perform, one would think, tolerably well and one would also think that they are sufficiently supervised. In the localities there are not always qualified leading workers and not everybody knows what is acceptable for us and what is not. As a result, if there is a bad performance in one place Blue Blouse as a whole gets beaten for it. And the centre gets it worse than everybody else, on the grounds that this is debauching the youth.[78]

But more fundamental and far more serious for the Blue Blouse was the trend towards the big play. The issue was complex. On the one hand there was undoubtedly growing dissatisfaction on the part of working class audiences with the 'superficial content and the primitive artistic form', the 'schematism and didacticism which typify the performances of the Blue Blouse'.[79] On the other hand,

The cry is raised that . . . in our time we need plays which simply provide entertainment. And as a result on the club stage we have *The Water Nymph, The Sunken Bell.* We have amateur group people undertaking productions which are clearly outside their capabilities getting carried away with the actor's pride, 'Look at me, I am playing a prince!' and not noticing that his prince is wooden and that he hasn't got the voice for the part anyway.

People are becoming soaked in the aesthetic skills of the past, they are drawn in by some leader, the moss-grown provincial actors, into trying to appreciate the 'beauty which belongs to all mankind', aesthetic canons outside contemporary time, outside society – this is the screen for essentially bourgeois aims – a mask behind which is the direction of a petit bourgeois. Uncritical acceptance of these skills or habits of the past, and we have an uncritical attitude already with us, means the rebirth of petit bourgeois and, under our conditions, clearly reactionary taste.

It is . . . ridiculous to try and brush aside agitational theatre. We should not make bad agitational theatre. Agitation is the way to a contemporary stage. It does not mean that a working man should not see an old play, a classical work, he should see and study it, he should be in command of the artistic forms of the past; but he should study them critically, not just cultivate them.

. . . More than once attempts have been made to reproach us Blue Blouse people for demanding hegemony for the living newspaper on the club stage. These attacks are cheap demagogy.

The club stage needs both the big play and vaudeville, variety, even circus attractions. We are not denying continuity in historical development and we know that without full command of the culture from previous epochs the building of the *new* culture will be imperfect. We are far from demanding at the present time that the art of the past be thrown overboard, but we are not going to mechanically imitate even the finest examples from that past.[80]

The Blue Blouse had their defenders. Representatives from the localities at a theatrical conference called by the Agitprop Department of the Central Committee of the Bolshevik Party reported that 'Living newspapers were far from dead, had not outlived their time,' that 'they are capable of moving workers' audiences through local themes.'[81] It was this quality which the Blue Blouse themselves singled out in a contribution to the production conference mentioned above.

The big play is constructed on generalization. . . . It can bring out this or that type of relationship, it can show the rabid economist, the bureaucrat, the hero . . . the audience can go away thinking: 'Yes, we've still got types like that, just look around you here, and you recognize the same faces!' Their thoughts are directed towards negative or positive phenomena in general.

But the living newspaper is concrete in the local character of its material. We have got general All-Union characterizations; these are in the things which are produced by the central Blue Blouse and sent out to the various localities . . . they raise important questions for this particular month, this particular time of year.

But even more concrete are the productions of the local Blue Blouse. While they take as their point of departure the models published by Moscow, the local Blue Blouses base their work on facts from the life of their own area. Here you have depicted not the bureaucrat in general, the hero in general, but the local ones everyone knows, Ivan Ivanovich or Ivan Petrovich. And the members of the audiences, as they go away, are not thinking merely about such types existing still and seeing how they can be opposed and unmasked by workers' public opinion, here they are learning to apply artistic methods in everyday construction work.

Living newspapers are doing the same job as wall newspapers; they prod public opinion, open up the faults and lash them pitilessly. The need for such work in the localities is enormous. But the experience of the localities is not rich . . . . Exchange of experience between the different places, studio-type work on forms by qualified personnel, systematization of methods are absolutely essential.[82]

The Blue Blouse admitted that mistakes had been made, experiments had sometimes been unsuccessful, unimportant details incorrectly pushed forward. They even agreed up to a point, with the criticism that clichés had developed in those clubs which imitated the Blue Blouse, that they had lost their initiative and were producing mere copies. But they argued that it would be shortsighted to blame the method, that the movement was young and had no blueprints for success and that overcoming these faults was largely a question of greater resources.

The Cultural Section of the All-Union Central Council of the Trade Union gives commissions to playwrights for writing special club plays. It organizes a professional model club theatre which is to serve as a laboratory and an instructional centre for club amateur groups.

Why can and should this be done in the field of the big play and not for the living newspaper?[83]

A school was essential, they maintained, for retraining leading workers and providing short courses for instructors and lecturers. They also wanted a regularly working centre, under the direction of the trade unions and the Party, and frequent liaison between this centre and the localities. In this way the basic principles of the movement could be systematically passed on and a more conscious attitude developed among the local workers which would help prevent mechanical imitation.

But the demands of the Blue Blouse for official recognition by the cultural institutions of the state and the unions continued to fall on deaf ears. Although district and regional associations of living newspaper were formed and attempts were made through letters and visits to bring about closer contact with the Moscow Blue Blouse, the links remained haphazard and tenuous.

Resolutions sympathetic to the Blue Blouse approach had been passed at the Party theatrical conference mentioned earlier. A firm line was necessary, they declared, against the uncritical imitation of old forms, deviations towards petit bourgeois ideology, and tendencies which denied the importance of critically absorbing and reworking methods from the past. But in spite of this verbal solidarity, in spite of their continuing popularity and their growing international reputation, the Blue Blouse were swimming against the tide.

By 1930 RAPP (the Russian Association of Proletarian Writers) and its associated bodies in the other arts dominated Soviet criticism. 'Using channels accessible only to themselves, they cleverly secured official support for nearly all their concrete recommendations, critical appraisals, and assessments of individuals.'[84]

Their programme, basically a rehash of the principles of the right wing faction within Proletkult, argued for an essentially reflective rather than dynamic art, for a positive true-to-life portrayal of Soviet reality in a style easily accessible to the broad masses. Although RAPP was itself dissolved in 1932 by the Central Committee of the Communist Party, its fundamental tenets were incorporated into what became official policy in the arts, Socialist Realism.

According to James's *Soviet Socialist Realism*[85] there were three main components to this twentieth century adaptation of the nineteenth century concept of Social Realism: *narodnost* – literally 'peopleness', popular in the sense that a work of art is close to the people, and expresses their most progressive aspirations as well as being easily understandable; *klassovost* – literally 'classness', pertaining to the class characteristics of art; and *partiinost* – 'partyness', the identification of the artist with the Communist

Party and its policies. Art in Soviet society must further the interests of the masses. To do so it must become an integral part of Party activity.

At first glance one might wonder why the Blue Blouse fell out of favour, since they would certainly have met these three criteria. Theirs was a popular movement in several ways: they used popular forms, changing and combining them with experimental techniques in a way that made them accessible to the unsophisticated spectator, their programmes were related to everyday issues and were full of local colour. At the same time they encouraged workers' self-activity, drawing thousands of young workers into revolutionary cultural work. They advocated a theatre imbued with proletarian values, and they supported the Party's campaigns on a variety of issues. In areas hardly touched by the revolution, where illiteracy and ignorance abounded, they used dramatic agitational means, first to inform people of the revolutionary process and its concrete meaning for them; then to deepen this understanding by showing the relationship between the local advantages the revolution brought to the people and the Party's national and international policies.

But there were fundamental differences. The Socialist Realist school promoted affirmative, entertaining and unifying art forms, an approach which glorified achievements but did not lend itself to the detailed criticisms of the Blue Blouse. This was in line with the growing Stalinization of the Party but it was also to some extent a reflection of the popular yearning towards an affirmative culture, hardly surprising after the 1905 and 1917 revolutions, a World War, civil war, war of intervention, NEP, and the additional sacrifice to come of fulfilling the first Five Year Plan in four years. In contrast to the idealized mirror of Socialist Realism, the Blue Blouse were in favour 'not of a photograph, but a construction'. They aimed to influence the 'brain of the spectator with all scenic means', preparing him for 'the perception of new social conditions'.[86]

> At the moment of the greatest possible reconstruction it would be senseless to occupy ourselves with external decoration. If you have walls in a flat that are soaked through with damp it is pointless to stick wallpaper on to them with a fancy design. This will not make it any easier to live in such a room. There is no point in deceiving oneself and trying to take refuge in half-hearted measures. One must tear down the pretty wallpaper, lay bare the patches of damp underneath and find ways of either drying out the walls or of rebuilding them.[87]

Such an approach was clearly out of step with the political developments taking place, in particular the putting into practice of Stalin's theory of socialism in one country, the attempt to propagate the triumph of the system, and suppression of all dissent as the work of 'foreign agents' or 'class traitors'. Far from the Socialist Realists' conception of big heroic historical canvases was the Blue Blouse vision of a dynamic agitprop variety genre. The differences were clearly spelled out by Osip Brik:

Great artistic forms exist in Russia only as survivals from another culture, the attempt to create monumental Soviet theatre is doomed to failure, since our time and culture is not monumental but transitional, and this transitional period of culture moves not with large but with swiftly changing, mobile, small forms.

The variety theatre . . . is not valued highly enough although it is the only genre capable of fulfilling the need for enlightenment, a need which the stationary theatre cannot fulfill.

. . . To the degree to which we do not conceive of cultural work as developing separately from political life, to that degree we must consider as living and progressive only those theatrical genres which are capable of uniting revolutionary cultural and political activity, and only the vaudeville genres can do this a hundred per cent.[88]

The Blue Blouse demanded leadership as well as support from the Party, state and union cultural bodies. At the same time Yuzhanin was emphatic that the Blue Blouse needed independence (in light of his experience of the 'committee period') otherwise it would not survive. And this meant the right to their own journal and their own centre. There was also a great deal of emphasis in the Blue Blouse on the rank and file membership: 'The club play is built from above, Blue Blouse, the living newspaper, was built from below.'[89] And as the resolution of the Party theatrical conference referred to above clearly indicates:

the club stage, linked with a particular point of production, with particular trade union organizations and the whole public opinion of the workers, has the possibility of getting closer to the masses, of more flexibly taking account of the cultural level, the particular demands of the workers of these given establishments and therefore exerting a more thorough political and cultural influence on the masses.[90]

Such potential might have been welcomed under different circumstances. Under those prevailing in the Soviet Union at the time it could not be realized. *The Russian Soviet Variety Theatre* (1917–1929) states:

The decline of the Blue Blouse was as rapid as its rise. This was facilitated by a complete change in its leadership. The collectives of Blue Blouse quickly lost their artistic physiognomy and became as A. Argo rightly wrote: 'ordinary small theatres doing sketches, theatricalized romances, one-act vaudeville. Just as the ripe fruit necessarily falls from the tree, lightly and painlessly, so the Blue Blouse met its natural end.' (A. Argo, The Word Sounds, p. 97)[91]

How painless the end of the Blue Blouse was in reality is difficult to judge. It is also not easy to determine exactly how much their decline was due to political/artistic disagreements with the dominant line, and how much it lay on their own shoulders. The official versions provide additional material, but as they were usually written by supporters of Socialist Realism they must be taken with a grain of salt.

The Moscow Blue Blouse (chief director B. Shakhet) . . . attracted attention for its immediacy, its youthful flair, its temperament, but it was distinguished by its considerable professionalism. Here different creative traditions joined together in a very complex way. On the one hand there is the influence of popular theatre . . . on the other hand, devices and forms taken from the festivals of the revolution. The Blue Blouse was also . . . to a considerable degree a variety theatre. However, within Blue Blouse there was a battle against the variety theatre. Variety was considered an entertainment genre and not a political-agitational one. (There is no mention of such a battle in the *Blue Blouse* – R.S. and K.M.) . . . Towards the end of the twenties and the beginning of the thirties Blue Blouse began to experience a crisis. The quantitative growth of groups was not accompanied by a creative growth. The collectives began to shut themselves up inside a narrow circle of specific devices and to move away from specific subject matter. Their themes began to repeat themselves. Entering the professional variety stage a number of collectives became professionalized and gradually lost their link with the youthful milieu which had engendered them. (Since the spec-ificity of their subject matter and their links with the class were very important to the old Blue Blouse leadership, it is likely that these criticisms applied to the movement after the leadership had changed. R.S. and K.M.) But the principal miscalculation preventing the general recognition of the Blue Blouse lay in its undoubted lagging behind the growing cultural demands of the working class audience. . . . In the period when a contemporary dramaturgy of a high standard had appeared the principles of the living newspaper and the Blue Blouse had outlived themselves and these collectives gradually dwindled away. Into their place stepped the TRAM. (From the *History of the Soviet Dramatic Theatre*)[92]

According to the *Soviet Encyclopedia* it had become essential for the Blue Blouse to be 'revised and reconstructed and for the artistic qualities of its programs to be strengthened.'[93] In contradiction of the account above from the *History* the Encyclopedia states that the Blue Blouse had rejected the techniques of the theatricalized agit-revue, a form used, of course, in the festivals of the revolution. This rejection, the authors conclude, coupled with the failure to develop new skills, led to the Blue Blouse's demise at the beginning of the thirties.

Russian Soviet Variety Theatre puts forward the most positive evaluation of the Blue Blouse movement:

> Despite a comparatively short existence of about ten years the Blue Blouse enriched variety with new and completely non-scenic themes. Forms and devices were elaborated which to this day continue to live and produce fresh shoots, not only in the variety stage, but in the theatre, circus, in the work of amateur agitational brigades, the direct heirs of the Blue Blouse. One can only describe as unforgivable the contemptuous silence about what it achieved in its time and what has become the possession of world art. The Blue Blouse and its development increasingly influenced variety and theatres of the small form. Among them were collectives from pre-revolutionary times trying not only to retain the best traditions of the revolutionary art but to apply them to the needs of the day.[94]

The TRAM (Theatres of the Working Class Youth) inherited many Blue Blouse characteristics although the two movements were in some ways quite different. They created large spectacles but also continued to work on the small forms which the variety stage, living newspaper, and Blue Blouse had done so much to develop. There were sixty to seventy TRAMs' in the USSR in 1929, and by 1932 three hundred. The Leningrad group which began as an amateur theatre was particularly interesting. Its worker-actors were so genuine and spirited that they built up a large following in spite of their lack of expertise.

The TRAMists maintained, according to the *History of the Soviet Dramatic Theatre*, that the essence of drama was 'not life but argument', their method 'dialectical materialist':

> A measured chronological flow of events was rejected, the action jumped around freely from place to place, episodes were linked with one another but 'polemically' in terms of objection or affirmation. . . . The episodes often represented . . . projections into the past or into the future, which would make it easier to assess the present.[95]

Memories were woven into the action or portrayed in parallel scenes which mirrored the main action, a technique which became known as 'TRAM-Flows'. 'Another widespread device used by the TRAMs was the contradictory "dialectical" illumination of one or another event depending on the character's relationship to it.'

The TRAM plays were constructed out of discussions, written collectively and polished by an individual member. (Eventually the movement developed its own dramaturges.) 'The actor turned into an orator, "an excited reporter", did not transform himself but simply conveyed his own relationship to the character.' The spectators were meant to be active participants in the action.

The Moscow TRAM's most important production was *Alarm* (1931). An agitational dramatized report, the play dealt with questions of military preparedness. Concrete examples supplemented the theses of the report, which were themselves scenically illustrated, and inserted by means of montage.

In spite of the fact that TRAM went further than the Blue Blouse in developing more complex montages, in spite of its greater potential to activate the spectator, it too went into decline in the early 1930s. The official criticisms made in retrospect are very similar to those made of the Blue Blouse: the performances were repetitive, schematic, superficial. 'The plot collisions of the TRAM plays became standardized, the schema of human relations and what are essentially the devices for characterizing them ossified.'[96] They were also accused of lack of culture and 'leftism', and of self-centredness, isolation and sectarianism due to 'an impatient confidence in the exclusive rightness of their artistic path and a certainty in the "providential" role of TRAM for the whole of revolutionary art.'[97] This was probably true to some extent and in this they differed from the Blue Blouse who seemed to have a more differentiated although critical approach to the art of the past.

In 1932 the TRAMS were reformed and their leadership replaced. In Moscow a group of people from the Moscow Art Theatre were put in charge. 'In the process of reconstitution everything specifically TRAM-like was liquidated, the TRAM collectives turned into more or less ordinary theatres.' Although tribute is paid in the official histories to the experimental work of the young theatres which 'strengthened . . . political . . . art, its partisan tendentiousness, one of the decisive principles of Socialist Realism',[98] the return to more conventional methods was inevitable.

In 1930 Glavrepertkom (the state censorship body) was already making cuts in Meyerhold's production of Mayakovsky's *Bath House* which according to Ted Braun resembled the agitprop shows of Blue Blouse. This was in accordance with RAPP's view that 'satire did nothing but harm to the cause of socialism and that art should only depict "real life".'[99] Braun relates how this attitude is lampooned in Act Three where the arch bureaucrat Pobedonossikov, and his retinue have just seen the play and have failed to recognize themselves in it. The walls of the auditorium bore rhyming slogans by Mayakovsky, broadcasting the slogans of the theatrical left, and ridiculing the bureaucrats, the censor, RAPP, the critics and the Moscow Art Theatre.[100]

In 1934 the First All-Union Congress of Soviet Writers – the organization replacing all other writers' unions and associations – adopted the policy of Socialist Realism. Subsequently the partiinost aspect was greatly strengthened. Membership of the Soviet Writers' Association became mandatory and a pre-condition was acceptance of the tenets of Socialist Realism. At a time when the party was so heavily dominated from above, partiinost meant in practice carrying out party policies unquestioningly, in the political as well as in the cultural sphere.

Looking back at the Blue Blouse

The Blue Blouse created a genuine and widespread workers' theatre movement which became a tool for the transformation of Russian society. Their contribution to the fight against illiteracy, their ability to respond swiftly to international and everyday questions, to agitate for concrete measures and provide the localities in which they worked with a dramatic forum where reactionary behaviour and beliefs could be exposed won them a large popular following. They struggled to re-educate the artistic tastes of this mass audience and succeeded in interesting them in new forms. Even their opponents agreed that the Blue Blouse had 'liquidated amateurishness, got rid, in the clubs where it works, of the vulgar, petit bourgeois play, turning the attention of amateur workers' theatrical groups and of audiences towards agitational presentations.'[101]

The Blue Blouse imaginatively utilized the entire range of devices which the previous period of experimentation with popular forms, mass spectacles and montage of attractions had yielded. The eccentric and grotesque styles pioneered by Meyerhold and Eisenstein were injected with earthy popular humour and wit which made them less abstract and immediately understandable and accessible to spectators without formal education.

But they had severe shortcomings. As far as we can tell from our knowledge of their repertoire, the evaluations of their critics and their own admissions, they hardly ever managed to shift from simple agitational material to more in-depth propaganda. (In 1923, the year the Blue Blouse was founded, the Party's 'Resolution on Agitation, the Press and Propaganda' called for a deepening in agit-prop work as the need for a 'more detailed analysis of economic and international policies requires a shift from traditional agitation to a more profound form of propaganda.'[102]) In spite of numerous resolutions at congresses and exhortations in *Blue Blouse* articles and editorials, the sketches remained short and one-dimensional agitki. They rarely went beyond the informational or beyond the simple juxtaposition of correct and incorrect ideas, behaviour or policies.

The spectator's learning process remained limited to a solemn acceptance or laughing rejection of the posed alternatives. The forms of presentation followed defined patterns which gradually became clichéd. The sharpness of their satire and the strongly visual staging helped to hide these weaknesses for a while but as the novelty of their work wore off they resurfaced.

This stagnation was partly due to their continuing adherence to the living newspaper formula. While it helped initially to break with the 'sujet' of the more traditional theatre, and provided a useful model for inexperienced groups, used over and over again it became something of a straitjacket. It had a lot of advantages: it was flexible and adaptable, made use of a variety of dramatic devices, appealed directly to the spectators. Different acting styles could be used in different sketches without clashing, the set as far as it existed, was extremely simple, mobile and cheap and therefore within the reach of amateurs with limited finances. The poster-type acting and declaiming of the living newspaper was easier for the amateur actor, and the form also facilitated collective writing without creating too much incoherence in the literary style.

This was extremely important, since there were very few qualified individual writers producing material for groups like the Blue Blouse. The colloquial language, often in dialect, made their texts accessible, the puns and ditties were amusing, but the texts were all too often crude, with blatantly moralistic or sloganistic endings, or pretentious imitations of other – better – writers. Collective writing did not necessarily overcome these problems, may even have helped perpetuate them, but it has the virtue of drawing on many minds, providing experience, stimulating and giving confidence to beginners.

The portraying of 'social masks', of stereotypes and cartoons, was all that was required by such simple dramatic material, and though this was carried out with great versatility and panache, the acting contributed to the one-dimensionality of the audience's learning process.

The music too, though it helped create a jolly atmosphere, was insipid, in some cases actually undermining. Unfortunately, the alternatives suggested by A. Lubimov in his lengthy contribution to the journal, although certainly an improvement, were hardly conducive to a really creative dialectic between what was seen and heard. Based as they were on the almost exclusive use of folk music and marches, with an extremely literal and illustrative approach to accompaniment, if they had been put into practice they would have done little to stimulate the imagination of the spectator. (It is a great pity that he did not take the music of such great contemporary composers as Stravinsky more seriously.)

But the movement was young, as the Blue Blouse itself so often reminded its critics, and operating in areas where the people involved had not had the benefit of absorbing, even if only to reject, the traditional bourgeois culture. After 1923 there were very few professional agitprop productions which could have provided a model. The conception of dramatic montage was still very underdeveloped. Eisenstein's notion of montage, which in its eccentricity went further than Meyerhold's, was still very abstract, the ability to take an audience through a complex learning process was developed later in his famous films.

So it was up to the Blue Blouse movement to find a way forward itself. This would have meant the evolution of a more complex form of montage. The revue sketches with their local details could have been placed in an overall political, economic and cultural context, thus generalizing the specific. The subject matter and characters might have received a more differentiated treatment.

However, the development of a dramatic approach like the montage is a historical process. Ossip Brik's article 'Training the Writers'[103] contains some very perceptive observations on the problem of developing new forms to express new themes. He pointed out that contemporary works of art with important themes were often less impressive than those with more remote or less significant subjects. The history of art is a history of continuous struggle between old and new forms. When new themes are suddenly thrown up, the necessary or appropriate elements of artistic creation, and methods of combining those elements, have not yet been developed. A discrepancy exists 'between the subjects which have arisen and the possibilities of writing about them.' After the October Revolution some writers argued that the new topical themes were only of temporary interest and 'art should deal with timeless themes of general human interest.' Others, more honest perhaps, admitted they did not know how to tackle them.

The critics divided into two groups. The 'Napostu' faction which took its name from the RAPP journal *On Guard* accused the writers who clung to their craftmanship of 'insufficient ideological strength'. They confused the author's ideology with the ideological effect of his work, believing that a piece of art 'could be completely decoded by analysing the author's consciousness'. Cultural politics, i.e. political pressure, would force the recalcitrant into solving the problems presented by the new themes. Those who refused were guilty of political sabotage.

Voronsky and his supporters defended the right of authors to independence and creative freedom. He represented the 'fellow travellers', the inheritors of the mainstream Russian literary tradition. Although not unsympathetic to the revolution, they kept their distance.

Brik believed both were wrong. For him, 'our cultural politics is not a question of exerting political pressure or exercising tolerance, but of training the authors for the fulfilment of these tasks.' A craftsman needs a technical plan before he can produce a chair from a piece of wood. The writer too must have what Brik termed a 'literary theme', a plot or scenic conception or structure, before he can create art out of social facts.

'Within the theme there takes place a fusion of the social fact and the methods of its portrayal . . . if the theme is inadequate, the fusion does not take place, the subject and its presentation will fall apart.' Artistic methods are developed in relationship to particular social facts, they cannot be randomly applied to any material:

> The many ways one can structure conflicts like jealousy and unfaithfulness, etc., were well known. But it was not known how to stage the opening of a factory meeting . . . or with which gestures and facial expressions a member leaves a meeting, angry about the attitude of the majority.

> It would be ludicrous to think that the authors have more compassion with the lover who has lost his loved one than with the worker who is angry about the behaviour of his comrades. It is not a question of compassion, but of the ability to portray these facts. . . .
> It would be wrong to assume that the author has merely to become more familiar with the life of the workers and peasants. . . .

> The problem is to evolve out of the particular living conditions of workers and peasants a viable literary construction in order to portray successfully the material conditions of the life of the workers. Without these purely technical experiments, without this literary draft no knowledge of the workers' environment would help.

The Blue Blouse made attempts to evolve such a 'draft' – slowly groping towards montage 'by destroying old methods and accumulating new ones'.[104] But they were at an early stage of development and needed a lot of practical help and encouragement. Although they approached the state and the unions again and again for ideological as well as economic sponsorship they got very little support. That they were able to survive as long as they did is a tribute to their determination to realize their political-cultural aspirations with whatever means they were able to muster.

When the trade unions finally did agree to sponsor them, they demanded a repertoire of long plays which entertain and confirm in their content, rather than the dialectical montage which facilitates constructive criticism, doesn't merely please and appease but is a dynamic process of investigation of social problems and behaviour. This is a reflection of the cultural policy taking shape at the time. Realism was more and more equated with a positive portrayal of the harmonious construction of socialism without the contradictions that still existed in Soviet society. 'The complete change in the Blue Blouse leadership' must be seen in retrospect as a result of this policy and the Blue Blouse's insistence on remaining a critical dramatic tool of the working class.

In spite of its relatively brief existence, the Blue Blouse spread across the entire Soviet Union, consisted of thousands of active groups, and had an astonishingly prolific repertoire. Internationally, their influence was enormous. Reviews of their work were published in the USA, Denmark and Germany, they toured workers' clubs in Germany, Poland, Scandinavia and China. Their impact on the German workers' theatre movement in particular was fundamental and long-lasting.

On tour in Germany

The Moscow Blue Blouse under Yuzhanin was invited in July 1927 by the German section of the International Workers' Aid to tour Germany for a month. The route was announced in advance in *Warning Call*, the organ of Workers' Aid:

October 5–6, Breslau
October 7–9, Berlin
October 10, Dresden
October 11, Chemnitz
October 12, Leipzig
October 13–15, Weissenfels, Halle and Wittenberg
October 16–17, Erfurt
October 18–20, Braunschweig, Hannover and Bremen
October 21–23, Hamburg
October 24–26, Düsseldorf, Solingen and Remscheid
October 27–29, Essen, Bochum and Duisburg
October 30, Cologne
October 31–November 1, Offenbach[105]

The objective of the tour was to stimulate the proletarian theatre groups in Germany, and that it certainly did. In most of the towns where the Blue Blouse performed agitprop troupes were formed almost immediately. The tour was so successful that it was extended twice and received overwhelming praise from the critics, particularly those writing for the left press:

The Red Star:
. . . a quick succession of entertaining and surprising scenelets which are highly topical and encourage the audience to evaluate the presentation from a communist perspective.[106]

The Fighter
This ability to grasp our contemporary problems with forms which portray them passionately and impressively is part of agitprop, of proletarian art. The more critically and satirically we do this, the more movement, imagery and sound we introduce and the less verbal our material is, the more successful our work will be . . . This is the path of the Blue Blouse which we can follow . . .[107]

The Fighter's review of the Blue Blouse performance in Chemnitz provides a vivid description of the ingredients which contributed to their effectiveness:

The entrée: a scene compiled of dance, marching and singing – 'The Locomotive'. The Blue Blouse form the image of the locomotive with their bodies, stomping forward relentlessly. Without understanding the Russian words the proletarians understood that this was a symbol for the task the Blue Blouse have made their own: to be one of the driving forces, a locomotive of the Revolution! Other numbers followed: 'Ten Years – USSR' – the way the living Soviet star emerges from the movement in the final tableau is a riveting process. . . . Then a humorous scene. A parody on those backward peasant elements which view the great achievement of electrification of Soviet Russia with mistrust, suspicion and superstitious fear. Three of such people are criticized with friendly coarse jokes. Another number, artistically the most developed . . . is a parody on the petit bourgeois foil songs of the pre-revolutionary period as still practised in the kitsch and petit bourgeois or completely counter-revolutionary 'art' production of the White Russian emigrés like the Don Cossacks or in the American-Russian films which have nothing to do with Soviet films whatsoever. A whole mixture of stale songs like the 'Rhine Girl' or 'Sailor's Love' and others, presented with changed texts and in a parodied, distorted form. The last number before the break was a propaganda scene for physical proletarian culture which is simultaneously a critique of bourgeois sports competition. First a dancing couple is shown, then a grotesque boxing match, presented ironically, and finally gymnastic exercises. The overall meaning of the scene, as reflected in the accompanying text, was that the workers will take over the bourgois techniques of physical training in dance and sport, but not bourgeois culture and its trend towards individualism.

The second part of the programme presented *chastushki*, short verse, usually of a humorous nature dealing with all the problems of working people. Biting scorn for all the shortcomings of the proletarian construction of Soviet power on the one hand, encouragement for the most important tasks on the other, whether it concerns electrification or the introduction of the metric system or any other sphere of the new way of life under proletarian rule. Special applause greeted a comrade caricaturing an old-fashioned peasant woman who complained terribly about the new approach to women under Soviet power, where the women do not merely cook and sew anymore but want to lead a free life with equal rights. . . .

The final scene was devoted to the Red Army . . . the costume changes take place on stage, with a quick touch the Red Army men transform themselves into Red Sailors or into Budyonny's team of riders; but at the end they change into the Young Pioneers, the future of the Revolution. The slogan of the entire scene says: 'We don't want war but we are ready to defend our socialist fatherland.'. . .

Five aspects appear to be the most important . . . for this particular art form. Firstly, that the performance dramatizes *reality* with all the phenomena and problems which are decisive for proletarians. . . . Secondly, an active fighting spirit permeates the entire rhythm of their presentation. Thirdly, one of the remarkable characteristics of their art is the complete collectivity of their performance. No individual ever makes himself stand out, it is always a collection of individuals in an overall presentation of complete unity. This aspect in particular expresses their unfathomably great difference from individualist, i.e. bourgeois art. The last two main features are the uniquely popular humour and biting wit with which they criticize, and the masterly discipline and expressiveness of their physical acting. Among the best artists of the German theatre one will hardly find anything that comes close to such a plastic and visual language of the body as among these proletarians whose art is an expression of their ideology and conviction in the true sense of the word.[108]

The *Red Flag* of December 18, 1928 summed up the effect the Blue Blouse had on the German movement:

The Russian Blue Blouse has set a trend in Germany. Its positive influence can be seen in the work of the best of our agitprop troupes, the 'Riveters', 'Red Rockets', the 'Red Megaphone' and the 'Red Blouses'. They do not mechanistically copy the achievements of the proletarian revolutionary cabaret from the USSR but have understood that the forms of the cabaret, short and manifold scenes, independent from each other and hard-hitting, are a more suitable form of revolutionary theatrical propaganda than the red 'revues' lasting a whole evening which prevailed before the tour of the Blue Blouse; the new forms are easier to act and are more interesting. . . .

The program of the Blue Blouse consisted of an uninterrupted montage of scenes, songs, music, dance, mime, acrobatics and gymnastics. Visual means dominated the performance. . . . Broad characterization of types eliminated all naturalistic details in acting, costumes, props and decor. The visual effect, the structuring of the entire performance on mime and acrobatics gave it such tremendous dynamic power which particularly influenced the style of the German agitprop troupes. They learned from the Blue Blouse how to make their performances even more flexible so that they could intervene in the daily class struggle with a maximum of topicality and concreteness. What impressed them most, however, was the collective approach of the Blue Blouse. Its members were trained in an all-round way – singers, actors, dancers and gymnasts at the same time, working with the precision of a clock and with the drive of a true collective.[109]

Having performed in twenty-five cities and industrial centres to about 150,000 spectators, the Blue Blouse not only inspired the formation of new agitprop troupes but also enriched their dramatic forms.

3 Living Newspaper

4 Blue Blouse – Props and Costumes

Echte Form von
Volkspoesie auf dem
Dorfe „Schnadahüpfel"

5 The *lubok* – cut-outs to act through

6 A scene about the Paris Commune

7 The 'Red Star–Finale'

8 The 'Caretakers' Couplet'

9 'Fordism and NOT' (the Scientific Organisation of Labour)

10 *Chastushki* (limerick) using the *lubok* (cut outs)

11 and 12, Scenes from the tour of Germany 1927

13 *above* 'The Recognition of the USSR'

14 *below Oratorio:* 'The Red Army'

15 *above* The 'NEP-Man'

16 *left* 'Physical Culture'

17 *below* 'Advertising GUM' (the famous department store)

Part Two

Hello! – State power! Workers' theatre in Germany

4 · The origins of German Agitprop

There are aspects of the proletarian struggle which become clearer through a play than through a speech for the working class because they *experience* the play. . . . We do not want to reveal higher art . . . but to stimulate workers to think. (A defender of the Bremen Free Stage, which the Social Democratic Party tried to close in 1909.)[1]

In 1847, the year in which the League of Communists was founded, Friedrich Engels wrote a one-act play which was performed by members and their families at a festival of the Brussels German Working Men's Association. Unfortunately, the play has been lost but we know that it dealt with the disastrous economy of a small German state. The feudal sovereign was toppled by a people's revolution which fought for an end to the monarchy and for a united republic.

Throughout the second half of the nineteenth century a number of didactic agitprop plays and sketches were produced. Topical and satirical, they were written by party functionaries or pamphleteers, by writers who emerged from the ranks of workers' organizations or by intellectuals who attached themselves to such organizations. Only two years after Karl Marx had completed Volume I of *Capital*, Jean Baptiste von Schweitzer attempted the first dramatic exposition of the theory of surplus value in his farce *Rascal. A Goose*, his 'Dramatic Dialogue on the Growth of the Female Labour Market' (1869), was printed in place of the lead article in the party organ *Social Democrat*.

These militant Marxist beginnings gradually gave way to the 'classless' promotion of 'pure entertainment' and 'great art' in organizations such as the *Volksbühne* (People's Stage). Such developments reflected the political decline of the Social Democrats from a position of class struggle to class collaboration.

There were a few notable exceptions. B. Strzelewicz and his ensemble *Gesellschaft Vorwärts* (literally Forward Association) performed his entertaining and agitational songs, couplets and short scenes at meetings of the Social Democratic Party (*Sozialdemokratische Partei Deutschlands –* SPD), for the Workers' Cycling League 'Solidarity', the Workers' Gymnastic League *Frei Heil* (Free Salute), for the Workers' Youth Education Association, and free trade unions such as the German Metalworkers' Association.

Strzelewicz's material was directly relevant to working class struggles. 'The Bricklayers' Strike in Dresden-Loebtau' was written after the imprisonment of the strikers. Working-class veteran Erich Erhardt heard the song in 1910 'and witnessed that Comrade Strzelewicz, who had sung "Workers' Silent Night" was arrested on stage and sentenced to a term in prison.'[2]

After World War I Strzelewicz joined the German Communist Party (*Kommunistische Partei Deutschlands –* KPD) and formed the Red Troupe – Dresden. Active in the campaign against compensating expropriated aristocrats they used painted cardboard cutouts representing types like the Philistine, Priest, Capitalist, Secret Police which were tied onto the actor. With this technique reminiscent of the Russian *lubok* the four-member ensemble was able to present a wide range of 'characters' or living images made up of a collage of cutouts. (In the late 1920s the Drummers – Breslau, 'First German Troupe of Worker Actors', took up this method using George Grosz-type caricatures.)

Prior to World War I the atmosphere of defeatism and reformism expressed itself in tragedies about disillusioned and isolated workers and their families. An exception was the one-act play *The Woman Factory Worker*, a contribution to the anti-war campaign among women. (The vast majority of anti-war demonstrators were women. They were also the main force in the mass strikes of munition workers which reached their peak after the Russian Revolution. On January 28, 1918, 500,000 munition workers struck in Berlin alone, most of them women.)

The forms used by the early German workers' theatre varied. Some were little more than speeches or oral pamphlets, others were laced with the crude but biting humour of the oppressed. The flexible songs and sketches of Strzelewicz contrasted with the scope of 'The French Revolution', the epic dramatic poem in twelve moving images by G. M. Scaevola, performed at a commemorative meeting on the fall of the Anti-Socialist Law, October 1892.

The war accelerated the breakdown of the great, united and balanced dramatic forms into a kaleidoscope of small forms which attempted to piece together a new world view. Initial experimentation with these new forms was dominated by the Expressionists. But even those among them who supported a revolutionary theatre like Hasenclever, Toller and Eisner were isolated from the working class. Their idealism and concentration on the individual did not lend itself to making social-political connections.

A new epoch of the arts

The Russian Revolution was followed by the establishment of a soviet republic in Hungary, uprisings in Poland and Finland and finally the November Revolution in Germany. In March 1920 a three-day general strike paralysed the Weimar Republic and 10,000 Communist, Social Democratic and independent workers joined the Red Ruhr Army to save the Social Democratic government from a putsch by the right.

The international character of these struggles inspired mass cultural events, celebrations of the collective revolutionary spirit and passionate calls for solidarity in defence of the revolution against the White Terror of the reaction.

Mass spectacles

Great collectives need to become conscious of themselves – for this they need mass meetings and festivals . . . demonstrations and manifestations of joy and sorrow, of determination, attack and defence. . . . It is the function of the arts to give these moments of heightened collective will their thrilling expression and solemnity.
Leipziger Volkszeitung (People's Press, Leipzig 14 August 1923)

Leipzig, 1920: *Spartacus*, the crucifixion at the cycling track – not the passive sacrifice and suffering of an individual, but the annihilation of the grassroots leaders of the Roman slave uprising. It was performed by 900 workers for an audience of 50,000 at a festival of the Leipzig trade unions. Josef von Fielitz, director of the Leipziger Schauspielhaus developed the conception for this mass spectacle and directed it at the request of the Leipzig Workers' Educational Institute which organized the event in co-operation with the unions.

Four historic pictures, illuminated by symbolic lighting effects, were brought to life by large groups on the grass of the arena, on rostra, and on a massive stage. They depicted the victory celebrations and Bacchanalia of the Roman ruling class, the misery of their slaves, their insurrection and finally their subjugation.

The performance was so successful that it was repeated the following day and encouraged the staging of further mass spectacles. In 1921 800 performers took part in *Poor Konrad*, a monumental evocation of the German peasants' war. A year later Ernst Toller devised *Pictures of the French Revolution*, with its somewhat exaggerated view of the role of the proletariat in a bourgeois revolution. Toller was also responsible for *War and Peace* (1923) and *Awakening* (1924), both of which were idealistic allegories with pacifist happy endings and no reference to the harsh reality of class forces.

The message of the mass spectacles was frequently a problem. Knellessen writes that the defeatist ending of *Spartacus* was a 'hint of the consoling certainty that sufferings and misery will eventually be overcome in the hereafter'.[3] The massacres of the White Terror and the murders of Rosa Luxemburg and Karl Liebknecht were still vivid in the memories of the audience, however. The crucifixions may have been intended as a warning of what happens when revolutions fail, a demand for more thorough organization, discipline and solidarity to ensure that the next major confrontation ended not in martyrdom but in victory.

In *Poor Konrad* however, as in Toller's productions, everyone was made equal at the end of the play. Death ruled over the defeated peasants and feudal lords who had massacred them and the conflict was resolved in Heaven. A pity, since the medieval drama was quite literally a weapon in the struggle of the peasants against feudalism. The original 'Poor Konrad' was an illegal Fools' Brotherhood from the Rems Valley whose performance was the signal for the peasants' revolt. The vanguard of the revolutionary peasants, the 'Strong Companions' had formed themselves into armed groups of players. In 1514 they performed their 'Shrew play' *Upright Fools – Judgement* by Gosselfingen at a festival which all feudal lords and knights of the area attended. During the performance, the peasants pulled swords hidden in the fools' swords and attacked their audience. If the 1921 *Poor Konrad* had linked up with this militant tradition, it would certainly have added another dimension to the performance and perhaps contributed to a more radical ending.

The weak content of the mass spectacles undoubtedly reflected the lack of revolutionary political analysis of the SPD which sponsored many of these events. It is also possible that the writers allowed the ideology inherent in the pageant form to dominate their rendering of history, resulting in a grand apotheosis as in the ancient religious pageants, or an uncritical celebration of achievement as in many secular pageants. At any rate the mass spectacle did not really develop in Germany although isolated events were held up to 1932. They were quite unwieldy as far as intervening in the day-to-day struggle, and uneconomical in terms of the expense and effort involved and the few performances given although they had huge audiences.

However, the impact of the collective nature of the spectacles both for audiences and participants should not be underestimated. Many young workers who were involved in these tremendous statements of solidarity went on to work in proletarian speech choruses or agitprop groups such as the well-known Leipzig troupe the Red Fanfares.

Proletkult

The foundation of a proletarian theatre will introduce in principle the idea of a proletarian class culture. Through its very existence it will propagate socialism in the proletariat against bourgeois cinemas and theatre, against bourgeois ideology. (Hermann Schüller, 1920)[4]

In 1919 a group of intellectuals, artists and workers formed the League for Proletarian Culture in Berlin. Influenced by the activities of the Russian Proletkult and the German publication of Bogdanov's *Art and the Working Class* and *What is Proletarian Literature?* and of Lunacharsky's *Cultural Tasks of the Working Class* they organized lectures, exhibitions and literature sessions. They looked forward to 'a new epoch of the arts, education and science, blossoming from the soil of labour.'[5]

In 1920 the executive committee of the International Bureau of Proletkult appealed for conferences and public discussion of proletarian culture leading to the creation of a network of Proletkult organizations and a world congress. The League responded by helping set up the first Proletarian Theatre in Berlin. In 1921 others were founded in Leipzig, Nürnberg, Mannheim, the Ruhr, and Kassel. With the exception of the Kassel Proletarian Theatre most of them existed only briefly or sporadically and never developed a coherent approach. Some of their programs would not have differed much from the cultural efforts of the Social Democrats.

The Kassel group, which became Proletkult Kassel in 1925, was a forty-strong company under the leadership of the Communist actress Ilse Berend-Groa. Although their repertoire was by no means consistently revolutionary, they worked in a systematic and collective way. In 1926 they produced *Yesterday and Tomorrow*, a series of twelve 'living images' with speech chorus and recitation, dedicated to the anonymous dead of the Proletarian Revolution. It highlighted the main events of the German and international workers' movement since 1848 and was performed at the KPD's March 1848 celebration. *Hammer and Sickle over Asia*, a sequence of scenes by Toller, Brecht, Gold, Lask and Komjat was presented in 1927. This was followed by Berta Lask's dramatic revue *Gas War against Soviet Russia* which was banned by the law courts, and satirical texts written by the group. After a publicly acclaimed production of Ivanov's *Armoured Train* in January 1928 they planned a realistic version of Shakespeare's *A Midsummer Night's Dream*, a unique venture for a workers' theatre. Unfortunately, the group was dissolved before these plans could be realized.

But it was Piscator's Proletarian Theatre which laid the foundations for a number of important developments in the workers' theatre movement some years later.

The Proletarian Theatre of Piscator (1920–1921)

With the exception of a few professional actors, ideologically close to us, we acted mainly with proletarians . . . people who saw as I did, the revolutionary movement as the centre and driving force of their creative activity. The very idea of the Proletarian Theatre led me to give decisive importance to the building of a collective which was a human, artistic and political community.

(Piscator, on the Proletarian Theatre)[6]

The essential features of the Proletarian Theatre were strikingly similar to those developed by the Blue Blouse in Moscow a few years later:

1 Simplicity of structure and expression.
2 A clear and definite effect on the perception of the worker audiences.
3 Subordination of artistic intentions to revolutionary objectives; the conscious emphasis on and propagation of the class struggle. Aiming to serve the revolutionary movement and be responsible to revolutionary workers. The executive of the Theatre elected by and from them was to ensure the realization of their cultural and propagandistic objectives. It consisted of representatives from the Independent Social Democratic Party (Unabhängige Sozialdemokratische Partei Deutschlands – USPD), the Communist Workers' Party (Kommunistische Arbeiterpartei Deutschlands – KAPD), the Communist Party, the Free Workers' League, the General Workers' League, the Workers' Rambling League 'Friends of Nature', the International League of War Victims, and the Council of the Unemployed, with support from the Berlin centre of works councils. All organizations pledged to the dictatorship of the proletariat were invited. The SPD did not send a delegate.
5 The decisive criterion in questions of style: will it be a source of clarification for the proletarian audience, or will it confuse and infect them with bourgeois ideas?
6 Revolutionary art can only emerge from the spirit of the revolutionary workers. The workers' drive for self-preservation necessitates that they liberate themselves in the artistic and cultural

sphere to the same degree as in the political and economic one. And
this spiritual liberation must be communist too.

In keeping with its agitprop aims the Proletarian Theatre broke out of
the established theatre buildings and took its production to halls and
meeting places in the various workers' districts of Berlin:

The masses were to be approached on their estates. Anyone who has
seen these halls with their smell of stale beer and gents' toilets, with
flags and streamers from the last beer festival can imagine under
what difficult circumstances we developed a new concept of theatre.

Mobility meant keeping technical equipment to a minimum.

The decoration was extremely simple. But in relation to the changed
tasks of the theatre the function of even this simple hastily painted
(by John Heartfield – R.S. and K.M.) canvas had changed. In
Russia's Day it was a map which clarified at one stroke the political
importance of the scene of action by showing the geographical situation. That was no longer simply 'decoration' but simultaneously a
social, political-geographical or economic sketch. It acted as well. It
intervened in the scenic events, it became a dramaturgical element.
With this a new aspect entered the performance: the pedagogic. The
theatre was no longer to affect the spectator emotionally only . . .
it appealed consciously to reason. It was to communicate elation,
enthusiasm, thrills, but also clarification, knowledge,
understanding.[7]

Russia's Day, performed at the commemorative meeting of the third
anniversary of the Russian Revolution, October 14, 1920, marked the
opening of the Proletarian Theatre. It was the first uncompromising
German attempt to place the theatre at the service of revolutionary
agitation and propaganda. Co-written at the request of Piscator by Lajos
Barta, a refugee from the White Terror in Hungary, and the theatre
collective, the play was a contribution to the international solidarity movement around the slogan 'Hands off the Soviet Union'. It describes the
war of intervention, inspired and supported by the Entente nations, and
the terror of the counter-revolution in Poland, Finland, Germany and
Hungary where after six months of Horthy's dictatorship 20,000 people
were murdered and 70,000 thrown into concentration camps.

With a subject of such breadth, all notions of traditional story-line had
to be abandoned. The structure is a dramatic montage of short scenes
connected by their common theme and the common enemy: the ruling
class figures such as the Officer, Diplomat, Priest, and even World
Capital. The Working Masses too were symbolically represented. Unfortunately, this undifferentiated approach also expressed itself in stereotyped dialogue and appeals to the audience which take the form of mere

agitational speeches with no scenic or gestic underpinnings. But in all probability the spectators didn't demand more.

The threat to the first socialist state moved revolutionary workers in all countries. In May 1920 German workers had prevented supplies being sent to imperialist Poland, which had invaded the Soviet Union with the help of England and France. The mobilized working class responded readily to caricature and crude sloganeering.

Even if they had required more convincing, there were neither the plays nor the writers to write them. Piscator was the first to recognize that literary production had not kept up with the advancing theatre either ideologically or artistically. The writers close to him were unable to break out of post-expressionism.

> It was always 'plays', plays of the time, segments of a picture of the world, but not the total, the whole, from the roots to the last ramifications, never the burning immediacy of Today, overwhelmingly emerging from each line of the newspapers. The theatre was still being left behind by the press, it was not topical enough, it was too rigid an art form, predetermined and limited in its effect.[8]

Piscator dreamt of a closer link with journalism. Believing it was only a matter of the manuscript rather than an entirely new approach to writing, he and his group tried to produce the written material themselves.

To make up for the lack of expressiveness in the texts he had to use, Piscator concentrated on developing 'a form of stylized theatre . . . uncompromising and like the Japanese theatre . . . with basic gestures that would be highly applicable to our propaganda and contribute to a reduction of the verbiage.'[9] The cartoon or poster style, personification of social phenomena, ideological and scenic simplifications of political issues, rapid scene changes, compressed demonstrations or presentations of events, and abstract, agitational dialogue all became part of the dramatic arsenal of the agitprop movement. In the absence of skilled revolutionary writers Piscator, like Meyerhold and other directors, concentrated on developing dramatic structures which were often far superior to the texts.

But the Proletarian Theatre broke new ground in yet another way. For Piscator the theatre as an enterprise had to change. He replaced the capitalist hierarchy with a collective approach. The directing team, actors, writers, designers, and the technical as well as the administrative staff were bound together by their common interest in the work. This equal relationship was extended to the consumers of the product, the spectators. An audience organization modelled on the Volksbühne was set up which soon grew to 5,000 members.

The speech chorus

Workers' organizations in the post-war years tried to enrich their meetings with artistic presentations. Song and orchestral pieces, choirs, and recitations were included in celebrations of May Day and revolutionary anniversaries, commemorative meetings on the death of Luxemburg, Liebknecht, and later of Lenin, and recruiting and propaganda meetings. They made a welcome change from the inevitable speeches.

Youth organizations introduced folk songs and dances, 'living images', and began the recitation of poems by choirs. Divided into solo and chorus parts the verses had to be structured differently. Gradually, the speech chorus became a new independent form.

Initially, choruses were performed by ad hoc groups, but soon stable collectives were applying themselves exclusively to choral work. By 1923 the KPD groups had become dissatisfied with general statements of socialist aims and ideals or flaming protests against the oppressors. They had to deal with the strategies and arguments of the bourgeoisie but also those of the Social Democrats. With revolutionary activity on the decline, works like the *Chorus of Labour* were intended to help the Party broaden its base.

> The speech chorus was created . . . to fill a whole evening in the framework of a Party event. It consists of standard and variable (topical) sections. The latter should be adjusted according to the local or current political needs. The more the chorus relates to personalities, events, local peculiarities . . . the more comments there are on exploiters and bureaucrats in the area, . . . the more references to excellent comrades and efficient factory cells there are, the better. . . . Satire is the main means of expression of the speech chorus apart from the seriousness of intensive communist propaganda. . . . Above all it demands from the participants tenacity and will power. For particularly difficult solo parts one can use professional actors, but only those with revolutionary commitment. It is best when only proletarians participate. Space: circus, large hall, sports hall; dress: workers' dress, no Sunday clothes or romantic scarves copying lumpen proletariat.[10]

The 'Chorus of Labour'

Author of the *Chorus* was Gustav von Wangenheim, leader of the Central Speech Choir of the Berlin KPD. (Formed in the summer of 1922, the choir grew from twenty-five to sixty members when it joined forces with the Proletarian Mobile Theatre.) The mediocrity of Wangenheim's text was partly compensated for by the attention paid to the precise orchestration of voices: 'the broad and slow base for the SPD, the short and metallic tenor for the KPD, the even shorter and piercing female voices supporting them.'

The 'one-two-three-four-five', supported by instruments, must have the broad sound of dull bells when spoken by the SPD, like short and shrill bells when spoken by the KPD. At 'Labour, labour, labour', the flags disappear and the main body of the choir forms a front towards the stage. During the rhythm of the labour process almost every line, every word, must be spoken by a different voice or section. Pace and rhythm are everything. The rhythm of 'hammer blows' is emphasized by the striking of anvils with hammers. The choir divides into two sections, the SPD striking slowly and clumsily, the KPD on the attack with its short, sharp blows – they face each other, having produced their flags and placards. . . . Just as the SPD falls on its knees in the parliament scene the arena is blacked out and the stage is flood-lit: we see a long green cabinet table with government representatives (grotesquely stuffed puppets). The short speech by the minister of the government food office in the style of a coalition minister – the speaker is hidden – is accompanied by the grotesque movements of a dummy controlled by visible strings. This is followed by a counter-speech by a Party speaker (the food minister's speech is selected by him according to political events.) When he says 'Cash laughs' his laughter is joined by the laughter of a large section hidden in the darkness, to achieve an eery effect. Both speeches are interrupted on certain cues by individuals and small groups, then by larger sections from the arena and the audience with interjections that escalate and lead to the storming and overthrow of parliament. When the children have finished their parliament song, the empty stage is flooded and we see a huge caricature of the local police president, a machine gun shooting out of his enormous mouth. We hear it firing. The effect of the middle-class scene is based on the weakening of the limp middle-class men and on the simultaneous escalation of the increasingly desperate screams of the middle class women. The long shopping queue of the women must not be comical but provocative and eery. In contrast to the 'Lord's Prayer' of the priests and quivering middle class, 'Our Communism' must be spoken in a hard and fighting tone. 'Kom – in – tern' and 'K – P – D' must sound like kettle drum beats.[11]

The agitprop and montage elements introduced in *Russia's Day* in rudimentary form were combined with powerful devices from the mass spectacles to make the *Chorus of Labour* both convincing and entertaining, in spite of forced rhymes and an absence of heightened language. But a literary experiment which backfired is the juxtaposition of the two prayers. The Communist ridicules the priest's attempt to make him believe in God's help in time of poverty and hunger and leads the chorus in repeating:

> Our Communism
> Which art in deeds
> Hallowed be thy name –
> Thy kingdom come on earth
> Not in heaven.
> Give us this day our daily bread
> Denied us by our tormentors.
> Lead us not into reform or morass
> But deliver us from evil.
> For thine is the kingdom
> And the power
> And the humaneness
> That may rule
> The Comintern
> The KPD.[12]

Faith, frozen into a centuries-old formula, forces itself onto the new content. In place of religion, blind belief in communism. And because as a prayer the original is stronger, the dominant ideology prevails, the unconverted are not convinced. This problem recurs throughout the *Chorus*: the spectator's potential for learning is limited and confined largely to the verbal level, the weakest aspect of the production. The characters representing the Social Democratic workers, peasants and petit-bourgeoisie change their minds almost miraculously, without doubting, testing or verifying the new approach.

In spite of these weaknesses the *Chorus of Labour* was a major step forward towards the loose combination of different forms. Entertaining and satirical agitprop material was utilized and the rigid stage-audience division broken down by placing individuals or groups of performers in the auditorium. These innovations were further developed by Wangenheim in the play 7,000, performed by the Steglitz Proletarian Speech and Performance Collective.

'7000' (1924)

Following the suppression of the Hamburg uprising a military state of emergency was imposed from September 1923 to March 1924. The KPD was prohibited and had to work illegally. Hundreds of workers were murdered, 7,000 imprisoned. The number 7,000 became a symbol for the terror of the reaction. Wangenheim's play was sub-titled 'An Outcry from the Jails and Penitentiaries of the German Republic. A Warning to the Army of Millions of the German Proletariat.'

> The plot concerned only with individuals was dispensed with – the suffering of thousands, which is also our suffering, was openly presented in all its brutality. The members of the choir sat amongst us. . . . In our theatre there are no passive spectators. One experience, one rhythm embraces actors and 'spectators' and sparks off consciousness and action . . . the direction of which is determined by the actor and the play, by the visual representation of images comparable to frames in a film. And what about the plot or action? To hell with it. We are the action, our anger, empathy, newly awakened will to sacrifice, our kindled preparedness to fight: 'We are coming.' Here is the action, in these three words.[13]

The mobilizing effect of *7000* was so strong that the audience did indeed join in:

> An actor in the uniform of the security police had to escort two handcuffed workers to the stage through the audience. The weak lights made it difficult to see straight away that the policeman was not a real one. The incensed spectators rushed at the 'policeman' and beat him, forcing him out of the hall. Finally, a team of Red Front League members was requested for these performances to cordon off the gangway from the entrance to the stage in order to protect the actor from the fists of the workers.[14]

7000 demonstrated the misery caused by oppression without explaining to the uninitiated the underlying reasons for that oppression. It marked the end of the development of the speech chorus as a mass agitprop form although it continued to have a place in workers' celebrations. Some Social Democratic groups experimented with dissolving static choral arrangements through massed movements, mime and dance, or combined choruses with drama to produce chorus-plays, but no significant developments resulted. (The Fascists also made use of the chorus to give their open-air mass rallies a stronger 'folk-community' character. Based mainly on myths and religion they were called *Thing-Spiele*, *Thing* being an ancient form of German self-government.)

However, formal elements of the speech chorus are evident in Brecht's *Lehrstücke*, and were used by workers' theatre writers like Friedrich Wolf. In 1929 the Red Megaphone developed Maxim Vallentin's speech chorus *When the Front Lines Wavered* into a collective lecture interspersed with short scenes, retitled *Third International*. And In 1930 the Red Blouse as the performers of *7000* were by then called, used a chorus broken up by songs in their scene montage *Free-thinker Revue*.

But there was another less obvious way in which *7000* influenced the agitprop movement of the future and that was in the carefully worked out context in which it was performed.

Programme of the commemorative meeting on the occasion of laying the foundation stone for the memorial for the victims of the proletarian revolution.

To make an immediate connection between the past, the present and the tasks of the future, the meeting had to start with the historic events of the day. The beginning is indicated by a drum roll. Then with the curtains still closed the string quartet begins the funeral march of the Russian revolutionaries, which is then sung by the mass choir. The curtain is lifted, the background and side walls are covered in black. Stage centre, on a big red base, there is a black coffin, covered by a red flag with hammer and sickle. Grouped around the coffin is the choir with red flags. After the song the choir stays on stage, the curtain remains open. In front of the coffin an actor reads the prologue 'The Grave' by R. Becher. With the last words of the prologue 'Prepare for civil war' a drum roll starts backstage and without a pause the singing of 'Warschawjanka' starts, the audience joining in. After this the curtain is closed behind a Party speaker. The last three paragraphs are read from Karl Liebknecht's final article 'In Spite of Everything'. When the audience joins in the singing of 'Brothers to the Sun, to the Light' the heavy mood of the beginning changes into one of positive commitment, a commitment to fight. The connection between past and present is made. After 7000 . . . the curtain is closed behind the Party speaker who asks the audience to stand up and repeat after him the oath of loyalty to the red flags raised in the audience:

> Hallowed by class hatred and class love,
> We are bound by free will to this vow!
> We believe in the red flag's victory,
> We fight for the dictatorship of the proletariat.

This is followed by the joint singing of 'The Internationale'.

The structuring of the program is all-important. Each part has to relate to every other part. Each contribution . . . must be examined thoroughly, to make sure it meets the requirements of our propaganda. Our cultural events must differ fundamentally from the stammering for liberation of the Social Democratic celebrations . . . Our audience should not only say, 'This was nice', they must be shaken, we must show them the political tasks.[15]

5 · Agitate! A movement evolves

Proletkult Kassel's *Gas War Against Soviet Russia*
It presented the victory of the united front. Not the victory of the
world revolution, not even the final victory of the proletarian
revolution in Germany. The conscious limiting of the subject matter
to a certain period in the great historic struggle between labour and
capitalism is what makes this revue politically significant. For this
reason it was able to present in dramatic form the topical slogans of
the Party!
                    Hessische Arbeiterzeitung (Workers' Press, Hessen, 8 July 1927)

In 1924 a bourgeois democratic republican system was being built in
Germany after the upsets of the revolutionary period. Hand in hand with
this temporary economic stability went the ideology of 'social partnership',
of the 'possibility in a boom period of overcoming class contradictions',
or the 'peaceful transition to socialism'. Propagated by right-wing Social
Democratic and trade union leaders, such notions were aimed at
preventing workers' resistance to exploitation and rearmament, since this
would interrupt the 'growth of prosperity'.

The KPD had to dispel these mystifications by uncovering the real
class contradictions in every important political and economic event. In
the elections of May 1924 the KPD won 3 million more votes than in
1920, while the Social Democrats lost almost 2 million. The attempt to
form a coalition government of Social Democrats and German Nationalists
failed. Parliament was dissolved and another general election set for
December, when currency was expected to be more stable due to support
from the Dawes Plan – the 'rising dollar sun' as it was called at the time.

The leading industrial cartels formed a consortium which donated huge
sums to the campaign funds of the bourgeois parties and the SPD. The
KPD had very few resources for electioneering. It was also at a disadvan-
tage because of its unpopular opposition to the dollars literally flooding
into the country. An illusion of prosperity was created which hid the fact

that control of German banks, industry and communications was falling into the hands of American monopolies. The mass media and cultural activities were dominated by the bourgeoisie. New and inexpensive ways of explaining the complex economic and political dynamic to the voters were needed. Mindful of the success of the speech choruses, the KPD began to explore theatrical means of agitation at a time when important developments were taking place in workers' theatre.

The first revues

Groups like the Steglitz Proletarian Speech and Performance Collective applied themselves increasingly to scenes. This was reflected in a new name. When they joined the German Workers' Theatre League (Deutscher Arbeiter-Theater-Bund) in 1926 they became the Proletarian Stage, Local Branch of DAThB – Central Berlin.

Meanwhile members of the KPD and its youth organizations began presenting satirical programs of short scenes and sketches. One of them, *German National Theatre*, written in September 1924 by unknown authors from Thuringia, was distributed in duplicated form by the Central Committee of the Party. The revue satirized the debate on the Dawes Plan in Parliament with fun-fair characters like the Barker, ironic dialogue, short scenes, and grotesque portrayals of the political opponents of the working class. And Piscator was entrusted by the KPD with a special program for the election campaign.

Piscator's RRR – Red Revel Revue

RRR . . . Red Revel Revue . . . Revolutionary Revue. Not . . . the show form imported from America and Paris. Our revues . . . had their fore-runners in the entertaining evenings I had arranged with the International Workers' Aid. . . . The revue form coincided with the disintegration of the bourgeois dramatic form. The revue has no unified plot and achieves its effect by utilizing every possible theatrical means. It is unchained in its structure and at the same time of incredible naivety in the directness of its presentation.[1]

First performed in November 1924, the revue was repeated thirteen times in various districts of Berlin during the run-up to the December elections. In choosing the revue form Piscator hoped to avoid the temptation to psychologize, and the barrier between stage and audience erected in plays. The extent to which he succeeded is clear from contemporary reviews and eyewitness accounts. The programme began with an overture by the workers' songwriter Edmund Meisel, composer of the original film music for Eisenstein's films *Potemkin* and *October*. (In Meisel Piscator had found 'a musician who understood . . . that music should not only illustrate and provide a background but continue the political line consciously and independently – music as a dramaturgical means.')[2]

When I entered the hall exhilarating music enveloped me: the 'Warschawjanka'! The spectators were packed shoulder to shoulder. Huge red drapes covered the walls and the wings. Next to the stage there was a large screen for slides. Big spotlights and projectors raise our expectations. 'Man, they're really up to something,' 'I hope everything works out all right', I hear a couple saying nearby. Suddenly there is a racket near the entrance. Everyone jumps up. Does somebody want to ruin our evening? But we laugh, realizing that the performance has started – 'from the back'. A worker on short time, let in free, and a wholesale butcher (with monocle, grey top hat and stick) who had to pay five Deutschmarks, enter the hall and approach the stage . . . and comment on each scene in their own slang. First a circus representing the election campaign of the bourgeois parties (in which they praise their election programmes in ridiculous costumes). Then a candidate of the KPD in prison clothes brought in by two policemen and handed over to class justice. (He is sent to jail for agitating for his party.) The fat bourgeois enthusiastically applauds each denial of free speech and the state attorney's demand for conviction. The proletarian interrupts with sarcastic remarks and incites the workers to resist. I notice how those around me grow tense. Pictures of German camps and prisons are projected, accompanied by a Russian funeral march. (Next, worker-gymnasts presented a club-swinging exercise, singing the club song – symbolizing the determination of the proletariat to fight.) This is followed by a cabaret song-sketch: 'The elastic eight-hour day' contrasted with the scene 'Who's to blame?' showing the consequences of 'The elastic eight-hour day' – a serious tram accident (the blame for which according to the scene, should not be attached to the driver, but to the fact that he is overworked).

Then Nanni, the Martian, telegraphs home: 'The Proletarians are mad!' (He reveals that there are creatures on Earth who slave and starve so that others can make money.) And now an operetta scene: a fight between a woman at the sink and her husband – 'What are they fighting about?' a woman near me asks. 'The woman won't let her husband go to the meeting,' answers another. 'Then she is mighty backward, I never complain to my husband, I'd rather go with him,' retorts the first. 'If the KPD would always organize evenings like this one I would always come too.' 'Do you think the political struggle is a theatre?' shouts someone else. 'Ssssh, be quiet!' (The election – a boxing match between the right and centre bourgeois parties and the SPD, in which the Communist, in the mask of Max Hölz (a leading KPD functionary – R.S. and K.M.) finally knocks them out – leads into the election speech of a Party speaker.) During the break in which a slide show with satirical posters and adverts is presented, I notice that well over half the audience are women. Many have brought their children, one is crocheting a cardigan. (After the break comes a cabaret scene from Berlin night life 'Everything's in Pieces'.) The fat one invites the proletarian into a champagne parlour. Gorging, drinking and in the company of half-naked wenches the 'hard-earners' entertain themselves with the help of patriotically inspired 'humorists'. 'You see how these scoundrels live,' I hear from many sides. (When a begging war-cripple is thrown out by the porter the workers storm the bar smashing everything into pieces.) One could see that the audience would have loved to join in. This is followed by struggle on the barricades and martial law. ('Revenge of the Bourgeoisie') Slides of the Noske atrocities are projected. (Noske was the Social Democrat in charge of the bloody suppression of the revolutionary movement of workers' and soldiers' councils in 1919. R.S. and K.M.) Lenin, Liebknecht and Rosa Luxemburg speak (leading into the 'Victory of the Proletariat'). Enthusiasm grows and leads to the singing of 'The Internationale'.[3]

Bourgeois education and art has a tendency to individualize, personalize, psychologize and thus internalize political problems, not to relate them to the overall social reality. In contrast, the *RRR* was meant to demonstrate the relation of events to individuals and to the social framework that gave rise to them and in which these individuals existed.

Thousands undergo this experience, you too. . . . It is typical for this society in which you live, you can't escape it – here is an example and another one! And this with the unscrupulous use of all possibilities: music, songs, acrobatics, on the spot caricatures, sports, projections, films, statistics, scenes, political speeches. . . . We made a montage from old material and wrote some new material. Much of it was thrown together, the text was unpretentious but this very fact allowed us to add topical material at the last moment. . . . Nothing was allowed to remain unclear . . . and, therefore ineffective. . . . The 'political discussion' dominating the factory and the street at the time of the election, had to become a dramatic element. We took recourse to the characters 'Compère' and 'Commère' of the old operetta and transformed them into the 'proletarian' and the 'bourgeois'.[4]

The process of making the subjective, the incidental, the historic moment visible as social phenomena in their historical context, and thus showing them as part of a social dynamic, of the struggle of class forces, became the fundamental principle of what Piscator called in 1927 the 'sociological dramaturgy'. In 1924 this meant in practice an early and unrefined form of montage, intercutting and combining different formal elements in an attempt to represent dramatically a complex and contradictory reality. Piscator and Brecht were later to develop it theoretically and practically into a much more differentiated scene montage, but the new dramaturgical approach had its roots in the revue movement of the early agitprop theatre. For us it is the yardstick by which the artistic achievement of the workers' theatre can be measured.

The Red Revels of the Communist Youth League

'A public meeting of the youth organization' – every functionary knew in advance that would be another flop. One could put up posters en masse – if one could not book a very special event – the young people passed them by, preferring to go to a dance, a cheap cinema or fairground next door. And the public meeting itself? A speaker strained himself in front of a dozen youth for an hour and a half. There might even have been a discussion. And then everybody went his own way.
    Then some comrades had an idea: what the fairground can do, we can do as well. We must try to find lively vivid forms for our political agitation like those found in the fairground: the barker who attracts the masses with his quick-witted remarks, the fun-house, etc. . . . The Red Revels . . . enabled us to approach the most indifferent young people and arouse their interest and enthusiasm.[5]

The first Red Revel of the Communist Youth League of Germany (Kommunistischer Jugendverband Deutschlands – KJVD) was written and performed by its members during the campaign for the Eleventh International Day of Youth. Inspired and assisted by the chairman of the KJVD and by the editor of *Junge Garde* (Young Guard) they evolved a sequence of independent satirical scenes linked by five sketchily developed characters – the Capitalist, the Prussian Junker, the General, the Priest, the State Attorney. The centrepiece of the revue was entitled 'This is the way in which young workers shall be drilled in the Involuntary Labour School.' It satirized the militarist education of youth in the 'Voluntary Labour Service' of the Weimar Republic, which provided cheap labour and strike breakers for the industrialists. The overall theme of the relation between monopolies and bourgeois politics, foreign policy and the threat of imperialist expansion and war was further explored in sketches such as 'March of Our Enemies', 'Racket in Parliament', 'Security Pact', and a scene about factory cells.

The nation-wide campaign for the referendum on compensation for the Hohenzollerns (German monarchs until 1918) and other aristocrats inspired a second Red Revel.

It was the first time that a systematic use was made of artistic means for political agitation on a large scale. . . . Proletarian performance collectives, speech choirs, progressive local groups of the Workers' Theatre League and other amateur players gave unstintingly of their services to the action committees for the referendum. They performed at almost every major event and demonstration, but also at thousands of street or village square meetings, as part of the agitation in housing estates and courtyards. Scenes, 'living images', speech choruses, songs and recitations, but above all revues supported the political speeches and appeals.[6]

Twenty million votes were necessary to win, 14.5 million were cast in favour of the anti-Hohenzollern lobby, 36.4 per cent of those eligible to vote. The police paid tribute to the effectiveness of the revues in the campaign, complaining that:

We cannot overlook the fact that the KPD has found a new form of agitation affecting broad masses and making police surveillance extremely difficult. The officer does not know the text and an unexpected word or phrase can suddenly put him in a situation where he has to decide whether or not the presentation violates the legal code, for instance, the law protecting the republic.[7]

The dramatic material in the Revels was continually being updated, collective writing and improvisation helped compensate for the lack of skilled individual writers. Political and artistic clarity was ensured by the leadership of more experienced members, and a direct link with the Party maintained via the political cadre assigned to the field of agitprop. The leader was responsible for selecting the best and most appropriate ideas produced by the collective. He or she would then 'refine and adjust the individual parts and rehearse the interaction and ensemble playing of the individuals'. By the last performance 'some scenes had changed completely with each comrade trying to improve and to incorporate new ideas.'[8]

We found out that it was not good when the script was ready by the time the rehearsals started, so that each player was just given his part to be learned by heart, and rehearsed. This is an outdated method which would only lead the comrades to perform tricks and empty routines. A pre-condition for a rehearsal is that the players are politically educated.

We call all those together who are prepared to participate, we explain to them the whole sequence of the Revel. Then we select the individual actors and give each of them a short synopsis, like: 'You will do a priest, you act this or that part, look up in the newspapers what the centrist parties' position is on this or that question and develop your part yourself according to our synopsis.' We had great success with this method. It prevents affectation and makes the comrades self-reliant and sure of their tasks. It makes it impossible to forget lines while acting as nobody has to stick strictly to the script. It prevents the formation of so-called 'actors' who in time become estranged from the organization. We have to emphasize again and again that 'artists' are not the best players, but the comrades who came from factory and organizational work and are politically completely up-to-date.[9]

The reliance of the workers' theatre movement on amateur performers was partly due to economic necessity: there was no money to pay salaries. Several important consequences flowed from this fact. Going to work every day meant the actors were familiar with the habits, humour, language and traditions of their working class audience. They also experienced the same problems, which gave them insight into the way their spectators approached the main issues of the day. And the fact that they were recognized as workers allowed them to make agitation and propaganda without coming over as outsiders trying to implant themselves into the working class.

Lack of money (and the need to be mobile) also affected stage design: Much can be achieved with very limited means. For instance, placards with the Fascist insignia accompany the march of our enemies. For international trade union unity we made a big placard with the well-known image 'Our hands clasped, their death', etc. . . . . It is also useful if one has a slide projector. This makes it possible to explain the scene with short headlines.[10]

This flexible and functional approach was applied to the incorporation of speakers, provided willingly by the Party. 'The speech is not made outside the programme but is part of it. . . . It can be split up and related to the various topics shown.'[11]

The success of Piscator's *In Spite of Everything*, a historical revue in twenty-four scenes and film clips performed at the Tenth Congress in July 1925, had already put paid to the arguments of those in the Party who were opposed to proletarian art. (We will be looking more closely at relations between the KPD and the agitprop movement later in this chapter.) With music by Meisel and design by Heartfield, Piscator and his co-producer Gasbarra combined professional and proletarian performers to depict the revolutionary activities of the KPD from 1914 to 1919 through an enormous montage of 'authentic speeches, articles, newspaper clippings, appeals, leaflets, photos and films of the War, the revolution, of historic personalities and scenes'. Piscator's work, which developed his conception of montage much further, provided invaluable models for the young Communists who had taken up the revue form.

The excellent audience figures for the first KJVD Red Revel led the organization's congress in October 1925 to recommend special 'Red Revels for large plants and for agitational work among country youth'. Soon the Party was to make a major effort to develop the existing revue groups into a movement of permanent troupes attached to its own agitprop section.

A new type of troupe – the Red Rockets (Berlin)

We started from a precise definition of our function, a combination
of agitation – in accordance with the tactical tasks of Communists –
and propaganda for the aims of the revolutionary proletariat. The
term 'troupe' was chosen consciously. It came to mean a militant,
extremely flexible and disciplined artistic collective of class fighters.
A new feature of this ensemble was intensive work with the audience.
During the breaks the troupe members went into the audience to
recruit for revolutionary mass organizations, to collect money for
'Red Aid' or to win subscribers for the Party press which was always
hard-pressed because of the bans. We made personal acquaintances
and provided an effective example of mass work. (From an interview
with Maxim Vallentin, leader of the Berlin Red Megaphone)[12]

At the end of 1925 a young actor called Maxim Vallentin was asked to arrange a cultural evening for the Liebknecht-Luxemburg-Lenin commemorations. With a group of young Communists from the Wedding he wrote and produced a collective lecture *When the Front Lines Wavered*. Encouraged by its success, and influenced by reports on the Soviet workers' theatre in the revolutionary German press, a stable Wedding collective was formed. In 1927 it became the first Agitprop Troupe of the KJDV.

The first program of the Troupe was *Alarm – Hamburg – Shanghai*, later published under the title *Hands Off China*. It called for international solidarity with the Chinese revolutionary army and an end to German involvement in the war of intervention led by Britain. Presented at the National Congress of the KJVD in 1927 it stimulated other young Communists to form their own performance collectives.

From 1926 onwards the movement grew steadily. At the end of 1927 the visit of the Russian Blue Blouse engendered so much enthusiasm that a true mass movement on a national scale developed almost spontaneously. By 1930 there were 150 KPD workers' theatre groups. One of the most active was the Berlin Red Rockets.

> Our troupes don't exist primarily to produce 'culture', to find 'new avenues in the theatre arts', our first and foremost task is to explain with our images and scenes, satire and vivid presentation to young people what words alone leave unexplained, to move where speeches fail to move. We must make them warm to our slogans, awaken and develop their class consciousness, their sense of belonging to the oppressed and exploited and their understanding that it is their duty to join our ranks and take part in the struggle. (Red Rockets, from 'How We Began')[13]

Autumn 1927: six unemployed members of the Communist youth organization wanted to improve the Red Press Days, the cultural festival organized by the KPD's main organ *Rote Fahne* (Red Flag) to attract subscribers. Inspired by the Moscow Blue Blouse they created a political revue which was performed in workers' meeting places. With money advanced by the Party they bought props, musical instruments and track suits, so that even their dress made a collective impression. The *Red Flag* sent them on recruitment tours and their extraordinary success turned them into a touring group, the Red Rockets.

In the summer of 1928 the Red Front Fighters' League (Roter Frontkämpferbund – RFB) organized to defend the left against counter-revolutionary and Fascist provocation, took over their sponsorship. They provided them with a truck and the Rockets were soon agitating and recruiting all over Germany. The *Workers' Illustrated* vividly described this new force in 1928.

> They are shopfloor workers and apprentices, using the little time and energy left over from wage-slaving to make theatre after work. They are their own writers, directors, actors, musicians and stagehands. Their art, and it is art, is a new, a growing art. Its roots are not in any particular theatrical school but in the life of an unbeaten rising class. What do they play? Everything that concerns the worker: scenes from his life, his daily needs, the factory and the revolutionary struggle. Our groups are not yet the great proletarian theatre of the future but they are its seeds. They are the vanguard of this theatre in a time of revolutionary transition in which the working class fights the rulers of the old society on all fronts. Therefore, this theatre is a fighting theatre. 'Red Rockets Illuminate the Night' is their group song and it has become a workers' marching song.[14]

The Red Rockets combined the revue form with techniques learned from the Blue Blouse, in particular their extensive use of mime and acrobatics. This physical expressiveness and big props lent visual support to texts which were both concise and specific.

We write and compose the material ourselves. Our repertory consists of thirty-four individual numbers, to which short topical local scenes are added. The troupe can play eighteen instruments, each of us is trained in speech and gymnastics. Some of us are cartoonists and singers and we try constantly to improve the quality of our work.[15]

An evening's programme

Duisburg, August 17, 1928

To the District President of Police, Düsseldorf:

Concerning the anti-war campaign of the Communist Party. As the enclosed programme shows a number of public performances by the Berlin cabaret group the Red Rockets took place during the anti-war campaign of the KPD from 1 August–19 August 1928 and the recruitment week of the RFB. The group consists of six male persons. Throughout, the staging and speeches caricatured sessions of the Imperial and Provincial Diets and the existing social order.

Notes on the individual scenes:

1 The Rocket Song – The entrance march:
   The oppression and exploitation of workers in Germany was juxtaposed in the first verse to the freedom of workers and peasants in the Soviet Union in the second. In the third verse workers and peasants were called on to unite, join 'Lenin's party' and break their chains.

The Red Rockets made several records of their own songs together with some from Russia, accompanied by a small jazz band or piano. The recording company was called *Arbeiter-Kult*, the closest German translation of Proletkult and was founded by the KPD. This shows how the influence of Proletkult persisted into the late twenties.

2 The Stupefaction Crusade of the Salvation Army:
   A group of three people in costume ridiculed the institution of the Salvation Army in songs and sketches, implying that the Army stultifies the masses. Several references to conditions in Berlin were made and the 'salvation' of several characters was mocked.

3 Political Couplets:
   The mock verses referred to: the arms industry, Parliament's consent to the building of battle-ships, and coalition, and other political questions.

4 The Political Musical Clock:
In a self-explanatory image a figure wearing top hat and tails representing Capital manipulated parties and social institutions presented as puppets, stressing their subordination to Capital in short statements. The puppets included: Steel Helmet, Reich's Banner, Swastika-man, the Centre (the clergy), the State Attorney (for the judiciary).

5 The Wonder Horse Called 'The Great Coalition':
A group of three actors showed a horse, the front half covered with a black, white and red flag, the back half with a black, red and gold flag. The horse had to jump a number of hurdles presented by the German nationalistic trainer. This is intended to ridicule the co-operation of the parties of the right with the Weimar coalition at the behest of right-wing capitalism. The first hurdle (a placard with the text 'Consent to the building of battle-ships') was taken with joy by the front legs, the back legs leaping it only after some hesitation and resistance. The second hurdle (a placard reading 'The banning of the Red Front Fighters' League') was taken with ease and enthusiasm. (It represented the co-operation of these parties in the fight against communism.) The third hurdle 'the eight-hour working day' was knocked over. (Supposed to show disregard for the workers' demands.)

The black-white-red flag represented the monarchic and militaristic parties, the black-red-gold the 'democratic' parties. The ban on the RFB was prepared in 1928 and became effective in 1929. As the Red Rockets were sponsored by the RFL they were also affected by the ban.

6 Political Jazz: The staging of songs like 'Gas'.

This song was written by the group in response to the explosion of a poison gas container in Hamburg in 1928. It is a parody of those whose wishful thinking about the new era of peace – in which battle-ships, tanks and bombs are only means to ensure peace – is interrupted by reality, by the explosion. The song ends with an appeal to the listener to join the RFB, to declare war on war. 'Only when the workers control the world will peace be undisturbed.'

7 Nigger Song:
The song was directed against the oppression of colonial people and the enslavement of the working class. It pointed to liberation through unity in the Red Front.

The song juxtaposes dancing 'niggers' who entertain the bourgeoisie with the approval of the press, with the press attack on 'negro atrocities' when the enslaved army of blacks rises up. A revue number itself, like Piscator's *RRR* it was critical of racist bourgeois revue entertainment.

The three soloists blacked their faces and tap-danced to add a visual dimension to the song.

8 Workers' Songs:
   They dealt with the liberation of the workers through the Communist Party.

9 Knock-out – a Boxing Match:
   The judge wore a comical hat, had a huge alarm clock and announced the rules in an ironic speech. Two boxers appeared in the ring, one draped in a black, white, and red flag, the other in a yellow flag. The flags are used to dry their sweat, fan them and to clean their seats.

The yellow flag was a substitute for the national colours black-red-gold, the use of which was forbidden by the Social Democratic police president of Duisburg on the grounds that it was an abuse of the national flag. This was explained during the performance by the leader of the group.

> (In the break between round two and three, the boxer representing the German National Party shouted at his opponent, 'This is being undermined by the Jews, it's rigged!')
> The phases of the fight which looked very violent, were repeated in slow motion. It became obvious that the punches missed their target, that the reactions to the impact of the blows were feigned. Finally, after hurling tirades of political slander at each other the boxers agreed that it would be easier to share the title, the ministerial chair, and fight the workers in a united way. They sang 'Unity, Justice and Freedom'.
>
> This was to caricature the mock fight of the non-communist parties and their eventual fraternization.

10 Songs Ridiculing the Constitution.

11 Pinkerton – an Opera:
   A work spy, boasting of his obedience to Capital and of his hostility to the workers, is exposed by a Red Front Fighter and beaten.

12 Capital and the Press:
   Mocking verses point to the dependence of the bourgeois and Social-Democratic press on Capital. Between each number a speaker from the group encouraged the audience to join the RFB.

> In the interests of the state, the provincial authorities should be instructed to make preparations for the prohibition of the staging of scene 9 of the program. The audience of 500 applauded the misuse of the national flag. The actors have been accused under the law 'In Defence of the Republic'.
>
> Signed
> The President of Police[16]

The police surveillance of agitprop troupes was so thorough that their reports are often the best source for the reconstruction of lost plays. What they neglected, however, was the artistic side of the presentation. The Wonder Horse, for instance, was used to comment on the policies of and contradictions in the coalition government without ever straining the image, and without falling into the temptation of getting laughs at the expense of the scene's political intentions. All the physical features of the Horse were used to depict the different attitudes of the two parties, showing which was more willing to compromise, on which issues they co-operated and on which they disagreed. Using circus training techniques they demonstrated: the Horse's spinelessness – a puzzle for the vets, its militarism – it stands to attention on the command 'Hindenburg' and marches in goose-step when it hears the national anthem, its see-saw politics – it becomes highly unsteady, rocking from front to hind legs, its ability to count politically – the horse puts its hoof down twelve times when counting the eight-hour day, etc.

The same use of biting satire expressed through vaudeville or music hall techniques applied to the 'Boxing Match'. The re-run in slow motion involved the audience in distinguishing the real political blows from the faked ones. Having to judge every move meant that the spectators also had to re-assess their own views of the contending parties.

Neither scene attempted a penetrating analysis and therefore the cabaret style was not overstretched as it would have been if it had been used to dramatize a more differentiated content. The emphasis on the visual made a lasting impact on audiences. Conventional verbal methods of agitation and education had proved insufficient. Language alone was not strong and compressed enough, the images formed by the actors' bodies and by functional props made the scenes easier to understand and more entertaining. (The fact that the group did a lot of street and open-air work also necessitated a visual emphasis. As they were often seen from a distance, but not heard the images had to carry the message.) The effectiveness of visual means is borne out by this letter to the Minister of the Interior from the president of the Berlin police in 1929. A Russian theatre group's visa application was rejected with the following argument:

As the experience of recent years has shown the visual presentation of communist ideas is a strong means of agitation and propaganda for the Communist International. I refer here to groups like the Red Rockets, the Drummers, the Red and Grey Blouses. Therefore, I think it questionable to grant a visa to the group as its undertaking will undoubtedly be less concerned with a presentation of unpolitical art than with a political propaganda activity in the Bolshevist sense.[17]

The revue form can present many issues, show the connections between them and put them into a political framework, providing the audience with an alternative perspective to that given by the establishment media.

However, when applied to a more complex ideological theme like religion as in the 'Stupefaction Crusade of the Salvation Army' its limitations soon become obvious.

The scene took up important questions such as the potential of religion to divert workers from the class struggle, which was regarded as insubordination to a Higher Authority. A worker who is egged on by his workmates to strike 'sees the light', co-operates with management and becomes foreman while the strikers are sacked. Also brought out was the religious presentation of the oppressing classes as the equal of the oppressed, forced to carry their own burden through life, and facing eternal judgment, where injustice would at last be punished; as well as the tendency to equate the struggle for a share of their earthly wealth with envy and greed. A housemaid in an aristocratic household comes to see the petty personal problems of her mistress as the greater burden of the rich. Her envy abated, the maid joins her employer in the distribution of Salvation Army literature. She is then made, quite unrealistically, to call the whole exercise a stupefaction campaign.

The mechanical and crude way in which this sketch related religion and ideology to economics, and the insulting treatment of the 'converted', who were made to speak in bad ungrammatical German, can only have offended the spectator with religious convictions. And the concentration on the profit-making side of religious institutions, symbolized by the Salvation Army's sale of its tracts which was supposedly an indictment of its 'material' interests, also misfired. The Red Rockets themsleves promoted KPD and RFB literature. It wasn't the sale of such literature that should have been contested but its contribution towards bringing about a better life for the working class. There was no real contest of ideas in the scene, the outcome was a foregone conclusion.

The songs were more successful. The group chose a lively popular melody for 'Gas' and parodied it to show how the general talk of defensive rearmament lulled people into a false sense of security. This jolly tune was rhythmically broken by the sounds of shooting every time the words 'deepest peace' were repeated in the chorus. The sugary frills of the melody were used to satirize the militarists' attempts to make the arms industry appear harmless.

The 'Nigger Song' went further in developing a musical structure that would make the spectator stop and think. Again, the song began with a parody on a cheerful tune: the dancing 'Niggers' entertain the Bourgeois with the approval of the press. This was interrupted – 'Halt, stop!' – and a more serious melody and staccato rhythm was used to illustrate the anger of the bourgeoisie when the blacks revolt. A third melody with more drive and fighting character supported the final agitation for unity of black and white workers in overcoming racial hatred as spread by the press and struggling to 'free themselves from slavery.'

This montage of musical forms was enhanced by the gestic singing of the group. Attitudes were projected in the very way the melody was treated, a note lengthened, a tune quoted. The critical juxtaposition of 'popular' music with an alternative musical form helped the spectator question not only the politics thus conveyed but the forms themselves. Rudimentary as it was, this notion of dialectical montage of musical elements which emerged in the workers' theatre movement was to be developed by Eisler and Brecht into a sophisticated cultural weapon.

Behind the scenes

The effectiveness of the Red Rockets can be partly measured by their success in recruitment for the KPD and RFB and the winning of subscribers to the Party publications. According to the group's report in 1928 they gave 184 performances in 100 cities to a total audience of 90,000. At 50 of them they recruited 648 members for the RFB. Twenty-five performances in Berlin-Brandenburg resulted in 42 new recruits for the KPD and 112 subscribers to the *Red Flag*. Fourteen performances in Pommern won 138 subscribers for the *Volkswacht* (People's Guard).

The tours of the Rockets were always planned three months in advance. The schedule was detailed but flexible enough to adjust to the changing political situation. They also attempted to arrange the sequence of their performances in keeping with their overall route.

One month before the performance a member of the group travelled to the district and discussed the details and peculiarities of the venue and publicity with the local KPD or RFB organizer. They also worked out together ways of overcoming police bans on the performances, an everyday problem for these groups and their audiences which was often commented on in the programmes themselves.

Working towards new political aims necessitated not only new theatrical methods but new working and organizational relationships as well. A theatre in which the interests of all the participants (the audience included) is at stake, had to replace the old bourgeois division of labour and power with a collective sharing of responsibilities. This did not rule out leaders, who were answerable not just to the group, but to the movement at large. The agitprop movement saw the group as the collective creator with an artistic, political and moral homogeneity, a new type of ensemble in which beginners were taught to learn and teachers learned how to teach. This collective control and the structural guarantees for the development of each member ensured continuity even during the times of greatest upheaval.

The Red Rockets' success led to police harassment. Their tactics ranged from taking personal details and intercepting correspondence between the group and the local organizations arranging performances, to the cordoning off of halls and a general performance ban covering entire provinces. Here is the answer from the Munich police to the group's application to perform in Bavaria.

Decision: The application for a permit for performances by the Red Rockets is rejected. Reasons: According to the application, the performances of the Red Rockets are in aid of a recruitment and propaganda meeting for the Red Front Fighters' League. This aid is to be in the form of scenes of crude comic character. According to present information the activities of the . . . Red Rockets are aimed at a partly hidden, partly overt mockery of the present Republican state, its institutions and representatives. This applies particularly to the scenes 'Wonder Horse', 'Knock-out', and 'Political Musical Clock'. Item Number 2 of the Program, 'The Salvation', is a mockery of religious beliefs. For reasons of public peace and order the application for this performance had to be rejected.[18]

The group's flexibility, courage, and working class support ensured in most cases that the show went on, sometimes disguised as a club performance, often involving a move to another hall which became a demonstration of performers, audience, and sponsoring organization. However, in 1929 after Bloody May when 200,000 workers were machine-gunned by the police on their May Day march, leaving thirty dead, the RFB and its sister organizations and allied groups were banned, including the Red Rockets.

The Rockets never commented on their difficulties, but the following excerpt from a group report by Left Column from March 1930 indicates the huge problems that had to be tackled by all the troupes. Left Column was formed in 1928 and saw itself as the 'propaganda troupe of the rambling section of the Workers' Sports Association *Fichte*' (Fichte was a progressive nineteenth century philosopher). The group's leader and main writer was Helmuth Damerius, who had already worked with the Red Blouse. Hans Hauska, a pupil of Hanns Eisler, composed their songs and accompanied the troupe on the piano. With the exception of Klering and Hauska the seven troupe members, three of them women, were all unemployed workers. Attached to International Workers' Aid and provided with a truck, they recruited 6000 members for this organization during one four-month tour. Returning from a six-week visit to the Soviet Union in 1931 – a reward for their excellent agitational work – they encountered the general ban on agitprop performances and returned to the USSR. There they worked as specialists in the Moscow combine Dynamo and organized performances for other foreign specialists working in the Soviet Union. Under the name 'German Theatre of Working Youth – Left Column' they continued the fight against Fascism from abroad.

Before we talk about the reasons for our success it is necessary to analyse the conditions under which we develop and the difficulties we are facing. Money? We haven't got that either. Where shall we find the money for the props, damn it? And then – Paul left the group . . . another change of cast. If the members were only more stable, this blasted turnover! And to top it off Hermann had to accept a trade union position and can't come any more – another one less. Praised be punctuality – somebody is late every time! Comrades, we have no rehearsal room and we have so little time. Comrades, with the best will in the world, we can pay you only half the agreed expenses, we made a deficit, the meeting was badly attended. Even comrades with whom we co-operate closely think 'an agitprop troupe only produces theatre, it's not so important.'

We had more than our share of this, but . . . one has to work in order to be able to work. . . . Some weeks we rehearsed six times and on Sunday. One year we had: 118 rehearsals, 86 performances, 33 discussions, 65,000 spectators . . . one ten-day tour for the KJVD through the Ruhr area, one eleven-day tour for the International Workers' Aid through Thuringia.

118 rehearsals are a lot and have made 86 performances possible. But it's not just 118 rehearsals, but thinking 118 times 118 what one can use for propaganda: in the theatre, the cinema, at work, when reading; not just for propaganda, for the group, but using the group . . . for the struggle of our class, for socialism.

You may think we are rather full of ourselves. Yes, this disease too, has claimed some victims. Of course one has to know what one can do but one must not rest on one's laurels . . . this alienates a troupe from the workers. . . . Even when successful we must continue to work . . . not become cocky, maintain discipline and not allow the troupe to become an end in itself – this is the secret, this is the way.[19]

Revolutionary commitment and a collective approach were the driving forces that kept the groups going. The pre-requisite of these qualities was political unity which was provided by their common membership of the KPD. Therefore, political disagreements within the Party struck immediately at the group's lifeline. And the 1920s were a decade of dissent.

Party leaders Brandler and Thalheimer were attacked as right opportunists at the Ninth Congress of the KPD and excluded from the Central

Committee. The left tendency of Ruth Fischer and Maslow took over the leadership but was criticized in 1925 as ultra-left. The Thälmann faction removed them from the Central Committee and took over the Party leadership. But they in turn took a left radical tack at the Eleventh Congress in November 1928 and expelled the 'compromisers' Brandler and Thalheimer from the Party.

The split – Stormtroupe Alarm is born

At the beginning of 1929 the Red Rockets experienced a political rift that reflected these struggles between right and left factions in the Party. After a number of heated discussions the group split. Those characterized as 'Brandlerist' – 'right opportunist compromisers' – continued performing the old programme under the old name. Those in agreement with the majority Party line also continued under the name Red Rockets, but planned a new and more up-to-date programme for the fifth national meeting of the RFB. It was never performed as the group was banned before the meeting, and their van, props and instruments were impounded by the police. The other group, now non-aligned, continued working, but was soon isolated from the revolutionary labour and theatre movement.

In the summer of 1929 the banned group reformed and resumed work under the new name Stormtroupe Alarm until the outbreak of Fascism. The seven men and one woman performed for the KPD and other revolutionary mass organizations, and after mid-1930 they were sponsored by Red Aid.

The police regarded Stormtroupe Alarm as the official descendants of the Red Rockets, and they had to overcome many legal obstacles. Their poem 'We Sound the Alarm' and their 'Fighting Song Against the RFB Ban' are scathing in their defiance of police harassment.

Reviews in the Party press show that the 'new' group was soon well-known and highly regarded.

The new agitprop troupe Alarm has revived the best qualities of the old Red Rockets: freshness, drive, vivacity and spirit, but without the drawbacks of the Rockets. . . . Everything is precise, clear, unequivocal – there are no remnants of political fuzziness and compromise. The eight comrades from Alarm do not only recruit. They provide valuable Marxist education.

and:

The troupe is not satisfied with cheap effects or relying on past achievements. Like the Red Megaphone, Left Column, Red Blouse and Red Rockets – Dresden, the group struggles not only to make our agitation and propaganda on the stage more popular but also to deepen it.[20]

The group's songs became very popular, among them their entrance march 'We are the Stormtroupe Alarm' and 'Proletarian Self-criticism'. The latter was remarkable not just as criticism of the dominant ideology and culture, but as a sharp parody on the way in which they have been absorbed by workers who consider themselves militant socialists when 'boozing in the bar'.

In this song the troupe was following in the footsteps of the Red Megaphone and Left Column. These groups evolved a genre called 'This Way or That Way?' which concentrated on family relationships and juxtaposed correct and incorrect behaviour. They ask: should a husband go alone to a political meeting, leaving his complaining wife to do all the housework, making her hostile to politics, or should he help her at home so that she can come with him: 'Communism and comradeship exist in marriage, too.'[21] Should a Party member who spouts about the need to organize the youth prohibit his daughter's participation in politics and strikes and beat her when she does not obey and insists on going to her factory cell meeting, or should he support her and the apprentices? 'Whether young or old – it's the same struggle, for the movement, for the Party, forwards!'[22]

The first three verses of Stormtroupe Alarm's 'Proletarian Self-criticism' describe aspects of the family life of three workers dominated by petit bourgeois attitudes and culture. There is the father Krause, head of the family and tyrant of the house

with a flat full of knick-knacks – a gold embroidered picture of two angels with the daily blessing inscribed thereon over the conjugal bed, a Venus in the loo, Lenin hanging lonely on the wall amongst nationalist military orders and wedding presents. But in the bar Krause is a Socialist, sweats class struggle, and curses bourgeois rubbish. Usually he eats himself sick, is pious and devout. It's not lip that counts, but practice!

In a similarly satirical style the next verse juxtaposes Lehmann's home life – his wife reading cheap love stories and dreaming of marrying a Baron, Lehmann himself listening to schmaltzy music – with his public bar talk of proletarian culture. The third verse shows how Schulze's daughter is moving up the ladder through her marriage to a civil servant. She hurriedly rejoins the church so she can have a church wedding. Schulze gets drunk at the celebration, bawls 'The Internationale' and beats his wife – an act in marked contrast with his pub speeches about women's rights.

The last verse sums up:

Schulze, Lehmann, Krause – you can see them in your own homes

– you can't win the class struggle with church, schnapps and incense. Fight stultification with proletarian culture. It's not the lip that counts, we want to *live* according to our principles.[23]

While the earlier parody of the Salvation Army misfired badly in the 'Stupefaction Crusade' the group's biting satire was spot-on when attacking the shortcomings within their own movement. Because of the fundamental solidarity between them and their audience the Stormtroupe could afford to ruthlessly explose their comrades' ideological weaknesses to laughter without turning those criticized against the group and revolutionary organizations.

The ending was also more convincing and productive than that of the 'Stupefaction Crusade' since the group's own practice offered a live demonstration of the alternative, and this alternative was an ongoing feature of the revolutionary workers' movement.

The development of the Red Rockets into the Stormtroupe Alarm, with their more differentiated and serious approach to the consciousness of the audience, was indicative of the shift of emphasis from the agitational to the propagandistic in the agitprop movement at large. This will be explored in Chapter 6, 'Propaganda – Coping with the Crisis'.

The KPD: linking politics and culture

The aversion to cultural educational work must be overcome if we want to break the ideological stranglehold of the bourgeoisie and Social Democracy on the working class.

(From 'Guidelines for the Educational Work of the KPD', January 1922)[24]

In the Soviet Union the attitude of most leading Bolsheviks to small-scale workers' theatre ranged from tolerant to antagonistic. In Germany the Party swung from active hostility to wholehearted support which largely explains why the movement blossomed in the late 1920s at the same time as it was withering in the USSR. In the early years however, even Piscator, a loyal Party member, was attacked for his pioneering work with the Proletarian Stage. The *Red Flag* warned:

The League for Proletarian Culture is mistaken in pretending that it is making revolution with its activity . . . the view that the value of art is that it is part of the proletarian struggle for liberation, that it can, in other words, be a substitute for the revolution, for class struggle, is a big mistake.

Having changed 'part of' into 'a substitute for' and grossly distorted the argument, the article came to the logical conclusion that:

> All forces which do not solely and exclusively serve the aim of helping the proletariat gain political power, even when they talk about freedom and brotherly love, do not have a revolutionary but a counter-revolutionary effect . . . every force that is withdrawn from the simple aim – seizure of power by the proletariat – strengthens the counter-revolution.[25]

This blinkered acrimony has to be seen in the context of the cessation of struggle following the unsuccessful November Revolution and the consolidation of the bourgeois democratic republic. The question of how the Party should respond was at the heart of factional conflicts which led to the expulsion of the left Communists who formed the German Communist Workers' Party in the autumn of 1919.

The KPD decided to revise its hostile attitude to the SPD and trade union struggle and thus increase its mass influence. The KAPD was pledged to 'the uncompromising fight against the counter-revolutionary institutions of parliamentarism, trade unions and statutory works councils.'[26] Their strategy was to speed up the revolutionizing of the consciousness of the working masses. They were therefore prepared to make an alliance with radical sections of the artistic intelligentsia. Their programme declared:

> Everything depends on helping the proletariat to the understanding that it only takes one energetic move to make use of the power which it already possesses . . . at the moment in which the objective conditions for the outbreak of the proletarian revolution exist, but the permanent crisis is not brought to a catastrophic escalation, or where this escalation occurs but is not grasped and carried through . . . to its final conclusion, there must be subjective factors at play. . . . The problem of the German revolution is the problem of the self-development of the consciousness of the German proletariat. A decisive factor for the acceleration of the social revolution lies in the revolutionizing of the entire spiritual world of the proletariat. Recognizing this the KAPD supports all revolutionary tendencies of science and the arts whose character is in accord with the spirit of the proletarian revolution.[27]

In contrast to this somewhat uncritical support the KPD regarded the mainly Expressionist progressive artists with suspicion, accusing them of individualism, pacifism and idealism. This judgment is understandable in view of the League for Proletarian Culture's programme: 'The revolutionary worker has recognized that the artist is his comrade, a proletarian like himself. . . . The army of brain workers is the intellectual proletariat.'[28] Like their Russian counterparts the German Proletkultists demanded autonomy. Since they were themselves 'workers' they didn't recognize the need for leadership from the working class and its organizations. The rest of their programme talked only about spiritual freedom and a loving human community but not about the class struggle.

One of the League's founders, Arthur Hollitscher, claimed that 'the education work of the socialist parties aimed too one-sidedly at the objectives of the party, did not engender revolutionary consciousness in the workers, but made them at best into docile party members and future cadres.'[29] There was undoubtedly some truth in this but there was also justification for the KPD's criticism: the League put much more effort into trying to change the stage than to change reality.

However, Piscator's Proletarian Theatre had representatives of revolutionary organizations on its executive. Not only did he and his co-workers consider themselves answerable to the proletariat, but Piscator made explicit references to the critical assimilation of the cultural tradition, unlike most Proletkultists. For him nearly all bourgeois plays expressed the decline of bourgeois society or demonstrated the principles of capitalism. To help the audience recognize them in their historical context, they could be preceded by a lecture.

In these plays the old world can still be found, with which even the least developed will be familiar – and we will find here too that all propaganda must begin to demonstrate the alternative with a criticism of the present. In this way a large part of world literature can be used in the service of the revolutionary proletarian cause, as the whole of world history has been used for the propagation of the concept of class struggle.[30]

This approach should have appealed to the KPD. But at the time the aesthetic theories of Franz Mehring and Clara Zetkin influenced the cultural policies of the Party. Zetkin argued that the proletariat is an emerging class which

cannot take its starting point and models from the art of a historically declining class. . . . Every emerging class takes its artistic models from the apex of the previous development. . . . In spite of our esteem for the artistic impulses and means of expression, with which the contemporary artistic tendencies enrich the artistic heritage, the art of the future will reach beyond them towards the classic art of the bourgeoisie in its search for guidance.[3]

The small fragmentary art forms with which the workers' theatre was experimenting were identified with capitalism's decline.

Gertrud Alexander, a Mehring pupil and the influential drama columnist of *Red Flag*, carried this position to extremes:

One cannot object to the idea of a proletarian theatre and one has to admit that there may be a demand for a proletarian stage, since the

Volksbühne is no real people's stage but a Berlin Theatre like all the others. . . . The programme (of the Proletarian Theatre – R.S. and K.M.) states that the aim is to express the proletarian communist idea on stage in order to make propaganda and have an educative effect, the object is not to enjoy 'Art'. In that case one should not choose the name 'theatre' but call it by its real name 'propaganda'! But the name 'theatre' . . . obliges one to produce art, an artistic achievement. Art is too holy to lend its name to trivial propaganda concoctions. . . . But to produce art always requires the bringing about of the creative personality, which can only be born, not educated. What the workers need today is a powerful art, which opens and liberates the spirit. Such art can also be of bourgeois origin, but it must be art.[32]

This hostile review denying that the Proletarian Theatre had any artistic value, provided ammunition for the Social Democratic police president of Berlin to withdraw the theatre concession in 1921, which contributed to the closure of the Proletarian Theatre. The next *Red Flag* review abruptly replaced this somewhat mystical, abstract notion of art with class struggle: 'these times of acute class struggle make contemplative and enjoyable art impossible. . . . The new art will not be born in the Proletarian Theatre, but in the factories, trade unions and in street battles.'[33]

Fortunately, Piscator and the rest of the nascent agitprop movement were not content with Zetkin's approach of waiting for the 'hammer blow of the social revolution as the liberating action' destroying 'the prison walls of the capitalist order, only beyond which on the island of the blessed in the socialist society, the mature expression of this cultural understanding will be possible.'[34] While he recognized that the proletariat as a class can only achieve its cultural liberation once it 'has constituted itself as the ruling political and economic power' he was not willing to wait for this event.

Until then our stage cannot be anything else but a revolutionary theatre, using its facilities for the ideological liberation of the proletariat, for the propagation of the social upheaval which will resolve the contradiction of the proletariat and with it also the theatre's. We had no illusions about the contradiction of our situation, but we did not regard these contradictions as an excuse, but rather as an obligation to hammer out our ideological line, based on years of practical experience, more clearly and precisely.[35]

Gertrud Alexander's inappropriate attack against Piscator succeeded because of the KPD's desire to win over the mass of USPD members towards a fusion of the two parties. They believed this could be achieved by a clear separation from the left communists of the KAPD, who were more heavily represented in the Proletarian Theatre and on its control commission. This is an example of a party's tactical considerations lending support to an underdeveloped aesthetic theory at the expense of a more revolutionary one.

In contrast to its attitude to the Proletarian Theatre, the KPD's initial criticism of the Volksbühne was, for the most part, careful and supportive so as not to alienate the large USPD membership. Once the KPD – USPD fusion had taken place in December 1920, some of the radical sections of the audience which had supported the Proletarian Theatre swung over to the Volksbühne. This forced the SPD leadership to invite Piscator as guest and later permanent producer in 1924. What was intended as a sop backfired, and Piscator's work radicalized the Volksbühne.

The Party changes tack

The Party's first National Conference on Education was held on the 6–7 August, 1922. It represented the beginning of an organized incorporation of the arts into Communist educational work and cleared the ideological ground for the development of agitprop theatre. For the first time an authoritative body in the Party recommended that its regional organizations give serious consideration and support to the agitprop groups springing up spontaneously all over the country – and regard this as Party work. This fundamental shift was undoubtedly related to the Party's need to extend its influence in the working class after the ebbing of the revolutionary struggle.

There was strong internal opposition which had to be overcome from those who still feared a return to reformist workers' education and regarded cultural work as a deviation from the class struggle. In rejecting all cultural activity they surrendered a sphere of the class struggle to the enemy without resistance. They also over-estimated the spontaneity of revolutionary processes, relying on the 'revolutionary instinct' of the masses, and underestimating the potential of art in helping to transform ideas and feelings into a conscious effort to change reality.

The official Party policy had already been printed in January 1922 in 'Guidelines for the Educational Work of the KPD'.[36] Drafted by a national education committee the pamphlet was the result of wide-ranging discussion in the Party press throughout 1921. It argued that the struggle for economic and political liberation had to be closely linked to a struggle against bourgeois ideology.

In revolutionary times the bourgeoisie doubles its efforts to bring the proletariat under its ideological influence, to confuse and split it with pseudo-socialist theories, with the help of petit-bourgeois democratic and social democratic parties. Schools and churches, science and the arts, the cinema and sport become powerful tools of a systematic and conscious counter-revolutionary propaganda – the more dangerous when operating under the banner of objectivity and neutrality.

In a complete about-face from the Zetkin position the Party now dismissed all attempts to give the proletariat a 'higher education' and link up with the classical bourgeois culture at its height. Such aims would only 'foster a minority labour aristocracy'. Without acknowledging it officially or internally the Party had incorporated the most productive aspects of the Proletkult and continued to do so up to the late 1920s. The goal of the Party's educational work was:

> not just to pass on knowledge to its members but help them to follow economic and political events independently, to view the . . . class struggle . . . in the light of Marxist principles, and to learn from successes, mistakes and defeats in order to translate this newly achieved understanding into revolutionary action.

Based on the working groups, cells, fractions, local and district organizations, three different levels of educational work were to be pursued.

1 The theoretical and practical training of a staff of party officials including editors, propagandists and travelling teachers.

2 Helping the mass membership become acquainted with the principles of Marxism, with the history, strategy, and tactics of the revolutionary labour movement . . . including training in propaganda work . . .

3 The winning of broad masses for the class struggle with popular means of propaganda and artistic presentations.

This new approach was soon expressed in the organization of popular propaganda on a local, district and national level. Each local group of the KPD elected a cadre or, preferably, a commission responsible for education in liaison with the local Party leadership. The tasks of this commission were: the preparation of courses, travelling exhibitions and lectures, organized in co-operation with other Party functionaries and trade union representatives, during which the participants were developed as lecturers and speakers; the creation and administration of a Party library, the sale of communist literature, of revolutionary paintings and post cards; and the organization of propaganda events, like slide shows or revolutionary artistic celebrations. Particular attention was paid to winning over proletarian sports and singing associations, dramatic clubs, freethinker and Proletkult groups, free school societies, Volksbühnen and travelling proletarian theatres.

The direction and control of all this activity was in the hands of the education and propaganda section of the national Party centre, which consisted of a commission and a full-time secretary. It issued instructions not only for the Party's actual educational work, but also for the work in parents' councils, the struggle in the schools and the teachers' movement, for work amongst intellectuals, academics, children, high school and school pupils. Apart from being responsible for Party literature, the commission provided the means for popular propaganda – slides, films, posters – and arranged model programmes for musical and theatrical performances. With its base in the working and study groups, in the cells and cadre meetings, the Party's educational activity reached its organizational peak in the central Party school, the central library and archives.

In relation to the theatre this change of policy had several far-reaching results. The Party's task now was to enter the Volksbühnen and German Workers' Theatre League 'and to strengthen the opposition, which has recognized that productions of the classics help to weaken the class struggle but which has no clear alternative, with a clear revolutionary programme for the theatre.'[37] A broad front policy was worked out embracing the 'declassed' intelligentsia who had aligned themselves to the revolutionary proletariat. The participation of large numbers of writers, artists and theatre professionals helped create new conditions for the development of a socialist theatre.

The Party was also concerned to promote 'self activity and initiative through seminar or study group teaching'[38] which encouraged students to question their educators and think independently. This led the agitprop movement to a collective form of political decision-making and artistic creation, and towards production and performance techniques which enabled the spectator to remain critical.

The 1922 conference ended without having reached full agreement but it laid the basis for a dynamic interaction with the agitprop and workers' theatre movement which was to last ten years. The more intense this interaction was, the greater a threat it became for the establishment. This is borne out by the relentless legal oppression and police persecution of every active individual and agitprop group linked to the KPD. The case of Josef Gärtner was fairly typical.

The accused, a thirty-eight-year old actor, was a member of the KPD at the time of his arrest. As early as March 1919, when he was a member of the Würzburg State Theatre, he participated in the foundation of the Spartacus League, leading the Group of Intellectual Workers. Elected as a representative of the workers' and soldiers' council to the executive committee of the governing council of the town of Würzburg in April 1919, he was court-martialled to one and a half years confinement in a fortress. After his release in 1920 he founded the Proletarian Stage in Nürnberg which was supported almost exclusively by Communists and soon prohibited by the Bavarian government. At the beginning of 1924 he went to Thuringia to produce proletarian cultural evenings. For this he was taken into preventive custody for three weeks. After his release he returned to Bavaria but was expelled in September 1924 because 'all police measures taken over the years to prevent Gärtner's communist agitation had failed to dissuade him from his subversive activities.'[39]

In Stuttgart Gärtner was put in charge of performances for the Communist youth organization. One of them was *7000* produced at a celebration of the seventh anniversary of the Russian Revolution and the anniversary of the KPD in Würtemburg in November 1924. For this he was charged with 'planning high treason'. The fact that Gärtner, having gained his freedom again, founded the Theatre of the Masses in 1926 shows how determined the members of this cultural movement were.

Radicalizing the German Workers' Theatre League

The DAThB began life in 1906 as the Charlottenburg League of Theatre and Entertainment Clubs. In 1913 with 66 clubs and 985 members it was renamed the German Workers' Theatre League. Although militant resolutions were passed at congresses it remained in the hands of a reformist leadership. Groups called 'Lily of the Valley', 'More Light', and 'Teutonia' performed a repertoire ranging from sentimental plays to Schiller's *The Highwaymen* and *Kabale und Liebe*.

Then in 1926 the leader of the agitprop section of the KPD's central committee Dr Duncker called a meeting of the leaders of the left groups. They decided that many of their groups, which had so far boycotted the DAThB, should join it, and they worked out tactics for the upcoming Ninth Congress. They could not prevent the re-election of the right wing Social Democratic chairman Alfred Jahn, a publisher who used the League to expand his firm's market. However, they won a number of important resolutions, the most important of which put the Communist Berlin district in charge of all preparatory work for the Tenth Congress in Berlin.

The Berlin district then held a conference at which the leader of the Proletarian Stage Arthur Pieck was elected as its head. For the first time revolutionary performance groups which had evolved outside the League participated in a DAThB conference. An appeal was made to all progressive artists to join the League. At the Tenth Congress in April 1928 the left opposition managed to isolate the reformist executive and take over the leadership.

Even the most staunchly traditional clubs had been impressed by the brilliance of the Moscow Blue Blouse whose guest tour had stimulated the formation of agitational troupes in most cities. They welcomed the new influx into the League which by 1928 was in numerical decline. And they saw in the imaginative preparations of the Berlin district a new way forward.

For the first time in the history of the DAThB progressive artists, theoreticians of proletarian culture, leading representatives of the labour movement, and working class actors addressed themselves to the League's activity in a concerted way in the Berlin district's publication *Das Arbeiter-theater* (The Workers' Theatre). They also organized an exhibition illustrating the successes and experiences of the Moscow Blue Blouse and a number of German agitprop groups. Piscator exhibited stage models of his productions *Rasputin* and *Flags* and showed for the first time Gropius' designs for his projected Total Theatre. Discussions and lectures by the writers Weinert, Toller, Mühsam, Becher, Lania and Gasbarra, and live performances by the Red Blouse and the Riveters impressed the delegates and contributed to the victory of the left.

Resolutions passed at the Congress were also indicative of the League's left tack: 'As long as we live in a capitalist society, it is our task to fight this "God-given" system of profit, of the army of millions unemployed, of the mass murder of war, of slums, of blackest church reaction.'[40]

Contact with proletarian writers and co-operation with the organizations of the proletariat with common goals were urged, and political topicality, a sharp delineation in content and presentation from the bourgeois stage, and strict discipline emphasized. The less committed membership was gradually radicalized, partly through the provision of agitprop material by the League's new publishing company Workers' Stage and the revival of the journal which had collapsed under the old leadership. Also called *Arbeiter-Bühne* (Workers' Stage) this periodical encouraged theoretical discussion and the exchange of practical experience. And in keeping with the view that the League should be seen as part of an international workers' theatre movement the name was changed to Workers' Theatre League of Germany (Arbeiter-Theater-Bund Deutschlands – (ATBD). In the space of a few years the DAThB was turned from a petit bourgeois workers' theatre association into a tightly organized agitprop arm of the revolutionary movement. It provided the necessary ingredients for the evolution of a more differentiated dramaturgy, and it played a leading role in the foundation of the International Workers' Theatre League in December 1929.

The Communist Youth League

A few months after the DAThB Congress the KJVD organized the first national conference of the leaders of the agitprop troupes in August 1928. Forty-nine members attended representing nine districts, as well as eight Party representatives, one a member of the Central Committee. Mistakes as well as successes were pointed out. Some of the KJVD's best officers had been performing and had neglected other important political work. At some events the performances had been given priority and the political speech relegated to the sidelines. At the same time,

> The agitprop troupes have proved to be the most effective agitational and propagandist means of our organization. They are not a substitute for political work but are a valuable complement to it. The troupes must direct themselves towards the factories and be particularly active in economic struggles and trade union elections. They must be small in number and flexible. They should stand up to any situation and be able to perform under any technical conditions. They should break with the old acting methods. The plays should be topical and uncomplicated. For special big events of a serious character the troupes should be able to change over to speech choruses.[41]

The demand for suitable agitprop material led to the publication of the monthly *Das Rote Sprachrohr* (Red Megaphone) in January 1929. Edited by the agitprop commissions of the KPD and KJVD it contained scenes, plays, songs, speech choruses, poems, essays, and information about troupe activities. It was published with interruptions until January 1933. Next to the *Workers' Stage* it became the most influential organ of the German workers' theatre.

To further centralize and develop their work the conference agreed to form a national commission of five leaders of the most important groups. They were to draft directives on subject matter and activity, and in turn the troupes were to submit reviews, songs, photos, reports to the commission. Local commissions were also to be formed with representatives from the KJVD troupes, the KPD, the Young Spartacus League, the RFB, etc. The establishment of links between the groups was encouraged, and plans laid for a second National Conference and a week-long school for troupe leaders. While emphasizing the importance of their own unification, the troupes were also instructed to join the ATBD, and provide leadership within it so as to prevent a sectarian split between the two organizations. In fact as the League became increasingly radicalized the KJVD began step by step to shift its cultural work onto the ATBD.

The improved organization of the troupes contributed to the astounding growth of the movement demonstrated by this report to the Twelfth Congress of the KPD in May 1929:

The workers' theatre associations can no longer meet the growing demand for performance groups. The Party itself has about 110 to 120 groups spread across the nation, the youth section has 62. The rapid growth can be illustrated most clearly by the example of the youth groups. In 1926 there were two, in 1927 four or five, in 1928, forty-two, and in 1929, sixty-two troupes. In contrast to the workers' theatre associations these are political troupes only, at least 80% of which are Party members. They are directly responsible to the Party, that is, to the district and sub-district committees. At present the central agitprop section is attempting to organize them nationally, a move which has been made absolutely necessary by the increasing importance of their work.[42]

Why only Red Cabaret?

The annual conferences of the KJVD troupes provided a forum for debate which in turn affected the DAThB. The dramatic theories evolved by the representatives of the most advanced groups were not worked out in fine detail, not were they the result of long and thorough study. However, two distinct dramaturgical approaches soon emerged.

The dominant tendency was led by the Berlin Red Rockets and Hamburg Riveters who concentrated solely on revue and satire. The Rockets even attempted to make revue the exclusive form for all groups at the first KJVD Congress.

The Riveters were a group of dockers from the Hamburg Proletarian Stage who formed themselves into an agitprop troupe immediately after a guest performance of the Moscow Blue Blouse. Dressed in dockers' blue cotton trousers and blue and white striped smocks they became famous for their gestic acrobatic performances and their sharp wit. They were reputed to be the German group that came closest to the Moscow Blue Blouse in the brilliance of their technique.

Conscious of the banality of available scripts, most of which had been produced by performers without a literary background, the Riveters demanded that revolutionary proletarian writers begin to fill the gap. They complained, however, that the writers understood the need for 'a clear Marxist-Leninist line' but did not appreciate the difference between writing for a 'professional stage a la Piscator, and for an amateur stage'. Worker-actors 'could never copy what bourgeois actors do just as no bourgeois actor can ever do what they can'. Scenes and sketches had to be three to ten minutes in length and require no more than ten actors, 'otherwise the organizational apparatus would become too clumsy and the high travelling costs would rule out guest performances in other places'.[43]

The Riveters wanted to break once and for all with the complex and cumbersome old forms which made such enormous demands on amateurs. They turned to satire because they believed their audiences, worn out after a day's drudgery, found it easier to follow. They likened their own work to the workers' press which reported the most urgent current events 'in short, clear, crass and unequivocal references'. The result was cartoon types in place of characters, tight, rhythmic language, abandonment of complicated costumes, set, and other equipment and an emphasis on vocal, facial and physical expressiveness – 'tools carried by every worker'.

One important doubt remains to be dispelled: 'Is this muse not too insubstantial? Should we not move and convert the workers with hefty morals proved in sad or impressive plays?' Of course we need to be serious – the bourgeoisie would not dream of propagating its ideology only in operettas and farces, but it has Schiller, Goethe, Hauptmann . . . (although it is undeniable that the workers and large sections of the petit bourgeoisie prefer the operetta, revue, the fairground and the cinema.) So why should we refrain from seriousness? . . . The only question of principle . . . is that concerning the effect of art. . . . Proletarian art is important because of its ability to create, change, undo or strengthen the connection between certain thoughts in the heads of the spectators, *by making them laugh or cry, it's all the same.* Whether you make, for example, the connection between *Hindenburg* and *ridiculous* via a joke, or a murder, has no bearing on the effect of the spectators' decisions.[44]

In his essay 'Virtues out of Necessity in the Workers' Theatre', Paul Signer, a contributor to the Tenth DAThB Congress, provided a theoretical rationale for the use of satire and revue. He argued that workers could be trained in speech and movement but not in the ability to empathize. But since dramatic action consists of clashes between opposites, workers could not just play themselves.

the worker-actor should make the short-coming, the inability to act the bourgeois, into a virtue, by showing him as he sees him . . . a class enemy . . . distorted by class hatred . . . he will consciously create a caricature . . . which will be pathetic or scurrilous . . . and will always have an imminent artistic value apart from the political one.[45]

But it was not only ruling class characters who were presented in a one-dimensional form. There was a general belief that workers just needed to be themselves on stage. Alf Raddatz claimed in another contribution to the Congress: 'We do not need to *act*, we only need to *be* to be effective. . . . We exchange the routine of the professional actor for our spirit and devotion to a cause which is ours.'[46]

A cartoon enemy and a bloodless kitchen sink picture of the worker – those who reacted against the individualistic psychologizing of bourgeois acting went so far in the direction of stylization or non-acting that they refused to consider any other approach. Throughout this period no real attempt was made to develop a dialectical approach capable of portraying contradictory social conditions and behaviour. The need for such a dialectic was recognized by Signer when he dealt with playwriting.

> The many-sidedness of the action necessary to achieve this aim depends not only on dispensing with the classic unities of place, time and action but also with constant characters. . . . But it differs from what is usually called revue today because the individual scenes are not just loosely related to each other by time and place, they are actually contingent on each other because of their content.[47]

But although he realized the lack of skill of the worker-actors was a brake on the complexity of the material, Signer did not make the connection between the quality of the acting and its ability to further or hold back the dialectic of the play. Poor acting was turned into another virtue: the collective character of the production, which further emphasized general rather than individual characteristics of figures portrayed. This was justified according to Raddatz by the historical stage in which the workers' theatre found itself:

> With few exceptions we are not interested anymore in individual experience, we are concerned with the destiny of a class. . . . When the revolution has created the economic condition for a happy life . . . we will come back to the artistic problem of individual experiences.[48]

The limitations of scripts and performers were compounded by the conditions under which the mobile theatre groups had to perform. This put the director of the troupe in a strategic position.

> Today here, tomorrow there, on stages most notable for the fact that their rudimentary equipment does not function. . . . Our directors suffer because they have to achieve a dramatic effect without the use of lights, decor and other scenic tricks. . . . However, whether this is a real shortcoming or not is questionable. For . . . the director has to draw . . . on performance skills, the movement, choreography and general direction of the ensemble. The director becomes . . . the balancing, synchronizing factor within the acting ensemble . . . the collective accord . . . the return to a theatre based exclusively on performance skills depends also on educating the audience to appreciate such a theatre, a task which will not be completed quickly, which has indeed only recently been consciously initiated.[49]

These essays reflected the working principles which prevailed during the agitational period and show up their numerous shortcomings. It was easy to make fun of your enemy, harder to show the danger he represented. The complex relationship between capitalism and the personal problems of workers which often got in the way of their participation in the class struggle could not be demonstrated by cardboard acting. Revue had proved more persuasive than pamphlets or speeches, therefore it was applied to all subjects, no matter what the context or level of consciousness of the audience.

At the First National Congress of the KJVD's agitprop troupes the leader of the Red Rockets, Nuko, distinguished between three types of groups:

1 Those who work too much in the style of old club performances;
2 Those who sweat to learn long speech choruses or plays and are therefore hardly politically active;
3 Those who consistently develop the system of the Red Revels. The first mistake is to be found in the less developed districts. The comrades are not politically independent enough to improvise and portray local and political events in their performances. They fall back on existing material which is usually bad . . . and unsuitable. . . . The second group of performance troupes developed out of the desire to create bigger, technically more complete scenes of an artistically high standard for great events, and . . . led to experimentation and to some fresh and often praiseworthy artistic approaches. But in general such events are not the task of our performance troupes. . . . An example is the Red Megaphone, Berlin. Once a good KJVD troupe, they started to experiment and were soon on the 'big troupe' route. We saw . . . their *Hello, Young Worker*. Some of it is remarkable. But a Leipzig group had more success and generated more enthusiasm with much more primitive means and with less preparation. They performed their scene dozens of times while the Red Megaphone only managed two or three performances. The clumsiness of their large-scale production . . . prevented more frequent performances, particularly at smaller events.[50]

The Red Rockets' attempt to limit dramatic forms to that of revue was not endorsed by the conference which agreed 'to make use of all possibilities in response to the situation and not to prescribe a particular form.'[51]

But in practice the approach of the Red Megaphone was scarcely heeded by the majority. Nevertheless, they did initiate an important and controversial discussion. In a short article entitled 'Prop' Maxim Vallentin, leader of the Red Megaphone recognized the excellent agitational work which had been done but pointed out that the agitprop troupes seemed unaware of the second syllable in their name.

Satire, the best method of agitation is not 100 per cent capable of describing the human condition. . . . To win people over we must be able to move, 'to electrify and shake up' (as the director of *Potemkin*, Eisenstein, says) . . . we must make the spectator ready for our historically justified demands . . . not only for the day to day demands. . . . Beware of one mistake, comrades, the use of the yardstick of agitational work in propaganda work. This leads down a blind alley.[52]

Hello, Young Worker, the Red Megaphone's first attempt to develop forms capable of portraying serious problems, was a combination of inter-related scenes connected by a speech chorus. Although Nuko called it big and clumsy it was only eight pages long. The desperation and suicidal impulses of a young worker were traced back to his deprived working-class childhood, his authoritarian school, his apprenticeship in which his relationship with the boss was akin to that of a slave to his master. Ordered to become a strike-breaker, his refusal led to his sacking, the dole queues, and finally to suicide or the alternatives posed by the mili-tarist, the National Socialist, the church, the Social Democrat, and the KJVD.

The speech chorus was used to comment on the action, make a clear and gripping appeal to the spectators and to draw conclusions, although the ending was left open. The scenes presented a differentiated picture of social processes which the chorus alone could never have managed. The serious problems of youth were approached historically and from different angles, leading to a deeper understanding than the average revue would have done.

Hello, Young Worker had none of the panache, humour and visual interest of the revue. It was serious throughout and mainly verbal, but the alternation of scenes and speech choruses gave it pace and it held the audience's attention. Vallentin said, 'It is the first attempt in this direc-tion. Hopefully, it will be superseded in a year just as the *China Revel* in 1927 was. It is already being discussed.'[53] And it was. The play demonstrated the need for a more thorough and multi-faceted treatment of issues: the revue 'tradition' had to be re-evaluated. This was recognized by G. W. Pijet, who reviewed the play in his essay 'Red Cabaret or Proletarian Drama':

Why only 'Red Cabaret'? In the whole of Berlin there is hardly a group performing a proletarian play. . . . Are three or four cabarets not sufficient? . . . Satire is good, and to finish off one's opponent with satire always shows ideological superiority. *There are, however, and this needs stressing, problems in our struggle where satire can not and never will be a means of propaganda.* Strike breaking, solidarity, the fight against the church (not with ridicule but with the struggle to win over the Catholic proletarian), or the Ruhr struggle in 1920 (its growth and disintegration into apathetic desperation), important problems of civil war. . . . And we should not be satisfied with lampooning and making our enemies look stupid anyway! . . . the proletarian drama will come slowly and to the extent and pace at which the Red Cabaret becomes insufficient.[54]

The attempt of the Red Megaphone to pioneer new methods and counter the neglect of propaganda did not attain the recognition it deserved at the time. There were a number of reasons for this. The guest tour of the Moscow Blue Blouse had given a tremendous boost to the cabaret tendency in the German workers' theatre. Secondly, the revue formula had been an unqualified success and an ideal solution to what the majority of troupes saw as the most urgent needs of the movement. They had been able to disguise or compensate for its weaknesses to an extraordinary degree. In comparison the first propaganda plays appeared feeble.

The revue style guaranteed a clear break with the past, while longer and more differentiated plays which put the emphasis on propaganda necessitated the critical assimilation of dramatic traditions. The agitprop troupes were repeatedly warned of the dangers of falling into the trap of bourgeois culture by their leading thinkers, among them Piscator himself. As there was no clearly worked out revolutionary theory to provide guidelines for the necessary leap forward in writing and acting which the new approach demanded, the fear grew that the workers' theatre might slip back into its early tendency to copy the bourgeois stage.

Then too, there were still whole areas which were 'unexplored' by the workers' theatre. The difficult job of agitation in the countryside, and in industrial sectors with little trade union or political organization, was made easier when the message was put over with the aid of humour. The first propaganda plays were certainly very serious.

But the most important reason for the conservatism of the movement lay in the general political climate. The change to an emphasis on propaganda could not be achieved by a single thrust forward but required the emergence of new political conditions. The demand for higher artistic and ideological standards became more pressing as the class struggle sharpened – at a time of world economic crisis and as the need for more profound propaganda on behalf of a united front against fascism became more urgent.

Audiences were also changing, in both a progressive and reactionary direction. This forced the agitprop movement to reassess its spectators' political awareness and the nature of the theatrical material with which it tried to affect this awareness. At the height of the agitational period recruitment figures alone seemed proof enough of the correctness of the work. (During the KPD election campaign, June 1930, the nineteen Berlin agitprop groups recruited 300 members for the KPD, 120 for the KJVD, 375 for Red Aid, 260 for International Workers' Aid and 66 for the Revolutionary Trade Union Opposition.)

Finally, it must be remembered that the agitprop movement was still very young and had been continuously engaged in hectic activity. Most of its members were workers carrying out what amounted to a full-time job after a day in the factory. This made it extremely difficult for them to step back from the heat of daily direct involvement and evaluate their means in a cool and critical way. The political forces which made this essential evolved between 1929 and 1930 and led to a new stage of the agitprop theatre.

6 · Propaganda – coping with the crisis

Campaign-style agitation must now be complemented with more thorough propaganda. . . . The sympathetic worker must be initiated into the deep-rooted causes of his exploitation, his question about the social connections must be given a serious and comprehensive answer.

('Mass Work – For the Political Mass Strike', *Red Megaphone*, April 1930)

The world crisis in the autumn of 1929 put an end to Germany's shaky economic stability. After the relative lull of the mid-1920s, the class struggle intensified. The impact of the crisis was particularly severe in Germany as she had to foot the bill for massive war reparations and the interest on foreign loans. The Young Plan, named after the American banker Owen Young, became a symbol for the state's attempt to burden working people with these payments, putting them at the mercy of both German and American monopoly capitalism.

In order to cope with the wave of strikes with which the proletariat tried to defend itself against impoverishment the state became more and more repressive. The Social Democratic government passed the Law in Defence of the Republic which paved the way for the erosion of democratic rights and the German constitution and, in the end, for Fascism. It was frequently used against the KPD and its agitprop troupes.

The working class bore the brunt of the crisis. In the winter of 1929 3.5 million people were unemployed and the rate of exploitation increased dramatically through the use of female and child labour, rationalization, organized strike-breaking contingents and factory spies. But at the same time many small and middle peasants, professional people and small entrepreneurs were facing economic ruin. In their desperation they looked for new alternatives.

The conservative, nationalist and Fascist politicians and their parties tried to provide these alternatives. So did the travelling theatre groups of these organizations. In an article entitled 'Don't Forget the Countryside, Comrades!' in the new organ of the ATBD *Arbeiterbühne und Film* (*Workers' Stage and Film*) Kurt Kläber stressed the importance of spreading agitprop work to the rural areas to counter the impact of the reactionary and Fascist groups: 'the Catholic agitational troupes alone worked intensively in 50 to 60 per cent of all German villages, the Nazis and Steel Helmet groups together at least 85 to 90 per cent, not just once a year . . . but several times.'[1] Although as Knellessen scathingly pointed out, 'The "cultural" efforts of the Fascists before their seizure of power demonstrates their tendency towards cheap imitation, lack of fantasy and frighteningly low intellectual level,'[2] they provided easy answers. Sophisticated methods were not needed to blame the Jews, communists, workers, or even International Capital and Bolshevism for the crisis.

But to prove them wrong and demonstrate the common interest of white collar workers, shop-keepers, and intellectuals with manual workers, and the need for unity between town and country, much more was needed. To begin with, the workers' theatre had to go beyond the usual venues. Performances at the meeting of revolutionary organizations for a public which was already politicized or at least sympathetic were not enough. To win over the many religious, indifferent or Social Democratic workers, peasants and the petit bourgeoisie, the agitprop troupes had to go into the countryside, housing estates and to the factories. Their plays had to combat the scapegoat policies of the reactionaries and overcome the divisions such propaganda sowed. The immediate struggle against repression and exploitation had to be linked to the long-term fight for socialism. The crisis made a thorough reassessment of the past hectic years necessary. The Third National Conference of the KJVD Troupes and the Eleventh Congress of the ATBD, held simultaneously in April 1930, provided the forum.

The *Red Megaphone's* 'Critical Review of Submitted Manuscripts' brought out a number of the movement's shortcomings. Not only was there a lack of initiative and danger of stagnation in the formal sphere, but there was a tendency for an agitprop cliché to develop. Forms which had been effective at a particular time and place were being applied uncritically to every new task: 'correct content can have a convincing . . . and thrilling effect only when it is not pressed into an already "proven" form but a new form is evolved from it, when the form does not kill but invigorates the content.'[3]

When the groups attempted to go beyond satire and make their material more factual or educative they ended up endlessly quoting facts and figures, delivering long lectures, or performing verbose and boring scenes. 'In other instances the desire to be entertaining leads to political superficialities.' Such weaknesses were particularly apparent when ideological phenomena like religion or 'press freedom' were dealt with. The *Red Megaphone* recommended that scenes be clearly structured, highlighting a few focal points from a number of different angles. This they recognized necessitated a differentiated and flexible method of analysis: the movement's formal problems stemmed from a mechanistic political approach.

This combination of political and artistic weaknesses was also raised in the main speech at the ATBD Congress by Hans Käbnick, leader of the Riveters. He pointed out the stark contrast between the harsh reality of the day and the performance material of the less politicized groups. Demanding that their material be more specific and aim at concrete results, Käbnick countered the arguments of those who only wanted to entertain, who protested that the ATBD was trying to get them to carry out party politics, those who feared confrontation with the police, or simply found it difficult to change to political cabaret. (Käbnick still stressed agitation rather than propaganda.)

But even some of the groups who were active in this fighting theatre made a number of political mistakes, as the KJVD conference revealed:

> Their factory work was often bad, if they undertook any at all and they neglected their main tasks among young workers, women workers and the masses of farm labourers and small peasants . . . those areas demanding the greatest effort, sacrifice and tenacity, and the most intensive application. The main reason for these mistakes was seen in the insufficient political training of the individual group members which was made particularly difficult by the fact that they were so badly overworked.[4]

While the troupes sometimes overestimated their importance and put their own interests before those of the organization, some of the district functionaries of the KPD's agitprop apparatus still tended to underestimate their potential and did not provide them with the necessary support. The Conference issued an instructive and detailed article 'How to Use an Agitprop Troupe' to rectify this problem. And they concluded that the educators of the spectators had to be educated themselves. Such training could not take place in isolation behind the doors of a Party school but through an ongoing interchange with their audience.

This led to concerted efforts to gather criticism from spectators. The Berlin Red Blouses, for example, collected 'in a short period more than 4,000 comments of workers . . . we learned from their judgments. . . . These critical notes, containing a wealth of suggestions, hints and ideas, are our most treasured possession.'[5]

This self-critical approach did not extend to the Party line which was accepted and propagated without question. This included the policy on Social Fascism, developed by Stalin in 1924, adopted by the Communist International and applied by the KPD in Germany from 1929 onwards.

The Executive Committee of the Communist International listed the crimes of Social Fascism in 1931:

> It sent millions of proletarians to the slaughter under the flag of the 'defence of the fatherland'. It helped 'its' bourgeoisie to carry out the military intervention against the Soviet Union 1918–1920. It saved capitalism from the proletarian revolution immediately after the war (Germany, Austria, Hungary, Italy, Finland). It actively helped the bourgeoisie to stabilize the capitalist economy. It put the working masses under the yoke of capitalist rationalization. Now, in the moment of deepest crisis, it makes every effort to save the capitalist system of exploitation and slavery from its approaching demise. The entire development of Social Democracy, since the War and the establishment of Soviet power, is an uninterrupted evolutionary process towards Fascism.[6]

The Party warned from time to time of the dangers of exaggeration and encouraged its members to differentiate between the 'Social Fascist' leadership of the SPD and its 'honest members at the base'. But since Social Democracy was now seen as the main enemy of the working class which had to be fought before the battle against Fascism could be waged, it became almost impossible for the agitprop movement to forge links with rank and file SPD members. This policy contributed to a weakening of the ideological attack on Fascism, which was growing rapidly, and facilitated its final victory.

But even within the confines of Party policy, the agitprop movement needed more political training if it was to have a sound ideological base for its artistic development. However, most groups were so over-worked they had no time to satisfy any of the growing number of demands made on them by the political situation and their own movement. The workers' theatre appeared to have arrived at an impasse. It was at this point that the Berlin Red Megaphone issued their 'Challenge to a Competition.'

'Into the Factories, to the Masses!'

> Dear Comrades! We hope that you will join us in a revolutionary competition, and we suggest the following conditions: The competition begins on October 15 and ends on December 31. In these six weeks we undertake to carry out at least eight performances at mass meetings, with the help of the Red Factory Councils, immediately after working hours. Costs for transport and travel to be kept to a minimum. All participating troupes should request a detailed report from the organizing body (nature and length of

program, number of spectators, a review by the organizers – as concrete as possible – date, factory and signature), and try to attain productive comments from the workers through skillful questioning. Judges will be a committee consisting of one representative of the feuilleton section of the Red Flag and of the agitprop section of the Berlin-Brandenburg district committee of the KPD and KJVD.[7]

The KJVD and ATBD quickly seized on this ingenious way forward. The KJVD conference included it in its 'Socialist Contract' which was fully endorsed by the ATBD Congress and countersigned by the international ATBD delegates, among them those from Britain, Holland, Czechoslovakia and Japan. The competition was extended by three months to the end of March 1930 and many other competitions were held in various German districts.

As part of their challenge the Red Megaphone came up with an important organizational suggestion. During their tour of the Soviet Union they had come across the shift system operated by the Russian TRAM groups. They decided to introduce it themselves to combat the alienation of their members – whose free time was completely taken up with rehearsals and performances – from the detailed work of the factory cells. Half the group was to be kept out of new productions. They maintained contact with the factories and passed on criticism, requests and suggestions. A second shift of members rehearsed the next programme. After a while the first team would return to performance and the second group replace them in the factory cell. . . . In this way the whole troupe was guaranteed contact with the masses and a concrete thorough political education. 'This is necessary because we think that each of our comrades must be able to substantiate his political views on stage, during a discussion with the audience or anywhere else.'[8]

It is difficult to know how many groups were able to implement this system. It demanded stability within the troupe and continuity of employment, scarce commodities during this time of crisis and red-baiting. However, with the sponsorship of the works committee the groups were able to perform to unorganized workers, apprentices and women at the point of production where class contradictions were starkest and where organizational follow-up was guaranteed by the Party's factory cell.

Supporting the revolutionary factory councils

Friday, a day like any other. Sleepily, one crawls at six to the underground. Everybody reads their papers – *Red Flag*, *Forward*, *The Attack*. Suddenly, a voice rings through the compartment: 'A wage packet has been found!' All heads are lifted. 'Do you know how much a worker earns at Siemens?' '9.80', '10.50', '6.39' are the answers from different directions. Ah, we know these voices! An agitprop troupe at work! 'The wages are to be cut even more! What are the reformist works councils doing? Mielke goes to sleep on the bog – while the red workers' councils are reprimanded! The Revolutionary Trade Union Opposition (Revolutionäre Gewerkschafts-Opposition – RGO – K.M. and R.S.) organizes the struggle!' the speech chorus booms. All of a sudden the whole compartment is alive. A lively discussion begins and is continued at work. Wernerwerk – the train empties. The stream of workers moves to the factory. The speech choir shouts from the platform: 'Forge the Red United Front! Strike against every penny of wage robbery!'

(From an article on Red Wedding in *Der Parteiarbeiter*, (The Party Worker) December 1931)

A wave of elections for new factory councils took place in the period leading up to the middle of 1930. It was an ideal opportunity for the Communist-dominated RGO to contest the Social Democrats' control. The Party's attack on the 'Social Fascist' leadership of the unions had inspired a counter-attack: KPD members were summarily dismissed from union positions. This led to the formation of the Opposition which created a deep split in the movement. Agitprop troupes played a crucial role in support of revolutionary factory councils and the KPD's cells. The Berlin Red Megaphones made the first documented attempt.

One example of many: we are asked by the editorial board of a . . . cell paper to attend a meeting of a factory which was weakly organized. . . . None of the workers wanted to show which side they are on, although most of them are sympathetic to the opposition, otherwise they would not have bothered to come. They are afraid of denunciation, repression and the sack. The . . . workers' council . . . mainly non-Party members with slight Fascist tendencies, come along to interrupt and heckle provocatively . . . hardly anyone dares to object in support of the KPD speaker. Then the council members who are being challenged speak: 'Anyone who does not like it here can go elsewhere; we did not fix the wages! What's the fuss all about?' The meeting hardly reacts. . . . We wait behind the curtain almost bursting with anger. But now our time has come.

First we present our trade union number. The comrade representing the bureaucrat quotes verbatim the impertinent phrases just uttered by the council members at the meeting in the appropriate moments of the scene – you should have been there! The workers –

usually so cautious – break into a veritable storm of applause. All their dubious 'good resolutions' not to give anything away – are gone. They have been taken by surprise.

Now they recognize each other as comrades and no one feels isolated except the council. Class consciousness visibly conquers the workforce, the cell receives important clues for its activity, three workers join the cell paper, two new members join the Party. . . . We often get more political satisfaction from performing to such a small works meeting than from a massive demonstration in Berlin where we do not have any opponents![9]

The production of *Black Plague*, a factory revue performed by print workers in September 1929, inspired the Red Megaphone to demand even closer links between the most active troupes and the cells of the most important works. They suggested that the troupes dramatize events of particular interest for the work force and that the content be provided by the cell committee. If this proved impossible the committee should form a small performance collective itself with the support of the street cells.

By June 1930 an evaluation of KJVD troupes' activity carried out by their journal *Red Megaphone* revealed that of the fifty groups which had completed the questionnaire only thirteen had carried out factory performances. However, one of them had managed forty! The journal recommended:

Each troupe . . . should see to it that a large factory undertakes to become its patron, that it co-operates with this, its factory, intensively and continuously; that it supervises the creative arrangement of mass meetings (including the use of other troupes too, as it will not be possible to perform the same programme to the same works); that it participates in the production and distribution of the cell newspaper; in brief, that it becomes the agitprop functionary of the factory cell![10]

The activity of the Düsseldorf troupe North-West Forward is an example of this systematic approach. The group was formed in the summer of 1930 by the actor Wolfgang Langhoff from the Düsseldorf Schauspielhaus and workers from the large factories in the city.

Three or four months ago the troupe North-west Forward Düsseldorf had been allocated the Phönix works of the United Steel Corporation by the district committee for agitprop work. . . . Phönix, the biggest works in Düsseldorf, had not been handled correctly by the Party street cell responsible.

In 1930 the RGO got the decisive majority in the works council. But . . . in the course of the year 900 workers were sacked or reprimanded. The majority of the Party cell, of the RGO factory group and of their supporters were out on the stones. . . .

First we organized a meeting between the troupe and the comrades from the works. We discussed only the situation in the works (production, the workforce, their political attitudes, the influence of the reformists, the influence of different renegades, etc.) This was done so that the troupe could get a picture of the works, which could then be used in the discussion with the other workers. Then we fixed a work schedule until the election of the works council. We arranged a cell meeting with the troupe each Monday at which the coming week was discussed and tasks were allocated. . . .

The main task of the troupe was: production and distribution of the works newspaper. Until this point it had come out irregularly. The last appeared three months ago and 120 copies were sold. . . . An editorial commission of works – and troupe – members was elected. The articles had to be written by cell members, were overhauled by troupe members who sometimes rewrote them, and provided cartoons and poems. The main emphasis was put on worker-correspondents from the factory. A leaflet announced each issue of the paper. We managed to issue the paper first monthly, then fortnightly, and to increase the number printed to 700. How did we organize the distribution? There are four gates. At each of them an unemployed troupe member was stationed with leaflets and the paper. Our comrades became known by the workers and discussions started with troupe members. In the paper we pointed out that each worker should write an article himself and send it to a troupe member. We received not only articles . . . but also poems.

Of course we organized mass meetings at which the troupe performed and sold Party literature. During the final weeks the activity had to be increased. We incorporated comrades from the street cell and held gate meetings with banners, speech choruses and speeches. Briefly, every possible means of propaganda was used. The result was a 2.5 per cent increase in Communist votes cast in the works council election, the RGO regained the decisive majority in the workers' council, in spite of reprimands and mass sackings. We achieved a tremendous increase in members for the factory cell and the street cell. We will continue to work with both, using all means at our disposal.[11]

The agitprop troupes also helped start chapters of organizations like Red Aid or International Workers' Aid inside the factories. At the same time they performed at the local unemployment offices linking unemployed and employed.

There was, of course, a danger that the troupes would take on so much organizational work that they neglected their dramatic tasks. By 1932 the Twelfth ATBD Congress had recognized this trend. It was not regarded as incorrect to undertake work which was not directly theatrical. But using it as an excuse to avoid coming to grips with the thorny problem of making propaganda was considered a mistake.

> We found that some troupes . . . did extraordinarily good factory work but when looked at more closely . . . it was a substitute for the work of the Party or the RGO . . . instead of a support and complement to it. The consequence . . . would be the self-liquidation of the agitprop troupes as a weapon of the class struggle with particular tasks. The Congress stated that this liquidatory trend is rooted in an unconscious retreat from the difficult tasks facing the agitprop troupes.[12]

The *AGFA Revue* was an attempt to meet these problems head on. First performed at a Red Factory Festival in March 1930, it anticipated the demands made at the KJVD and ATBD congresses for a deepening of the workers' theatre, the move towards the factory, and the overcoming of schematic forms. It broke with the revue cliché, concentrating on one subject. The mainly female cast from the AGFA works presented rounded characters who changed and learned in relation to the events portrayed. The audience was able to learn with them.

The play opens in the canteen during the breakfast break which is only supposed to start when the bell has stopped ringing. It rings for a very long time. With this apparently trivial tactic the women calculate that the firm robs its 1,000 employees of 825 marks annually. They also complain about the foreman's bonus swindle and amorous advances. Their class consciousness is contrasted to that of a reader of the 'Moth Post', a pun on the reactionary *Morgen Post* (Morning Post), who hopes to hook a rich husband with marriage ads.

The second scene in the director's office, juxtaposes the revolutionary opposition to the union bureaucrats of the Factory Workers' League which has been given shares in the company. They begin to identify their interests with those of the autocratic rulers of the chemical concerns. In the third scene on the shop floor the employers' dictatorship in Germany is contrasted with the dictatorship of the proletariat in the Soviet Union through a comparison of the use of technology, the treatment of sick workers and general social conditions. The final scene turns into a mass meeting and according to an eye witness account in *Red Flag* was

> the most effective propaganda for the coming factory council elections. . . . Uniting stage and hall . . . the last scene caused a mighty revolutionary response from the ranks of the workers. This is no play anymore – everybody present is completely involved in the meeting. . . . Hardly ever have we witnessed such a thrilling and forceful performance. . . . It is important that this new kind of revolutionary factory play . . . is developed on the largest scale![13]

The 'Moth Post' reader Paula was included to allow the 'apolitical' spectator to relate to a character who goes through believable changes during the course of the play. (Paula finally joins the revolutionary forces.) The portrayal of real people rather than types also affected the language. Apart from the sloganistic ending, the dialogue was simple and down to earth, based on concrete arguments. Although very verbal and lacking in literary compression, the language was praised by *Red Flag* for its authenticity and its avoidance of literary 'tricks'. The acting too was termed unpretentious and truthful. It appears that in breaking with one-dimensional cartoons the group had fallen back on the other half of the movement's underdeveloped acting theory: 'Actors have to identify with something whilst the workers simply continue living their lives.'[14] This might have been a necessary stage, but it would hardly have brought relief to a dry play with little visual appeal. Still, the relevance of the *AGFA Revue*'s subject, and commitment and enthusiasm of the performers, helped to compensate for these short-comings.

In courtyards and on the countryside

The activity of the agitprop troupes was by no means confined to industry. The first troupe to respond officially to the Berlin Red Megaphone's challenge was Red Wedding who suggested that the competition should include propaganda in housing estates and courtyards. The journal *Red Megaphone* hailed the idea: 'With this artistic propaganda we can approach social strata (housewives and the proletarianized petit bourgeoisie) we cannot reach with Party or works meetings.'[15]

Red Wedding was a group of apprentices, young workers and unemployed youths who were members of the KJVD and the workers' sports club 'Fichte'. The troupe was formed in the Wedding district of Berlin in response to the May Day massacre in 1929 when 13,000 armed police attacked 200,000 demonstrating workers. The Social Democratic police president Zörgiebel authorized the use of airplanes and machine guns against the workers who had erected barricades in the Wedding. Thirty workers were killed. The troupe's entrance march, 'Red Wedding', written by Erich Weinert and composed by Hanns Eisler, is a militant and defiant commemoration of the massacre and became a popular anti-fascist fighting song. It was translated into Russian, English, French, and Yiddish and was secretly sung in concentration camps and by the International Brigade in Spain. Here is an eye witness report of one of the many courtyard performances by the Red Wedding group published in *Red Flag*:

6 Koslinger Street. A large tarmac yard is surrounded on all four

sides by . . . boring walls five stories high. The agitprop troupe
Red Wedding has spread leaflets announcing that it will carry out
agitational activity on estates and in courtyards from August 1 to
September 14. An old lorry is used as a stage and they begin. 'Left,
left, left, left! We are beating the drums!' With loud-speakers placed
at three different windows the Workers' Radio League (A mass
organization with its own magazine *Der Arbeitersender* (Workers'
Transmitter); interested in the technology of radio, members listened
collectively to German programmes from Moscow and attempted to
influence German broadcasting – R.S. and K.M.) transmits red songs
and accompanies the troupe's song. Not one of the hundreds of
windows remains closed. Two hundred workers are crowded into
the yard. 'Great! Bravo! Red Front!' comes from the windows.
'Everybody to the demonstration on August 1!' The whole yard joins
in the chanting. In a few minutes the troupe has collected 10.89
marks. Now to the demonstration. . . . The troupe performs on the
Rodel Hill. Hundreds have come with the demonstration and people
converge from all sides. All those who wanted to snatch a whiff of
fresh air in the park have become part of a Party rally. The entire
area round the hill is packed and people stand on the street as far as
the church. 'Left, left, left, left, in spite of Zörgiebel's police! . . .'
'Everybody to the Winterfeldt Square, every red election aide of the
KPD!' The troupe collects 36 marks in five minutes for the election
fund. Bravo, Red Wedding . . . in the courtyards, in the parks,
wherever the proletarians are . . . keep going.[16]

According to Asja Lacis[17] over 300 courtyard performances in support
of Party candidates took place during the 1930 election campaigns. In
one twenty-five-day period 349 election performances of all types were
given, including 86 in villages and towns, 31 in factories, to a total of
280,000 spectators who contributed 2500 marks towards the election fund.
Groups like Red Wedding became very flexible and had a varied program
to suit every venue including restaurants, cinemas, the underground,
factory gates, demonstrations, outdoor swimming pools, allotment garden
colonies, even a delicatessen.

Only a few groups worked successfully in the countryside however, in
spite of the urgent need to win over or at least neutralize the increasingly
desperate peasantry. Under the pressure of debts and expropriations by
the banks they were easy prey for the Fascist and conservative propaganda
machines. Under the influence of agent provocateurs some committed
individual acts of terror often directed against revolutionary organizations.

The impoverishment of the peasants and their drift towards terror was
the subject of the didactic play *Landed Property* performed in 1929 by the
Red Scythes who agitated mainly in the country. And in 1932 Friedrich

Wolf's Performance Troupe South-West performed his play *Peasant Baetz* which also dealt with terrorism against expropriation, in a last-ditch attempt to woo the peasantry. It was set in Schleswig-Holstein where Fascists led bands of right extremists against Jews and Communists under the slogan 'Peasants, Bureaucrats and Bombs'. It put the plight of the peasants into the overall economic framework of the crisis and juxtaposed socialist solutions to those of the Fascists.

Most of the agitprop troupes consisted of factory workers to whom the mentality and problems of the peasants were quite unfamiliar. Then too, for years the church, the landlords and Fascists had been calling the city workers the peasants' enemy. A number of adjustments and considerable sensitivity were required to approach the country population with convincing revolutionary propaganda. The *Red Megaphone* published an article by Ernst Putz in 1930 which stressed the need for the creation of special sketches which would take into consideration the objective conditions of the peasants and the way these conditions shape their consciousness. It also emphasized the importance of demonstrating with concrete examples that the source of oppression and exploitation was the same for both workers and peasants, and a united front was therefore essential.

The troupe North-West Forward, which had worked so successfully with steel workers in Düsseldorf, attempted to put such ideas into practice with good results:

The Lower Rhine district committee of the Party gave us the task of working in the area left of the Rhine. . . . First we made a plan, deciding in which places we would perform in halls, and where we would perform in squares or in the streets.

In most cases if there were local comrades we arranged for them to receive us and lead us through the village. In every village we went from street to street advertising the performance with speech choirs.

Mostly we performed in the open. After the music we performed speech choruses or songs. This was followed by a speech after which we recruited and sold literature. Sometimes we arranged the performances at the end of mass, in front of the church, or at the fair in the afternoon.

We returned to almost all the villages and towns after two months. Everywhere we noticed that the local groups of the Party had grown by 100 to 300 per cent and more; or that the local groups started by us had developed considerably. At times we had a hard struggle against the influence of the Centre Party. At our first visit to Kevelaer, a place of pilgrimage, we were chased out of the village. When we returned after a few weeks we had a very good indoor meeting and recruited successfully. In Weeze the priest had the alarm bells rung which caused a large crowd and we were able to sell our literature.

In many villages we held rallies with 300 to 400 participants. But the decisive fact is: we made big inroads into the stronghold of the Centre, the revolutionary movement is advancing in this area and cannot be stopped.

Comrades . . . relate to the situation of the peasants, tell them that we want to help them out of their misery and we will win the confidence of the small and middle peasants and be able to organize them.[18]

Police repression

From 1930 onwards the activity of the troupes increased by leaps and bounds. In the nine months from August 1930 to April 1931, the Berlin-based groups alone performed 1400 times, to a total of half a million spectators, recruiting 6,000 members for the proletarian organizations. The Hamburg Riveters won a competition with a burst of activity. (We are not clear if this was the competition initiated by the Red Megaphone since other contests were also held in the agitprop movement.) In eight weeks they collected 255 marks for the Party, recruited 294 members and subscribers for the KPD, KJVD and their press, and 35 for sympathetic organizations. With 33 performances they reached 21,658 spectators.

The German ruling class was seriously worried by these developments. This can be seen from the bourgeois press which reported that troupes of workers were invigorating Communist campaigns with factory performances which demonstrated the 'life of the workers and the proletarian struggle with the most revolutionary realism possible.'[19] An even better gauge of the impact of the agitprop movement's work was the legal measures taken against them.

Although the Weimar Constitution did not provide for theatre censorship the law 'For the Defence of the Republic' and the emergency laws introduced direct censorship by the police from 1930 onwards. Performances were supervised by uniformed officers who could break them up or dissolve them at any moment if they thought the content was subversive and against the interests of the state. In 1931 the Social Democrats passed an additional measure called 'The Law to Fight Political Excesses'. It enabled the police to issue a general ban on agitprop performances, as this excerpt from a sixty-eight page police report indicates:

The KPD strongly supports the agitprop troupes and with good reason. There is hardly any Communist event or meeting held without a performance by an agitprop troupe. One can deduce from statements by prominent leaders of the KPD that the . . . troupes have caused a considerable growth in the numbers of people attending meetings and brought about a substantial increase in Party membership . . . short cabaret scenes, sketches, one-acters, etc. . . . are much more apt to convince the audience of the correctness of communist principles than the most effective speeches. Nothing has such an inciting and stirring effect as . . . these agitprop troupes. . . .

In the interest of the state itself and to protect the public the state must use all its powers against . . . the agitprop troupes. . . . For this purpose the Law to Fight Political Excesses provides an effective measure . . . it is justifiable to assume that the performance of an agitprop troupe will contravene Paragraph I, section 1–4 . . . and to place a pre-emptive ban on the performances. . . . This ban makes the most effective and evil agitational tool of the KPD impossible.[20]

Paradoxically, the repressive measures had the opposite effect, at least for the time being. The troupes began to camouflage their performances, making them less directly political and seeking 'cultural' sponsors. They also increasingly avoided superficial and defamatory representations of their enemies, and therefore had a greater effect on a wider audience! This was acknowledged by the 1931 National Conference of ATBD troupes.

Unwittingly the bourgeoisie corrects our methods of work. The primitive ridicule of representatives of the church and the government – something we have been fighting against for a long time – will now be punished with imprisonment . . . we are not allowed to state explicitly anymore, but we may hint. And it's an old law that one can achieve much greater effects by hinting. . . . The audience understands and has the pleasure of thinking through what was only inferred.[21]

After a few months of internal re-organization, they went on the offensive. Demonstrations were organized against the ban. Representatives of the major factories and 6000 unemployed actors supported a rally organized in Berlin.

But the workers' theatre movement was not content with protest. It attacked police persecution in its very plays. The Berlin Red Blouse for example, explained in their scenes what to do in case of arrest, while North-west Forward demonstrated in its *Drum of the Red Front Fighters' League* how to escape the police bans with wit and the right tactics. Perhaps the troupe which was best at coping with police surveillance was Red Forge.

The Red Forge – taking on the state

Hello, State Power!
At the beginning of the show a member of the group welcomes the audience with the salute 'Ready to fight'. He is interrupted by a pistol shot. A police officer followed by a plain-clothes man . . . calls reinforcements from the middle of the hall. Four policemen burst in with their truncheons ready. . . . They take positions in the four corners of the hall, guarding the exits. On the command 'Fire!' they shoot into the hall. Now the officer asks the plain-clothes man to take a seat. He sits down beside the real plain-clothes man who regularly watched the performance. The audience laughs. After this scene the realistic basis for the performance is established. The audience watches the following scenes with a heightened interest.
(Reconstruction based on police report 'Noteworthy Slogans and Agitational Methods of the KPD', 1930)[22]

The Red Forge was formed by young KJVD workers in November 1927 after a performance of the Blue Blouse in Halle. They wanted to help forge a united anti-fascist front, hence the name. Their entrance march was the Russian fighting song 'We are the Forge', well-known among German workers, which they illustrated with blows from huge wooden hammers. They wore cheap black track suits which could be transformed into simple costumes by adding a few effects. As the district committee of the KJVD Halle-Merseburg was unable to support them, they had to buy all their props and costumes with their own low wages until they had a small group fund.

They performed for the first time in December 1927 and soon became one of the best troupes in Germany. Together with Red Megaphone they won a competition of agitprop groups, organized by the KJVD for the National Day of Youth and the Second National Agitprop Troupe Conference in 1929. As a reward both groups were sent on a guest tour of the Soviet Union, where they took part in the campaigns 'Twelve Years of Victorious Russian Revolution' and 'Ten Years Communist Youth International'. Red Forge gave twenty performances for 20,000 workers and peasants and were praised for their collective and incisive acting which helped bridge language barriers. Upon their return they devised a programme 'in which we showed what thrilled us in Red Russia and what the consequences of this for the German proletariat are.'[23] It was performed thirty times to 14,000 workers.

In the summer of 1930 Red Forge was given patronage by the Communist factory cell of the Leuna works at Merseburg, and the police repression of the troupe increased. Part of I. G. Farben, which later supplied gas for the gas chambers in the concentration camps, the plant was the biggest producer of nitrogen in the world. Twenty-five thousand had once been employed there until rationalization threw thousands onto the streets. The works was known throughout central Germany as the 'Leuna prison' for its subsistence wages and high accident rate. The employers had . . . their own legal department, an arsenal, a force of works police, and an enormous number of company spies. Red shop stewards are sacked en masse, each meeting is shadowed. This is the Leuna works – "our factory" '.[24]

For two months the Red Forge worked closely with the factory cell, working out a schedule and preparing a special Leuna programme.

And then we started . . . in dozens of performances we agitated to the Leuna workers in halls, meetings, the factory housing estates, open spaces in front of the plant – we encouraged them with our plays to join the struggle. In the beginning the spectators were few, but then the audiences grew and grew. . . . More than once we had to escape police raids but our plays had made an impact. The mere mention in a leaflet of the participation of the Red Forge caused the utmost interest within the works. Discussions were held everywhere. We finished our propaganda for the elections of the Imperial Diet with a mass rally in the market of Merseburg. During the lunch break an aeroplane dropped thousands of leaflets over the Leuna works. This caused a real stir. Four thousand workers met in the canteen: 'The Communists are great!' Everybody was bursting with enthusiasm, with the exception of the management. The rally in the evening was one of the most important demonstrations by the Leuna proletariat. Thousands of ears rang with our speech choruses. The police wanted to intervene but a triple ring of two thousand workers protected our performance. An hour later our lorry raced undisturbed to Halle whilst a massive torchlight demonstration shook the streets of Merseburg. Leuna is awakening, the RGO advances! In spite of a ruling class judiciary, a police state system, and terror the Leuna works are a red fortress![25]

Although there were no Leuna workers in the Red Forge the group was able to produce a montage of speech chorus elements, dialogue and narration which revealed a detailed knowledge of conditions inside the factory. This was made possible by their close interaction with the factory cell, and the revolutionary trade union opposition. Ideas were also taken from the press, both left and right wing. This raw material was collectively transformed into scenes, either by several members working together, or an individual producing a plan and submitting it to the others for improvement. The pre-requisite for this approach was that all members were politically trained and up-to-date. Eventually almost every troupe member was involved in some way in the writing process in keeping with the group's principle that it was wrong to breed specialists. A wealth of ideas was produced, if they could not be immediately used they were often incorporated in a later programme. Their scenes were quickly produced and relied heavily on topicality and witty improvisations. Serious scenes posed more difficulties as these depended more on language, and the crudeness and lack of compression of the texts could not be disguised by a strong visual presentation.

The Leuna Program usually began with 'Hello, State Power!' which the police claimed endangered public safety and order since it was deemed likely to incite the spectators against them! According to Arthur Pieck, they retaliated with 'three confiscations (slides and police helmets), the breaking up of the performance, one trial (seventy Deutschmark fine), one arrest, three trials pending.'[26]

It was followed by several scenes contrasting the conditions of workers in Germany with those in the Soviet Union. Then came 'Leuna!' the centrepiece of the program, written in rhythmic, concise rhymes. A short choral introduction described the 'hell in the Leuna workhouse'. This was followed by three short sections separated by the unrolling of banners and the clash of cymbals. The first showed the Social Democratic chairman of the works council agreeing to the sacking of Communist militants with the 'Leuna King'. The second depicted with its escalating rhythm the speed-up and rationalization which had led to 7,500 redundancies and 1,000 accidents a year, 30 fatal.

The third section appealed to the Leuna workers not to allow the products of their labour to be used for military ends against the Soviet Union. The nitrogen, nitric acid and phosgene gas they manufactured could easily be used for the wholesale production of explosives and poison gas in case of an imperialist war of intervention against the Soviet Union. This is the only documented play from this era in which workers were asked to fight for the right to determine what they produce, and for which purpose, a demand that points towards production for use and not for profit. The final chorus drew this conclusion and called for a mass strike to end the Leuna workers' servitude.

The very success of the Leuna actors led to their being so overworked that they even lacked the time to update their material. This was a problem which for them lay at the heart of the 'programme crisis' in the workers' theatre. In spite of police repression they performed three to five times a week. Their report 'A first-class touring month', states that they performed nine times one March in six different cities for a total of 2,680 spectators, made 47 KPD recruits, and won 54 subscribers for the *Workers' Illustrated Paper*. The individual audiences ranged in number from 80 to 1,000.

Gradually, however, the agitprop movement was beginning to develop less sloganistic and stereotyped programmes with which it could approach the less politicized sections of society, programmes which related specifically to their situation and their state of consciousness. Although the revue or cabaret sketches still predominated, more and more scenes were being written which placed equal emphasis on agitation and propaganda. Tentative attempts were made to evolve dramatic structures capable of unravelling the complexities of political life, the world economic crisis and its effects on individuals. From 1929 to 1931 the movement tried to branch out and to affect the widest possible audience in an effort to build the united front. In the years from 1931 to 1933 the requisite theatrical tools were forged – the scene and song montage resulted.

The Red Megaphone and montage

The scene montage . . . transforms the stage into a living dialectical interplay of social relations and contradictions. . . . It demonstrates the antagonistic nature of two worlds, the socialist and the capitalist.
(Review of the Red Megaphone's *For Soviet Power*, October 1930)[27]

As the German economic and political crisis deepened, the necessity for convincing alternatives became more pressing. The grim statistics were outlined at the ATBD's National Troupe Conference in 1931.

Five million unemployed, three million on short time, 2.6 million impoverished farm labourers . . . 10.5 million families who are condemned to starvation . . . every day 18,000 workers are sacked and 3,000 have their unemployment benefit stopped . . . and twenty are forced into suicide. Every day Mr. Krupp earns 43,000 marks. This is the 'People's Republic'. In 1930 69 workers were murdered by the police and Fascists, 5,200 injured, 1400 jailed. In January of 1931 alone 19 workers were murdered. . . . This is the 'Road to Socialism'. Welfare expenditure has been cut by 2.5 billion in the past two years, the workers' income was reduced by 6 to 7½ billion last year. 12 to 14 billions escaped taxation through the export of capital in one year. Siemens pays 14 per cent dividends as before. This is 'Patriotism'. More is spent for the maintenance of a police dog than for that of an unemployed person.[28]

The agitprop movement had to show people the connection between their impoverishment and the profit-motivated economy, between Fascism and war and the media which moulded public opinion. And they tried to point to an alternative: the USSR.

To win over those thinking differently, we must respond to their world of ideas: the 'strong man', the 'German people', 'colonies', 'Jews', 'the great and the small', the 'career' of the clerk, the 'existence' of the small shop-owner or trader, the fear of 'expropriation' of the already expropriated middle class, the 'tradition' of the bourgeois newspaper reader, the peasants' hatred of the 'city', the 'spiritual weapons', the 'freedom of thought' of the intellectual, the hope for 'recovery' of the Social Democrat's party, his vague notions of unity of the proletariat, the 'Moscow Gold', the standard argument of all counter-revolutionaries. We must show up the untenability of these concepts so that they will find no place in any brain anymore.[29]

The workers' theatre had to take stock to see if it was up to fulfilling this battery of tasks. The crisis had taken its toll of the movement too. Income raised at meetings had been reduced, more and more members were unemployed themselves while those who did work were exhausted by the ever more intense exploitation. Economic hardship was accompanied by a severe repertory crisis which expressed itself in the emergence of rigid clichés and political superficiality. These short-comings were traced back to a lack of Marxist-Leninist training and organizational bonds with factories, outmoded working methods and the inability to keep up with the revolutionary movement.

To remedy these weaknesses the system of patronage was extended and the ATBD ran one and two week training courses for its members and instructors. Participants studied the theory and technique of workers' theatre as well as political economy, historical materialism, the history of the workers' movement, its revolutionary strategy and tactics, ideology and Marxist aesthetics and the Five Year Plan. A lot of attention was paid to an exchange of experiences between the collectives, concentrating on subject matter and the principles of a division of labour.

The turn towards Marxist education and the attempt to make their scenes more 'scientific' had its own short-term problems.

Some troupes . . . perform Marxist formulae in as boring a way as a pupil repeats a drilled lesson. But . . . the dead letter, the drilled formula is not only the worst enemy of any vivid scenic effectiveness but also an enemy of Marxism, a living world view. . . . We must spurn the dry didactic play, void of life and feelings![30]

It was the Berlin Red Megaphone who showed how to overcome this weakness. One of its members, Elli Schliesser, analysed the development of the movement in an essay entitled 'Looking Back and Looking Forward'[31] at the ATBD's National Troupe Conference in 1931. Her critique became a definitive working guide for the troupes in general and the Red Megaphone in particular.

Looking back and looking forward

In the early years, she reminded the conference, the majority of texts were produced by writers at a desk with little practical knowledge of the daily work of the troupes and the strengths and limitations of their members. The plays which resulted were long-winded and bombastic, and not always topical, the characters spoke a paper language. The necessity for flexibility demanded by the struggle and the growth in numbers and quality of the troupes meant that the writers either had to leave their desks and immerse themselves in the troupes, or literary skills had to be developed by the group members themselves. The collective production of texts and the conditions of the struggle favoured satire and cabaret. ' "Ridicule is deadly," it was thought – and that was correct – but this was taken further and still believed: "Ridicule alone is deadly – ridicule achieves everything!", and that was wrong!'

The seriousness of the situation demanded a stronger emphasis on propaganda. In answer the Berlin Red Megaphone produced its collective lecture *Ten Years Comintern* which generated an electric atmosphere in its audiences and stimulated an 'exuberant' and yet serious and systematic development among the troupes. 'Unfortunately, most troupes saw it as a ready-made form; every political task that could not be handled by means of satire was pulled over this newly-found boot last.' The essence of the new form was not understood: the dispassionate language of the speaker could be alternated with the 'passionate intensity of somebody who is right in the situation', the framework of the lecture could be broken up by lightning scenes. But these scenic germs were not developed further, they too rigidified.

A kind of 'dualism' came about: the belief that one worked either with vivid scenic means . . . but politically superficial – or in a politically serious way, but then in a deadly, dry and boring way. Whilst in theory a separation of agit and prop was considered impossible, this separation was happily carried out in practice: recruitment without education and education without appeal, this was the direction in which the cliché would have led.

Again, the Berlin Red Megaphone broke the cliché with its programme *For Soviet Power* which pointed the way towards the dialectical play. Schliesser then warned her comrades to be careful that the movement's pragmatism, which had so far been understandable because of insufficient experience, did not hinder the vital process of theoretical clarification.

And here we arrive at the most essential shortcoming of our working method so far. We have shown: the Capitalist (mostly with a big belly and a money bag), the (party) Official, the Law – abstractions, concepts which, even in our heads, were not the starting point of a thought process but the final result. We did not represent our thought process on stage – thus developing the concept in the spectator in the same way . . . we threw . . . fixed concepts at his head . . . we can't just declare these forms wrong – as they were a necessary stage of development. They only become wrong when the causes leading to their coming about disappear and the old forms remain out of tradition and laziness. We must look for forms which enable us to make the relations of class forces visible. . . . Away from the cliché, but not back to the 'Old Theatre', the 'Naturalistic Drama', forward to the dialectical play!

The innovators

The revue *Hands Off China*, with which the First Agitprop Troupe helped trigger off the German agitprop movement in 1927, departed from the usual revues by concentrating on one subject only. The policies of the imperialist nations and the liberation struggle they were meant to defeat were illuminated from different angles in a curtain-raiser and five short, poignant scenes. This 'agitational play' as it was called, retained the punchy satirical quality of the revue but was more coherent and gave a deeper insight than the popular 'Revels'.

Again they were the first to provide an alternative to the satirical revue with the serious *Hello Young Worker* in 1928. This play, also focussing on a central theme, made technical demands which highlighted the group's artistic shortcomings. To overcome amateurishness in movement and speech technique the group participated in an intensive training programme from June to November 1928. Ideological, acting and organizational questions were all included. In an interview given in 1969 Maxim Vallentin remembered:

> We took the topical political message as the sole reference point . . .
> and we expressed our arguments in everyday German that was
> incisive and mobilizing, in the language of our working class, not in
> a naturalistic dialect, but in a clear and gestural way; the words were
> meaningfully articulated with realistic commitment and disciplined
> élan, strictly in accordance with the content.[32]

In the spring of 1929 the Red Megaphone presented their first collective lecture *Third International*, also called *Ten Years of Comintern*. Substantial sections of Vallentin's speech chorus *When the Front Lines Wavered* were interspersed with scenes concretizing and illuminating the central theme, a juxtaposition of revolutionary struggles with the opportunism of the Second International. The chorus was further loosened by the recurring 'Song of the Comintern', composed by Hanns Eisler, who worked with the

Red Megaphone for two years. During this time he developed a unique song style which led to an increasing use of song by the workers' theatre and in particular by the Red Megaphone who later wrote song-plays.

The Red Megaphone saw the evolution of the new form as the result of a change in the function of theatre. Eisler expressed this idea clearly in relation to music:

> History teaches us that every new style in music does not derive from a new aesthetic standpoint and does not therefore represent a revolution in the artistic material; the change in the material is inevitably caused by a historically necessary change in the function of music in society in general.[33]

Because they were aware that these changes in the function of art were an expression of ideology, the Red Megaphone made it their job to criticize bourgeois ideology as they saw it presented in mass media and in the opera, theatre, church and state institutions.

The only traditional revue sketches the Red Megaphone ever produced were criticized for their flippant and superficial parody of political opponents which led the spectator to dismiss them laughingly without recognizing their menace. The group took heed of this. Without abandoning the weapon of satire they presented a historical kaleidoscope of German mythology and contemporary political figures in the style of a fairground which was thought-provoking as well as amusing. It was entitled *The World of Wonders of the German Philistine*.[34]

Four wax figures were transformed as they walked in waltz time round the stage, responding to the commands of a 'quick change artist' representing the coalition government. The 'Wagner-Siegfried', blonde hero and fighter par excellence, became the cabinet minister Scheidemann, 'defending the interests of the monarch', and then the police president Zörgiebel, responsible for the Bloody May in *Berlin-Wedding*: 'May has come, bring out the Saracens.'

Gretchen from *Doctor Faust* was 'the blonde ideal of the German virgin, with woollen stockings, braids and a swastika – but she's forced to have an abortion.' She turned into the Social Democratic Bohemian rambler, marching for peace, playing the guitar and 'hoping to change the world with romantic songs.' The Wandervogel was then transformed into a Social Democratic city councillor who accuses working-class families on the radio of neglecting their children, argues for more authoritarian education, and accepts bribes.

The Pope was portrayed as a conjurer who turns a sheep bone, 'already gnawed by the dogs', into a holy bone from St Anton of Padua and then into one and a half million gold marks – donated by pilgrims to the sacred relic. He becomes a liberal and then a Social Democratic priest, praying for the status quo.

The fourth and final figure was Friedericus Rex, the German Kaiser, enjoying his millions in compensation and annual income granted him by the republic. He changes into the President of the Reich Ebert, another 'fat Fritz' saving the fatherland from Bolshevism, and then General Field Marshall Hindenburg who guarantees the future of Germany through imperialist expansion and the building of battleships.

These different permutations were commented on by the whole troupe in rhythmic jazz rhymes, while the characters themselves spoke in both rhyme and prose. Their speeches were linked by the barker and by the troupe's repetition of the statement: 'The German Public is cheated and betrayed.' At the end the chorus ask why the German public is so gullible. The answer was given in a song describing how after a long day's labour the workers' leisure time is filled with the establishment radio, film, press and sport, his questions answered in a way that will make him accept the inevitability of yet another imperialist war against the Soviet Union.

This was contrasted with a final speech chorus agitating the IfA (Interessensgemeinschaft fur Arbeiterkultur), the umbrella organization for all forms of workers' culture. (The IfA was founded in October 1929 and lasted until Hitler's take over.) 'Revolutionary workers and artists' were 'committed to overcome the remains of bourgeois mis-education, to fight relentlessly against kitsch and trash, within their own ranks too.'

(The Red Megaphone were in fact not alone in attempting to counter the effect of bourgeois media. Left Column produced a sketch called 'Film' in late 1929 which parodied the cheap romances, eroticism, detective stories and crime, nationalism, militarism, and sentimental portrayals of poverty and stardom churned out by the movie makers. The promotion of such motion pictures was juxtaposed to the censorship of progressive films: 'Our answer to trash and censorship – People's Film Association'.[36] Written by Damerius and composed by the Eisler pupil Hans Hauska – who later worked with Brecht at the Berliner Ensemble – it combined mime, music and text in a kind of Moritat which linked up with the tradition of living images used before World War I and later in the mass spectacles and speech choruses following the November Revolution.)

In August 1929 the Red Megaphone toured the Soviet Union for five weeks with the Red Forge, co-winners of the KJVD competition. They prepared an anti-imperialist war programme which they performed twenty-six times in ten cities. They also gave eighteen lectures, visited factories, agricultural co-operatives and universities. Everywhere they went they talked about the struggles of German workers and met with representatives of Russian workers' theatre groups with whom they found they were in principled agreement in spite of differences in conditions and tasks.

The Russian worker audiences, used as they were to the Blue Blouse and TRAM, received them enthusiastically. Their dress and props must have struck a familiar chord. The Red Megaphone wore 'dark blue boiler suits without visible buttons, pockets, or collars so that they could be turned into different costumes with just a few additions such as belts, military decorations, etc.'[36] Their costumes and props for a ninety-minute show were so minimal they could pack them into one suitcase, a hat box and a cloth cover. That left the members at least one hand free for the megaphone.

This tour strongly influenced the Red Megaphone and through them the German movement. In addition to the organizational suggestions they brought back with them it led to the celebrated scene montage *For Soviet Power* which they kept in their repertoire until their dissolution in 1933.

For Soviet Power

One evening there was a wall newspaper in our rehearsal room, covered with the colourful front pages of pamphlets on the Five Year Plan and the Young Plan, published by the International Workers' Publishing Company. A hefty arrow pointed to the heading: 'Every comrade must have read these pamphlets for our USSR programme.' We organized revolutionary competitions committing ourselves to the reading of certain pamphlets by a certain time. After one week the first suggestions for scenes and ideas for the plot had already appeared on the wall newspaper. A plot commission was created to work on these ideas and produce new proposals.

(Report by Elli Schliesser, January 1931)

The troupe's own experiences as well as written material were incorporated in the course of a number of group discussions which resulted in a skeletal plot. The programme began with an entrée announcing the revolutionary contract made with Leningrad TRAM which had led to the making of this scene montage. A short historical survey followed since the group maintained that socialist construction could only be understood in the context of the wars the USSR had had to fight. This review was interrupted at the point when economic chaos had been overcome and reconstruction begun. The audience was brought back to contemporary Germany and asked to choose between poverty and class struggle. The Russian workers and peasants had chosen the path of revolution in 1917, this was the link to an episode describing 'the Five Year Plan . . . the struggle for proletarian work discipline, the competition of shock brigades and collectivization, the roar of columns of tractors, burying beneath them the last remnants of the bourgeois class.'

The second part compared the lives of Soviet citizens with those of German workers, showing the effects of proletarian dictatorship and the

Five Year Plan on maternity provision and abortion, nurseries, schools, apprenticeships, and working conditions. The chauvinistic demagogery of the National Socialists was contrasted with the liberation of 112 nations of the Soviet Union.

The third section depicted the crisis of capitalism and the crusade against the USSR and predicted that the white mercenaries would be 'trapped between the front of the Red Army and the front of the international revolutionary proletariat which is ready for the defence of its only fatherland'. The audience then joined in the oath 'We give our blood for Soviet Power!'

Schliesser went on to described how the skeleton became flesh and blood with the use of a typical example, the 'Slacker Scene'.

When we visited Soviet factories the Russian comrades often told us: 'One of the greatest difficulties we have to overcome is the making of disciplined worker-cadres from the peasant masses streaming into the cities.'. . . . An evening's discussion led to political clarity on the scene and defined the material that had to be worked into it. (We learned from the pamphlets mentioned above, that in many Soviet factories an undisciplined worker was cured by his workmates, who made fun of him by erecting a puppet, which looked very much like him, and once he had been taken down a peg or two, they discussed the problem with him.) . . . We began to improvise next evening – a new experiment that bore surprisingly good fruit. An extraordinarily humorous and hard-hitting text resulted, taken down in shorthand by a woman comrade . . . but . . . it had too many weaknesses to be the final script. We incorporated a comrade who has the ability to arrange the words so that they rhyme at the end of the lines. We gave him the text . . . and the melody to which we wanted it to be set. Next day we got the text back in verse form. During rehearsals ambiguities and shortcomings showed up and . . . we had to rewrite whilst rehearsing. A word about the production of our songs: in parts one and two we used exclusively Russian melodies; the three melodies of the third part were composed by us – don't misunderstand, *not* by a troupe composer, but by us, collectively. We surrounded the piano and spoke the text of a song until each of us could sense something of a melody in it. . . . The suggestion of each individual was tried out in all its permutations – and after two and a half hours we had a melody of which we were extremely proud as it was 'flesh of our flesh'. . . . The entire one-and-a-half-hour long program was produced in this way. . . . We aimed at a higher degree of collective work among the troupes than had been practised until now. Because we allowed the public access to our rehearsals we had comrades from other troupes at almost every rehearsal, and non-actors too. We profited enormously from this co-operation – we received constructive criticism and suggestions for improvement – so that one could almost say: *Our USSR program is a collective production of the First District of the ATBD.*

For Soviet Power was presented as a model for the movement at the national troupe conference in 1931 and the Twelfth Congress of the ATBD. The left press was unanimous in its praise especially of the use of montage. It was also recognized that this new approach to structure was no coincidence: 'The immense complex of issues simply split asunder the framework used so far.'[38] The 'Pioneers of proletarian theatre' as the *Red Flag* (October 31, 1930) dubbed the Red Megaphone intercut narration, collective speaking, scenes, songs, mime, dance, sound effects and bold headlines projected with the aid of megaphones. These elements were no longer interchangeable and independent or only loosely connected, they were very much related to each other, dealing with one subject at a time from different angles but always with reference to the central aim of juxtaposing historical and social conditions in the USSR and Germany.

The collective lectures were used in a similar way to film and slides in the epic theatre, providing a documentary complement for a particular event or development. Even these sections, the longest in the programme, were interrupted by mimed visualizations at particular points.

ALL: 1930 . . .

> The Young Plan makes us free –
> Free? Of whom?
> Mr von Börsig stated years ago:
> 'We have 50,000 Germans too many!'
> Today Minister Bredt says:
> 'We could be the richest nation on earth
> if 20 million Germans could disappear overnight.'
> And the *Börsenzeitung* (stock exchange paper) thinks:
> 'One should make short shrift after all
> And shoot 100 ringleaders!'
> The Young Plan makes us free!
> Free are you, proletarian, freely you can choose.
> If you are a charge hand
> A foreman,
> A works council member,
> Then you can drive and denounce,
> Then you can opt for corruption, class treachery.
> But consider:
> The smallest technical innovation,
> The slightest simplification of the production method,

Will enrol you, in this system,
Into the army of unemployed millions.
Then you fall from rung to rung
Down the entire ladder of unemployment benefits.
Till they say:
(*The collective lecture dissolves into a mimed scene, the speakers opening up to make room for a drum serving as a counter behind which one of the actors sits and says to the worker standing in front of it –*)
'You've been paid off, we can't help you anymore.'
Free are you, he today, tomorrow you,
Free from work,
Free from rights and protection
Free from shelter and bread,
Free are you, proletarian, freely you can choose:
Burglary (*This is mimed.*)
Murder and robbery (*mimed*)
The rope (*mimed*)
Or?
Struggle, Class Struggle, Solidarity, Revolution!
Choose![39]

The physical expressiveness of the five men and three women who performed *For Soviet Power* helped to compensate for the rough language and sometimes stilted rhymes.

They collapse into a heap of corpses, march across the stage as victorious columns, crawl on their bellies along the stage floor, mime the sabotaging of machines and the surpassing of the quota of the Plan . . . changing costumes in split seconds, peaked caps, officers' caps, red scarves and hats . . . singing Soviet songs and beating the rhythm with their steps.[40]

Every member played an instrument, which was sometimes freely transformed into a prop. The mandolin, for example, often doubled as a machine gun.

The guiding principle for the structure of the montage was not a historical sequence of events as it was in Piscator's *In Spite of Everything* or the troupe's own *Third International*, nor was it the development of a central character as in Brecht's *The Mother*, begun in the same year as *For Soviet Power*. The sequence of dramatic events was determined simply by the learning process the Red Megaphone hoped the audience would go through, and it is this that makes the production unique. By shifting back and forth at carefully chosen points between the two social systems, events and conditions which appeared distant to the audience were made tangible. The spectators were able to re-evaluate, compare and choose before joining in the final song in a demonstration of solidarity.

This demanded the active mental and emotional participation of the audience. The dialectical effect was further heightened by the inclusion of a speaker. The Communist MP Ernst Schneller took part in numerous performances of the program.

> The play receives topical reference points, the crucial moments . . . are emphasized and the lecture's crucial aspects are represented by the play. As a speaker I always attempted – without falling into a teacherly tone – to elucidate the main tendency of *For Soviet Power* and the most important slogans of the play to create heightened interest for . . . the programme. The lecture is only one part of the programme . . . and should not be an independent act.[41]

'Reach into Life' – the song montage

The twelfth and last congress of the ATBD took place May 1 and 15 in 1932. The organization had already begun to prepare for illegal work. In spite of this it was growing rapidly. One hundred new groups had joined during the previous year, including a number of professional unemployed actors' collectives. The four hundred member troupes had recruited 63,000 members for revolutionary organizations in one year. It was in this tense but militant atmosphere that the Red Megaphone made their next important theoretical contribution 'Reach into Life'.

The early abstractness of the agitprop troupes was directly related to the fact that they seldom reached those sections of the masses beyond the influence of the KPD. The more they were able to realize the slogan 'Into the Factories – to the Masses', the clearer became the necessity of relating to the consciousness of each individual member of the class to show them their

> relationship to the struggle of the entire class (to so-called 'high politics'), to make them conscious of how they come up against the most varied forms of capitalism every day without ever having spoken to the Capitalist X, how not one minute of their lives goes by without their having been affected by political events. . . . the troupes must learn 'to grasp the full human life', to demonstrate . . . the great laws of the class struggle through the minutest daily experience of human life. They must learn not only to talk about the class struggle, but to *give it shape* by dramatizing the life of its representative, the human being.[42]

The means to achieve this could not be 'newly conjured up' from within the proletariat itself. The bourgeois heritage had to be critically analysed and its most valuable elements appropriated. The danger of being swallowed up by bourgeois art, of aping it instead of evolving an independent proletarian art, should not deter the workers' theatre from this historical task.

This was the first time that the assimilation of the cultural heritage had been explicitly demanded by an agitprop troupe. It laid the groundwork for gestic and realistic acting and the development of more complex scene montages. The group did not arrive at these conclusions primarily because of artistic considerations, but because they had a better grasp of the political situation, the way it was viewed by audiences, and finally of the means by which the spectator's views could be changed.

The Red Megaphone were able to face up to one of the most difficult tasks of the agitprop movement; ending shows on an optimistic note without falling into the trap of the 'happy end'. The essence of this knotty problem was formulated by the ATBD at its National Conference in 1931:

> the situation in which we acted was not ripe for the chasing away of
> the capitalists, the tasks facing us were the organizing of the masses
> . . . propagation of strikes . . . to show the role of capitalism and of
> bureaucracy in the class struggle – independent of the size of the
> belly and the cigar. The possibility of an artistic impact is not reduced
> by the correctness and depth of political content but is created by it
> in the first place.[43]

At a time of increased repression the delicate balance between an honest portrayal of sacrifices and hurdles ahead, and inspiring audiences to take up the fight called for an approach that was both sensitive and mature. In their attempts to meet this challenge the Red Megaphone turned increasingly to music. With the help of Hanns Eisler they produced montages of scenes and songs which enriched the already strong visual quality of their work.

The *Song of the Red United Front*[44] was produced in mid-1931 and printed in the June edition of the *Red Megaphone* with a recommendation from the editorial board that the troupes utilize the opportunities provided by the verses for lightning scenes. The passing of the emergency decree in March 1931 and the increasing repression made performances of long plays more and more difficult. For development of the scenic ballad, short episodes, combinations of song sections and lightning scenes gave the groups the necessary flexibility and mobility to get round the tightening police control. The *Song of the Red United Front* is made up of five episodes, each consisting of four verses set to the same melody. The chorus draws the conclusions of the individual episode, while maintaining the overall theme of the need to build the united front on the basis of one's own concrete experience. This was the first time the united front was made the main subject of an agitprop production.

Unity is also dealt with in episodes demonstrating the need for mutual support from different sections of the working class, proletarianized peasants, and the middle classes: the evicted tenant, 'cut off the dole', gets support from his neighbours and the removal man and together they form a front against landlord, bailiff and police. The demonstrating apprentice, chased by the rampaging police – 'A dozen heads are split, many a bone is cracking' – is hidden by a greengrocer. The impoverished small peasant – 'pawn tickets sticking out everywhere' – has his impounded cow rescued by city workers. The workers, facing sackings and wage cuts, strike in spite of the machinations of the trade union bureaucrat – 'negotiate!' – they beat strike-breakers and sustain the strike with the help of the unemployed. The 'attacking Nazi storm-troopers' are confronted by the Red Defence corps, formed by SPD and KPD workers.

At certain points without breaking the overall rhythm, individual singers stepped out of the troupe song and economically acted the behaviour and attitudes of the characters in the episodes.

The fact that the episodes dealt with the problems of different individuals, as representatives of entire social strata to which the spectator could relate in accordance with his or her own class position, had several advantages. The group could show what the objective reasons were for the support given by certain sections of German society to political movements by connecting 'the concrete life of the individual . . . to the struggle of the entire class.' (The Fascists were actively recruiting among the social sectors portrayed.) The group could 'relate to the world of ideas' of these individuals and show them as the result of particular conditions. In this way the prejudices and false ideology which were obstacles to the formation of a united front could be exposed.

And finally the episodic structure based on five different characters made it possible for the spectators to learn about struggles which they had not directly experienced. Had this been done through a central character it might have led to an artificial stretching of the character in order to accommodate the pedagogic function. (Brecht pointed out this danger in a conversation with Friedrich Wolf, leader of Performance Troupe South-West. Having to show 'an inner change' in a character 'or a development to the final point of recognition . . . would often be unrealistic, and in my view a materialist presentation necessitates that the consciousness of the characters is determined by their social being and not dramaturgically manipulated.'[45] By selecting stages of a central character's development, this manipulation of consciousness could be avoided or minimized as in Brecht's The Measures Taken and The Mother, Wolf's From New York to Shanghai and Peasant Baetz, Wangenheim's Mousetrap, and the AGFA Revue.

The scenic ballad helped translate abstract slogans into real life situations, thereby overcoming the schematism of many agitprop scenes. It was also particularly suited to speedy updating and improvised street and courtyard agitation. Before the police became aware of the troupe the performance would be over.

The few recordings which exist give us some idea of the power of the Red Megaphone's rendering of songs like the 'Solidarity Song' by Brecht and Eisler which they performed to drum accompaniment with the backing of 4,000 worker athletes and choirs. The 'Komsomol Song' simply and collectively sung, is based on a Russian melody and reveals considerable agitational force derived from the group's long experience of speech choruses. Perhaps the most differentiated performance was that of the 'Red Flag Song' written to support the paper during one of the many bans imposed by the state. This ardent but often quite subtle appeal alternates between solo male and female voices sometimes speak-singing, with the whole group joining in on the fourth line of the verse and parts of the chorus. The carefully phrased but urgent propaganda sections of the solo parts could be combined with the powerful agitational appeals of the chorus.

The group produced a number of scenic ballads similar to those used in the *Song of the Red United Front* which were published in a special edition of *Red Megaphone* under the title *Mass Strike*. They were loosely connected, no attempt being made to form a coherent program, but they were all contributions to the campaign for the formation of a united front from below. The 'Song of the Lesser Evil', the 'Song of the Crisis and Rationalization', the 'Strike Song' and others tried to relate the industrial action of workers to the fate of clerical workers, shop-keepers, the unemployed, small peasants and farm labourers and juxtapose their conditions to those in the Soviet Union.

A concrete example of the group's political clarity was the significant correction made when the *Song of the Red United Front* was republished in 1932. Two verses of the last episode of the 1931 version were changed so that the 'black-red-gold mobile commando' became the 'Nazi stormtroopers' and the original lines linking the Nazi leader Frick and the Social Democrat Severing were replaced with a call for proletarian mass defence. The main attack was no longer against Social Democracy but against Fascism, a recognition of the damage done by the Social Fascist theory in practice. This came about partly because of the group's close contact with ordinary people and their putting into practice the principle of developing social concepts anew in the heads of the spectators instead of throwing conclusions at them. (There were other attempts to get away from this damaging policy. Arno wrote a montage of six scenes in 1930 called *Nazis among Themselves* which took a worker through the experience of the SA and showed how and why he finds his way back to his class. The Stuttgart Performance Troupe South-West also developed an unsectarian approach in its scenes and plays.)

In 1932 the Red Megaphone expanded considerably. It grew to fifty members and formed four brigades. The Children's Brigade was made up of adults which performed a programme for children, the last production of the Red Megaphone. (There was a widespread children's theatre movement in Germany, mainly connected to the Communist children's organization Red Pioneer and partly affiliated to the ATBD. Most groups were called 'Red Drummers' after the Pioneers' journal *Rote Trommel* (Red Drum), but the most advanced was called 'Lenin'. They existed before 1927, but grew rapidly after the tour of the Blue Blouse to around sixty groups by 1932. They performed living newspapers dramatizing excerpts from *Red Drum* as well as speech choruses. Particularly active during elections, their success and recruitment figures led to arrests, house searches and bans by the police.) The Touring Brigade performed the USSR programme in Saxony, Thuringia, and Rhineland, the Active Brigade performed *Mass Strike*, smaller items like *Song of the Red United Front* and the USSR programme. The Reserve Brigade had the task of education and the rehearsal of new material. After the return of the Touring Brigade the troupe formed smaller units which performed the more flexible material, in suburban inns, factory and tenement court-yards and in streets and squares.

Even after the appointment of Hitler as Chancellor in January 1933 the group continued giving performances disguised as closed meetings for members of organizations not yet banned or as events held by 'theatre associations'. Some members were forced to emigrate but the rest continued illegal work with members of Red Wedding. It was not until 1936 when a wave of arrests made this co-operation impossible that the group ceased performing. Several members had been interned in concentration or forced labour camps. Those who had emigrated fought for the liberation of Germany from Fascism in the Soviet Union, Czechoslovakia and England as actors, broadcasters or soldiers in the Red Army.

Impact on the movement

Although Nuko of the Red Rockets blamed the 'long' production *Hello Young Worker* for the few performances the Red Megaphone gave in 1928, the group had performed longer material eighty-five times to 65,000 spectators in one year by 1930 in spite of police repression. But no less important than the troupe's own factory work was its influence on the rest of the agitprop movement. In 1930 having already instituted open rehearsals they took on the patronage of the Young Guard of the Berlin KJDV, whose members ranged in age from 13 to 19.

A few months later the *Red Flag* (April 17, 1930) acknowledged the positive influence of the Red Megaphone on the troupe's production *Karl Liebknecht's Youth Are Marching*. Their mainly satirical revue material had been deepened by speech chorus elements and short scenes, they had become more precise: 'The structuring of the scenes gives their plays . . . impressive lucidity and an element of surprise.'[46] Having been 'towed' to a higher standard the Young Guard in turn helped fourteen children of an allotment garden colony to form a Young Socialist League group.

The Red Megaphone then recommended that the more qualified of the twenty-five Berlin troupes should each take in tow a group of average ability so as to close the gap in political and artistic standards. They were already aware that the police might make it impossible for them to operate and it was essential that experience be shared and the utmost flexibility developed. The troupes were to observe each other's rehearsals and if possible participate in each other's work. Before long the less experienced troupes would be able to lend a hand to even younger ones.

The Hannover troupe Left Attack openly declared their indebtedness to the Red Megaphone in overcoming their repertory crisis in 1931.

After failing to produce something new, jolted by a notice in the *Red Flag*, some comrades travel to a performance by the Red Megaphone. There we received our best advice so far . . . 'The programme must be structured dialectically.' 'The content must not be pressed into a form.' All this was thoroughly discussed by the troupe. The next programme for a free-thinker event already bears the essential traits of this new form . . . the crisis has been overcome.[47]

The Red Megaphone was so concerned to overcome the clichés that bedevilled the movement that they refused to provide detailed stage directions for the individual scenes in *Mass Strike*. 'The . . . form of the presentation must result from collective discussion. . . . The short notes should not be seen as dogma but as suggestions, stimuli. . . . We do not want schematism, rigidity, but liveliness.'[48]

There is such a striking similarity between the later work of the Red Megaphone and the work of Friedrich Wolf's Performance Troupe Southwest that it seems likely the Berlin group also strongly influenced the Stuttgart collective. Formed in February 1932 they were able to·reap the benefits of the older troupes' experience. Their analysis of the agitprop cliché in relation to the audience's consciousness was almost word for word the same as that of the Red Megaphone. They learned rapidly and made extensive use of montage and music in the three plays they produced.

The revue sequence *Where Are the Front Lines Drawn?* used songs like 'Class against Class' (the troupe's entrance song), the 'Proverb Song', and the 'Song of the First Commandment' ('Thou Shalt Labour'), and was performed mainly at factory meetings. *From New York to Shanghai*, a two-hour scene montage with choral music and masks showed international opposition to the imperialist war in Asia. The Chinese agitator Wang linked the two dozen scenes set in cities all over the world. Their last production *Peasant Baetz* was what Wolf called a dialectic workers' play. Simultaneous scenes showed the common interest of town and country, which was also expressed by the main song 'Arbeiternot ist Bauerntod' (literally, 'Workers' Plight is the Peasants' Death') composed by Eisler. The troupe participated in the election campaign of the KPD, performing 67 times for about 45,000 spectators from May 1932 to March 1933 when their seventh performance of *Peasant Baetz* was banned and Wolf was forced to emigrate.

The Performance Troupe South-West, one of the most advanced in the movement, had in Wolf a professional revolutionary writer. One of his plays, *Tai Yang Awakens*, had been staged by Piscator. Wolf took part in the great director's production team which gave him valuable insight into Piscator's approach to montage. He gave full credit to Piscator and the workers' theatre movement for their contribution to the development of dramatic structures:

> We must stress again and again that all the left wing plays of the professional theatre – be they 'analytical' like Wangenheim's *Mouse Trap*, or one of Brecht's 'epic' plays, or my own – that all these plays of the 'big form' are unthinkable without the pioneering work of the agitprop troupes and Piscator. The essential formal components of our plays – the short scene, the scene montage, the distancing narration and report, the simultaneous scenes . . . the bursting of the boundaries of the proscenium arch and the incorporation of the audience as co-actors and co-workers into the play – they were all fought for by the agitprop troupes and Piscator in hard ideological and practical labour.[49]

These formal breakthroughs were spearheaded by the Red Megaphone, whose reputation had become international. (The Salford Red Megaphone in Britain called themselves after the Berlin troupe.) But they were also the result of a truly collective effort by the entire agitprop movement. The achievements and weaknesses of individual groups were continually discussed and analysed at conferences and in journals. This ongoing interchange was made possible by their understanding of the need for a dynamic relationship between theory and practice.

7 · Towards a popular theatre

The creative forces of the proletariat can only develop fully in the cultural field in general, and in the theatre in particular, after the seizure of power by the proletariat. This does not preclude, however, the possibility that we can pass through important stages on the road to this seizure of power and does not prevent us from forging ahead with the preparations for the victory of the proletariat with all the energy at our disposal.

From a resolution in response to Piscator's speech at the 1932 Moscow Olympiad of the revolutionary workers' theatre.[1]

This resolution was passed towards the end of an important period of activity during which the foundations were laid for a major break-through in revolutionary theatre. *Russia's Day*, the mass spectacles and the *Chorus of Labour* affirmed and celebrated the strength and unbroken fervour of the mobilized workers and soldiers of the early twenties. These productions also warned against the bloody repression and political manoeuvering which were to rob the working class of its gains.

Following the November Revolution a shaky republic was founded in a hurried attempt to paper over the cracks caused by ongoing class confrontations. Restabilized capitalism, and the bourgeois and militarist parties which supported it, projected an image of normality to which many people began to resign themselves. Piscator's *RRR*, the Red Revels of the KJVD and the satirical revues of groups like the Riveters and the Rockets appeared to be the ideal weapons for tearing the cloak of democracy into shreds and exposing the militarism, exploitation and Social Democratic class collaboration hidden beneath it. The need to be mobile and topical led to short, punchy, and flexible sketches like those of the Red Forge, Red Wedding and North-West Forward. Most of their programmes remained relatively simple combinations of interchangeable scenes or songs arranged in a loose sequence.

The escalating crisis and the ideological turmoil it left in its wake demanded a thorough economic and political re-evaluation from the Party and its troupes. The bourgeoisie and the Fascists presented the recession as a 'national' disaster and put forward nationalist solutions. These had to be countered by an explanation of class society and the antagonistic forces within it before the masses would accept class solutions. To cope with such complex arguments, analytical dramatic structures were evolved by the Red Megaphone, the Performance Troupe South-West and some of the professional revolutionary actors' collectives.

In retrospect this development from a dramaturgy of proletarian self-affirmation to one of exuberant attacking agitation and finally to one which offered convincing alternatives on the basis of painstaking analysis seems straightforward enough. Less obvious are the reasons for sudden individual breakthroughs, for temporary stagnation or retrogression. How did the movement respond to innovations, or the lack of them, why did different groups take different paths, how did dramatic methods overlap and why did agitational and propagandist forms continue to exist side by side?

To try to answer these questions it is essential to look at the relationship between the workers' theatre movement and the KPD. The Party was much more than an organizational backbone for the agitprop troupes, it was also a source of political assistance and pressure, and it interpreted and defined aesthetic traditions and theories. In accordance with its assessment of the historical conjuncture and the militancy and political awareness of the working class, the Party worked out its tactics and strategy, which were translated by the Party's central agitprop section. The resultant theoretical aims and practical tasks were carried out by the theatrical movement. The Party's own political traditions, composition and development was thus fundamental to the agitprop movement.

Since the murder of its founders and leading theoreticians Luxemburg and Liebknecht, the KPD's policy was dominated for a number of years by left sectarianism. This led to an often admirable stance against class collaboration, but also to an extremely inflexible, even counter-productive sectarianism which alienated proletarian SPD members and resulted finally in a split in the trade union movement. The only strategy the Party had at this time was for a revolutionary situation. It maintained this strategy even during a non-revolutionary period like the mid-1920s.

The KPD's initial support for the great dramatic forms of the ascendant bourgeoisie as argued by Mehring and Zetkin led to a lack of support for, if not open hostility to, attempts to create a proletarian culture using smaller fragmented forms from the disintegrating culture of capitalism in decline. But when the Party observed that the assimilation of 'great art' as practised by the SPD led to a passive acceptance of ruling class values and to reformism, they rejected *all* cultural activity. The alternatives offered by Piscator and the proletarian theatre were ruled out. Anything which did not contribute directly towards the seizure of power was seen as a distraction from the life and death struggle ahead – it was even considered counter-revolutionary.

But the need for cultural expression continued in spite of the Party's official attitude. As it happened the emergence of workers' choirs, revue and agitprop collectives coincided with the Party's need to grow and extend its influence. Gradually, educational and artistic activity came to be regarded as an integral part of the struggle against exploitation. At last the Party swung behind the self-activity of the worker-actors, even incorporating them into its agitprop apparatus. In accord with the Party's uncompromising course of confrontation, they produced an attacking, fighting theatre.

At first this change in policy was felt only on the practical level. The theoretical and dramaturgical implications were not explored. The growing agitprop movement had to evolve its own dramatic theory, one reason for the crudeness of so many early efforts. The only thing that was clear was what had been rejected: the elitism of the 'legitimate' theatre. Contemplative dramas and glittering entertainments had become reified and solemn or extravagant and fashionable occasions. Culture was a business, the hierarchy of stars, managers and directors were themselves subject to the ever-present pressure from the box office. And as there had to be a connection between these objectionable features of commercialism, individualism, and artistic decline on the one hand and bourgeois dramatic aesthetics on the other, the theories and practices of playwriting, stage design, directing and acting too were rejected as bourgeois.

It was easy enough to substitute general principles for what had been thrown out. The workers' theatre was to be a dynamic mobilizing cultural force performing for proletarian audiences in their own meeting halls. The groups were to be non-profitmaking collectives closely linked to a revolutionary organization which provided political leadership. This was institutionalized in the person of a troupe leader who was sometimes also the artistic director of the collective. Whether or not the two functions were separate, those who held these positions were subject to collective criticism and control as were all members. This system, combined with the development of a collective playmaking process, gave the troupes a political and artistic cohesion and discipline which enabled them to operate under heavy police pressure.

But when it came to finding alternatives to the old dramatic tradition, rejected by the Party in a completely undiscerning way, the movement encountered great difficulties. The once militant dramatic tradition of the SPD was also opposed, and remained untapped. There was no ready-made 'proletarian' or revolutionary dramaturgy. The theoreticians were no help, so the practitioners had to find a solution themselves.

They found it in the 'low' forms of popular entertainment: the fairground, the circus, the travelling showman and street singer. From them came the device of directly addressing the audience, the knockabout style, the barker, the satire and parody, the music – simple, humorous and anti-illusionistic. These small forms derived not from the time when capitalism was at its peak but from the time when it was struggling against feudalism. When the clergy took its propaganda plays outside the church to widen its influence, the forms became secularized. The ascendant bourgeoisie adopted them to promote its interests. And in turn the workers used them in their struggle against capitalism.

In the revue the workers' theatre had found a form capable of replacing the long and complex bourgeois drama. To make up for shortcomings in writing and acting important innovations were made in the staging of scenes and the visualizing of abstract concepts with the help of revolutionary artists like Piscator and Eisler. But before long stereotypes developed: no matter what the content the revue was the vehicle. Apart from the reasons already given for this stagnation, there is a less obvious political one.

The Party maintained its strategy for revolution at a time when capitalism was restabilized, and agitation for the revolution should have been complemented, if not replaced by, propaganda for a long hard struggle. The prolongation of an exclusively agitational political and theatrical approach beyond the point when it was politically justifiable led to a cliché – ruthless attack and the ceaseless promotion of revolution in a predictable pattern.

The revue had helped the audience decide between two policies or systems. Now the spectators had to be provided with a Marxist method of analysis which they could apply independently to issues both in and outside the plays. More complex and more realistic scenes and acting were required. Experiments with speech choruses, revue and the model productions of Piscator and the Red Megaphone led to the scene montage but the development was slow and the new form was not adopted by all groups.

Writing and acting remained the weakest areas. Some plays were little more than sloganeering, others veered unselectively towards the naturalistic language of everyday speech. In the acting cartoon types or model workers prevailed. All these shortcomings severely limited the possibilities of stimulating the audience's thinking in a truly profound way.

At the roots of this lack of progress lay two basic misconceptions about the nature of art. First there was the view that form as such has no content, and therefore that old forms could be used to express new content, which led back to naturalistic writing and acting. Secondly, there was the contradictory view that rejected the old forms as bourgeois, but did not see the need to consciously create new ones. They would spring more or less automatically from the new content and the intentions of the new cultural force, the working class. This led once again to clichés and sloganeering or naturalistic dialogue and acting. Both approaches proved inadequate.

The need for an alternative meant coming to terms with the 'heretical' notion – to dogmatic Marxists – that form carries content, that, like all methods of production, artistic production too must be analysed with regard to its particular function within a particular context and society. For example it was important to know at which historical stages art was seen as contemplative and passively reflective, or as dynamic and mobilizing and which forms were produced to carry out these functions.

This process was begun by a few troupes, in particular the Red Megaphone. The main criteria for selecting propaganda forms were popularity, clarity and entertainment value. 'Popularity' was redefined as that which made complex problems easy to understand and handle and made learning enjoyable. As demonstrated by the Red Megaphone, language and acting became both realistic and gestural, able to quote social attitudes. The link was made with popular traditions and with the most modern analytical forms. Asja Lacis explained why this did not happen earlier:

> Officially, the functionaries of the amateur theatre had assumed from early on that the bourgeois heritage would be respected and critically applied. In reality, the study . . . of this heritage was badly neglected. Even worse, the amateur theatre was in opposition to the professional revolutionary stages like the Piscator Theatre, partly because it considered Piscator's strategy of subversion of bourgeois culture wrong, partly because it rejected the professional theatre as such. Piscator, on the other hand, who once had done so much for the amateur theatre was at this stage hardly interested in its development. The result was that the artistic level of the amateur theatre could not be raised to the level that would have been possible under the given conditions, and that the professional theatre also missed out on useful achievements by the amateur theatre. This antagonism between the two forms of revolutionary theatre was overcome in 1931–1932.[2]

In 1932 the ATBD began to integrate the revolutionary collectives of unemployed professionals among whom were directors, writers and actors who had previously worked with Piscator or the workers' theatre movement. The International Workers' Theatre League changed its name to International Revolutionary Theatre League, reflecting the unification of the amateur and professional movements. This increased co-operation meant a qualitative improvement as well as a widening of the cultural front. The unevenness in standards was eroded to such a degree that Brecht did not detect any break in the method or level of skill in *The Mother* when 'amateur actors performed next to Helene Weigel.'[3]

And in Brecht, Wolf and to some extent Wangenheim in addition to the best amateur writers who originated in the agitprop troupes the movement at last had the playwrights it had lacked for so many years. They were in turn able to make full use of montage which the workers' theatre had developed to a high standard. The movement was ready to make a great leap forward. As Wolf put it, 'The developing agitprop theatre will become the professional theatre of the working class.'[4]

Politically, the workers' theatre produced a repertoire that covered all the important issues of the day, reflecting the history and struggles of the workers' movement over a span of more than fifteen years. This fact alone is a tribute to its vitality. It was however, only one weapon in the armoury of the working class, although probably the most advanced. There were associations promoting revolutionary films, radio, music, dance and literature, as well as those engaged in physical culture. Together with a wide range of educational and propaganda institutions they created a counter-culture that began to challenge the dominance of bourgeois cultural institutions. (The performance of Brecht's *The Measures Taken*, for example, in which mass choirs of Berlin workers participated helped to radicalize the German Workers' Singers League. In 1930 it was under Social Democratic leadership. It 'consisted of more than 14,000 associations with a total of 560,000 members.'[5]

At this stage the Social Fascist policy was laid to rest and the movement focused on the genuine article. The Fascist state responded with an all-out attack, using 'legal' means and physical force. The movement's representatives were eliminated, imprisoned or had to flee. Hans Otto, one of the leading figures of the ATBD and a fine revolutionary professional actor was tortured to death as a warning to the agitprop troupes of the fate they could expect if they defied the Fascists.

The ATBD shifted the direction of its work to the decentralized sub-organizations on the provincial and district level. The holding of conferences and the publication of journals became impossible. Debate and communication between the groups became dangerous and the movement disintegrated. Small pockets persisted until forced into emigration or underground. The priority of those who survived became the preservation of the backbone of the workers' movement, the Party, which was under the heaviest attack. Those who could not fight from inside Germany continued the struggle abroad, often adding the gun to their cultural weapons. The songs of the Spanish International Brigade are an example of this fighting tradition. The tradition was buried but not eradicated. In his notes to his most explicitly agitprop play *The Mother* Brecht wrote:

This type of non-Aristotelian play, applying principles of presentation of a new, epic theatre, makes use of the technique of the fully developed bourgeois drama on the one hand; on the other, the technique of the small proletarian performance troupes which . . . had developed a new and unique style for their proletarian purposes.[6]

It was Brecht and Eisler in particular who developed the incomplete theory and practice of the agitprop movement and integrated them into a systematic revolutionary dramaturgy.

18 'Behind Bars!': Red Troupe sketch agitating for freeing the political prisoners, 1926

19 Boleslaw Strzelewicz, founder and director of the Red Troupe, Dresden

20 Agitation against compensation of expropriated aristocrats, Red Troupe 1926

21 The band of the Red Rockets, Berlin 1928

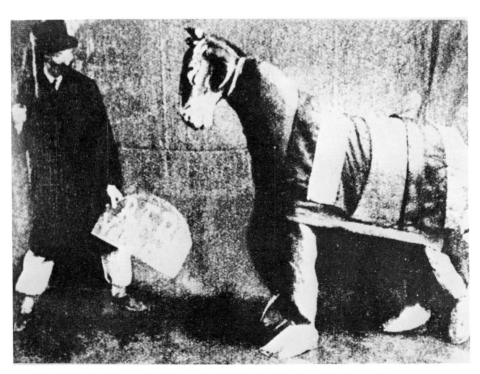

22 'The Wonder Horse called Great Coalition', Red Rockets, Berlin 1928

23 *above* The Red
Forge, Halle
1929

24 *left* Red
Wedding, Berlin,
during a
courtyard
performance,
1929

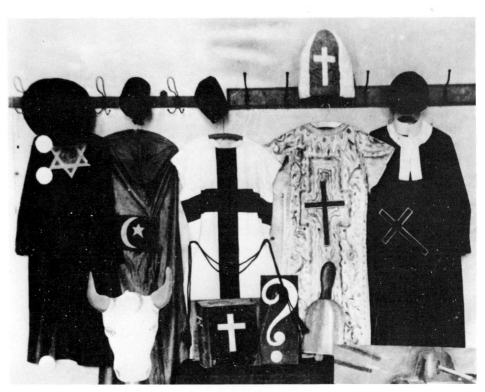

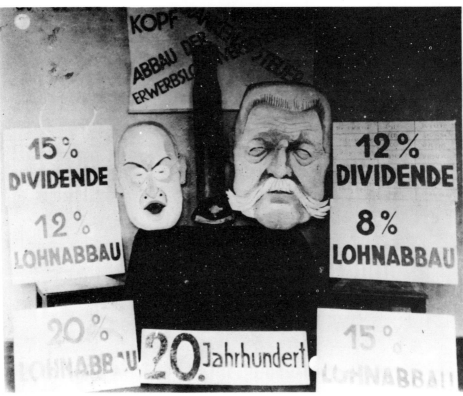

25 *opposite and above* Props and Costumes for the 'Freethinker-Revue' of the Red Blouse, Berlin, as impounded by the police in 1931

26 *left and below* Portrait studies from 'In Spite of Everything!' by the Red Rats, Dresden 1932

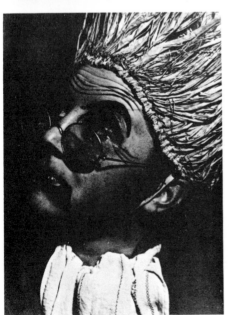

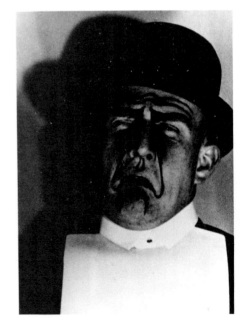

27 *above and left*
Text illustrations
from 'Hands off
China', by the
First Agitprop
Troupe of the
KJDV – 1927,
later the Red
Megaphone,
Berlin. The texts
mean: 'Entrance
for Chinese and
Dogs prohibited';
'Entrance for
Capitalists and
Dogs
prohibited!'

28 Street agitation for the workers' press, Red Rockets, Dresden 1929

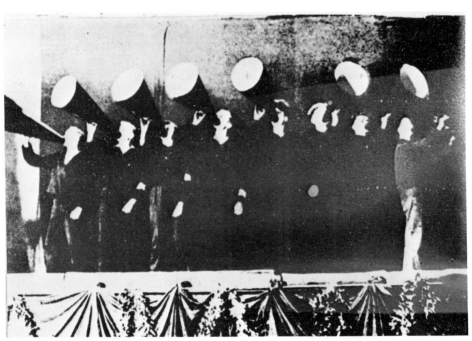

29 The Megaphone-Chorus from 'Hello, Young Worker!', Red Megaphone, 1928

30 'For Soviet Power': members of Red Megaphone singing, 1930

31 The Children's Brigade of the Red Megaphone, 1933

32 *left* Maxim Vallentin, founder and director of the Red Megaphone – GDR, 1983

33 *below left* Elli Schliesser, after 1945. The main theorist of the Red Megaphone, nicknamed 'Karl Marx without Beard'. She survived years in Auschwitz and the march to Theresienstadt, keeping others' spirits up. When colleagues came to collect her from a mental clinic, she mistook their limousine for that of the fascists who had arrested her. She ran to her room, locked it and burned herself to death

34 *below right* Edith Vallentin, founder-member of the Red Megaphone – GDR, 1983

35 From the Film 'Kuhle
Wampe'. The Red
Megaphone is
performing 'The Song
of the Red United
Front', 1931. Elli
Schliesser on front stage

Part Three

Theatre of attack:
Workers' Theatre in Britain

8 · From Luddite melodrama to the Workers' Theatre Movement

They would have made us slaves, nay worse; but then
We struck to show them that we still were men.
And all who value worth and manliness
Have sympathized with us, except the Press –
The Press! that engine to enlarge the slave,
Can it refuse when truth and justice crave?
Alas! Oppression sways the venal pen –
Corruption backs the master – not the men!
But time will come when these things will not be –
When heaven will give success to honesty.
And those who worked at Nelson's Monument,
Add Woolwich too – by slavery unbent,
Shall with their brethren raise a noble name
That tyranny shall daunt, and treachery shame.
Oh! may the members of the Houses be,
As were the builders, foes to tyranny.

(A poem by a striking stonemason who helped build the new Houses
of Parliament, recited at a benefit for the masons at the Victoria
Theatre in 1841.)[1]

On April 24, 1926, just a few days before the General Strike, the
Hackney Labour Dramatic Group gave its first performance in London.
This was the beginning of a Workers' Theatre Movement in Britain which
was to last ten years, until, as one veteran put it, 'It was overtaken by
history'.[2]

A long and lively tradition

Like its counterparts in the USSR and Germany, the British Movement
sprang out of a long tradition of radical theatre. In 1832 for example a

Luddite melodrama called *The Factory Lad* by John Walker was performed at the Surrey Theatre in Blackfriars, a working class area. In 1833 it was advertised in a list of playscripts in the *Poor Man's Guardian* so it may have been used by working men's reading circles, may even have been performed by amateur groups. The play was unique in that many of the speeches strongly resembled statements in the *Guardian*. The fantasy, comic relief, and happy ending associated with the genre were abandoned in favour of realism, an unresolved ending and economic arguments.

> WESTWOOD: . . . To compete with my neighbours – that is, if I wish to prosper as they do – I have come to the resolution of having my looms propelled by steam, which will dispense with the necessity of manual labour, and save some three thousand a year.
>
> ALLEN: And not want us, who have been all our lives working here?
>
> WESTWOOD: I can't help it. I am sorry for it; but I must do as others do. . . . Turn you out are words I don't understand. I don't want you, that's all. Surely I can say that? What is here is mine, left me by my father to do the best with and that is now my intention. Steam supersedes manual labour. A ton of coals will do as much work as fifty men and for less wages than ten will come to.[3]

Although one of the workers kills the 'villain' Westwood, it is by no means certain that virtue will have its reward. The final curtain comes down on the image of 'the soldiers with their muskets levelled at Rushton'[4] whose fate is thus left undecided. The play was probably aimed at the skilled artisans and small masters who were the Surrey's regular pit audience, men who might have felt the effects of mechanization and the factory system themselves.

Other examples of topical plays with a radical slant which dealt with the underprivileged include *The Barn Burners*, performed in 1833 at the New City Theatre, and Southey's *Wat Tyler*, which was used to raise funds for the working class Society for the Protection of Booksellers in 1836.

Chartist benefits were held at the Standard Theatre in the 1840s. Just up the road from the Surrey, the Rotunda, a theatre from 1835, served as headquarters for Owenites and Chartists who also organized campaigns for the licensing of illegal working class saloon theatres. Several Chartist leaders wrote plays themselves, the illegal unstamped anti-establishment papers printed theatrical news and criticism, and Home Office agents were assigned to watch the Rotunda.

Towards the end of the century Ibsen was produced for the first time in London at working men's clubs in the East End by Eleanor Marx and Aveling. Theatre was used to propagate the cause of the suffragettes and the aims of the new labour parties. *The Clarion*, an Independent Labour

Party newspaper, was founded in 1891, and Clarion groups organized to promote the paper and other socialist literature. A National Association of Clarion Dramatic Clubs sprang up, which in 1912, set about compiling a library of plays on labour and socialist themes such as women's rights, recognition of the union, and evolution. The Newcastle People's Theatre which still exists today, although it is no longer a socialist propaganda theatre, began life as a Clarion Club offshoot of the British Socialist Party in 1911. By the 1920s the ILP and the Co-op had hundreds of dramatic groups and socialist choirs. Shaw was the most popular playwright and pacifism a recurrent theme.

The Socialist Sunday Schools, 'faced with the common difficulty of how best to convey the Socialist Message to the children, and through them to the wider community',[5] turned to drama. In 1907 for example a play called *Brotherhood* was performed at the Paisley Sunday School in Scotland. The characters included 'a bankrupt Private Trader, a Working Man and His Wife, an Ideal Philanthropist, a Minister, a School Teacher, a Bottom Dog, and a Socialist Student'.[6] They related their troubles to each other, showing up the iniquitous system of modern society. Consequently, Lady Goodwill was converted to socialism and handed over Brotherhood Castle to those who needed it. In Perth, Frank Simpson wrote *When Dreams Came True, a Fairy Tale for Children – And Others*, which was published by the Socialist Prohibition Fellowship in 1920.

For all their utopianism such plays were consciously written to educate both the young pupils and their adult audiences, as Simpson's sub-title clearly indicates. And for at least one member of the future Workers' Theatre Movement it was the start.

Alice Jones's parents were members of the Social Democratic Federation, later the British Socialist Party and the largest contingent in the Communist Party of Great Britain. She was active in the Socialist Sunday School Movement from the time she could think and walk. She remembers reciting 'working class poems'[7] by such writers as William Morris at her school. Later she and her future husband, Jack Loveman, provided piano and violin music at Labour Party meetings. Still teenagers, they joined the Young Communist League. Soon they were being coached by Mrs Tom Mann, wife of the famous syndicalist trade union organizer and orator, and leader of the London and Deptford Labour Choirs. According to Alice Loveman, 'She was very keen, a lovely singer, and she took half a dozen of us YCLers every week and trained us to sing sea shanties, Negro spirituals. . . .'[8] They put on a 'Red Concert' at the Working Men's Club in Greenwich and included in the programme a sketch Jack wrote called 'Dubb's Reduction':

Henry Dubb was a cartoon character, representing the dumb type of worker. The boss wants to reduce wages, and if he can only persuade Henry to take a reduction the others will follow. Much to his amazement Henry refuses and actually leads a counter-demonstration. The thing was written in a mixture of Shakespearean blank verse and ballad form. I don't think it's necessary to say any more than that.[9]

The Lovemans then joined a theatre which was probably linked to the Plebs League, a Labour College movement formed by dissidents from Ruskin College in 1909. Tommy Ashcroft, editor of the Plebs magazine, took part. The Lovemans remember performing Upton Sinclair's *Singing Jailbirds*, a play about the Wobblies, the Industrial Workers of the World, at the Infirmary in Bethnal Green where there was a Communist mayor. During the General Strike they represented the YCL on the Lewisham Council of Action, and temporarily gave up their theatrical activities. Later they were to work with the Deptford 'Red Blouse' troupe and the Red Front group in Streatham.

Meanwhile in East London Tom Thomas, the future founder of the Workers' Theatre Movement, was responding to quite different influences. His father was a staunch trade unionist, the President of the London Society of Basketmakers, but politically a Liberal. His grandmother was an Ulster Unionist, and the only newspaper in the house was the *Daily Mail*. Thomas soon grew to loathe the *Mail's* ranting against Liberal reforms alongside fulsome descriptions of country house parties:

When I sang in the Church choir 'He hath put down the mighty from their seats and exalted the humble and meek, He hath filled the hungry with good things, and the rich He hath sent empty away,' I looked at the occupants of the pews, and it was clear to me that He hadn't done any of these things and it was about time that somebody else did them.[10]

Thomas's sense of injustice was aroused when he saw neighbours evicted for non-payment of rent, their poor belongings thrown out in the rain. His own mother scrimped and saved and took in lodgers to pay for rent and food. In an attempt to understand what was happening he turned to books. By the age of fourteen he had read Shaw, Wells, and Galsworthy, while his studies of the theory of evolution caused him to leave the church. He joined the anti-war Herald League, and after the Russian Revolution became a socialist, joining first the ILP and then the Labour Party.

Thomas first became interested in theatre at the Queen's Road Evening Institute where he was taking courses in commerce and literature. (Adult education was an important influence on other members of the Workers' Theatre Movement. Charles Mann, son of Tom Mann, thinks he got the idea to form a group when he went with his mother to see an offshoot of Ruskin College Players doing Shaw. Bram Bootman got his start in

Toller's *Masses and Man* in the early 1930s at Toynbee Hall, a university settlement in the East End of London.) He joined the Queen's Players, acting in Shakespeare and Shaw, and began attending the West End Theatre. Struck by the triviality of the plays, he deplored the fact that working class characters were invariably shown as 'born idiots or contemptible lackeys'.[11]

New plays, a new audience

There seems to be a great rush of organizations broadcasting their propaganda by means of plays and sketches and some branches of the ILP are enthusiastically entering into the production of socialist pieces. People will come to witness a play when they would never dream of coming to listen to a speaker. The only wonder is that the propaganda value of the stage has been so little taken advantage of in the last few years.   (*Labour Leader* June 1, 1922)

Labour Party meetings were often dreary affairs and Tom Thomas soon decided to liven things up with a bit of theatre. He enlisted the help of his wife and a few friends and in 1925 or 1926 at the regular monthly social of the Hackney Central Labour Party they performed a one-act play by Gwen John about a pit tragedy, which he had found in the library of the British Drama League. It was enthusiastically received and was repeated at several other socials.

Thomas became convinced that the labour movement was neglecting a powerful means of influencing people by putting over socialist ideas in a palatable form. In 1926 he started the Hackney Labour Dramatic Group. With the support of the Hackney Trades Council, they made their debut at the Library Hall, Stoke Newington on 24 April with four one-act plays: *A Woman's Honour* by Susan Glaspell, Shaw's *Augustus Does His Bit*, *The £12 Look* by J. M. Barrie, and *Unemployment* by C. K. Munro.

After the General Strike, Tom Thomas joined the Communist Party, in protest at the betrayal of Labour and trade union leaders. (The Hackney Labour Dramatic Group was renamed the People's Players.) He spent hours in the British Drama League Library looking for plays with working class subjects, and an analysis of the class system based on wage slavery which had neither prevented war nor delivered the 'home fit for heroes' promised the war's survivors. He found no such plays. Thomas soon realized he would have to write them. Till then the group had to be kept in training with whatever progressive pieces did exist.

In November 1926, Čapek's *R.U.R.* about a robots' revolt (a programme note explained that 'Robot' meant 'Worker') was produced, to be followed by *Mrs Warren's Profession* and an adaptation of *The Adding Machine*. The following March *Stanley Baldwin's Pipe Dream*, *Passaic* by John Dos Passos, and Joe Corrie's *In Time of Strife* were presented in Camberwell. The *Sunday Worker* gave a favourable review to the work of the Scottish miner turned poet and playwright:

> Corrie's play gave the dramatic side of the domestic problem that confronts all workers' families in attempting to resist the employers' attack on their wages and standard of living. This is real labour drama and just the type of play that a workers' theatre group can perform with real enthusiasm and feeling.[12]

A week later the *Sunday Worker* also printed an appeal from Tom Thomas for the launching of a £500 theatre building fund. There is no indication that any contributions were ever received.

By the middle of 1927 the People's Players had about 20 members and new plays were being written. A worker called Bernard Woolf wrote an election playlet called *Lady Betty's Husband*. Tom Thomas had completed a play about Chiang Kai Shek, at that time considered an anti-imperialist hero. He also wrote a sketch for the Hackney Young Pioneers, the Communist Party's youth movement, entitled 'Bessie Burton's Father'. It was about a girl who is taunted because her father has been arrested in the General Strike. She defends him, wins over the other children, and calls them all to the next Pioneers' meeting.

The Ragged Trousered Philanthropists

Ten years earlier, at a Herald League meeting, Tom Thomas had purchased a copy of *The Ragged Trousered Philanthropists* by Robert Tressell. 'It was a book which cried out to be made into a play, and when I re-read it I realized that it had the material not just for one play but a dozen.'[13] He set about adapting it for the stage, intending his dramatic version to be 'as unashamedly propagandistic as the novel'.[14] He stuck closely to the story – except at the end. The book he had bought was an adulterated version then in circulation which concluded with Owen coughing up blood from his tubercular lungs and deciding to kill himself and his wife and child. In fact this passage had been lifted from the middle of the original manuscript and substituted for Tressell's optimistic ending. In altering it Thomas was actually remaining faithful to the author's intentions.

The play was produced in 1927 in just three weeks. The first scenes were in rehearsal while the final ones were still being written. It was a huge success.

With it the group was able to perform to working men's clubs of every sort, to Labour Party gatherings, to strikers and to the Hunger Marchers. As much as £8.10s. was received for a single performance to a club audience, and by means of these receipts the group was able to equip itself with a great deal of scenery, and a portable electric switchboard with dimmers and floods (built by an electrician comrade of the group), which was an essential part of the programmes which followed.[15]

The People's Players also donated £150 to various strike funds.

An indication of the play's impact on its working class audiences can be gleaned from an incident at the Mildmay Radical Club. The bar steward warned the players that they must finish at a quarter to ten because the bar would close at ten 'and they must have their drinking time. So I'm telling you. . . . I'll ring a loud bell and if you haven't finished by then they'll all walk out on you.'[16] The actors decided to chance it. At a quarter to ten the bell rang out, but not a single soul left for the bar.

One of the most memorable performances took place at the Manor Hall, Hackney when a column of Hunger Marchers from the North marched in to applause from both actors and audience. The play went on to a rapturous reception from the packed house.

Five years later the *New Red Stage* was to attribute the success of Thomas's adaptation to:

its closeness to the life of the workers, which won for the ideas contained in it the acceptance of any worker audience. However hostile at first, the homeliness and familiarity of the working class humour, dialogue and action won the attention and support of a worker audience.[17]

The poor tea-boy Bert White's opening line was 'I don't think much of this bloody tea.'[18] It brought delighted laughter from an audience which did not expect to hear their language from the stage. The censor was less amused, he ruled that

a play with more than three 'bloodys' in it could not pass him. A keen argument ensued, with the result that we were officially allowed fifteen 'bloodys' in the course of the performance, which allowance was usually exceeded in the course of the first three scenes!![19]

The Ragged Trousered Philanthropists was a turning point for the Hackney People's Players. The audiences which had come to see *R.U.R.* had been Labour Party members, contacts, and supporters for whom 'it was rather nice . . . to have somewhere to go on a Saturday night'. Now they had an entirely new audience, who 'would normally have come to hear a music hall performance'.[20]

Its weakness lay in the fact that after this telling exposure of capitalism the audience was told, and voted usually with a tremendous 'Aye' that 'Socialism is the only remedy for unemployment and poverty', without however, having any light thrown on the crucial question of HOW Socialism was to be won.

As a result of experiencing and discussing this weakness the message of the next programme of plays was much more definite in character.[21]

The demise and rebirth of the Workers' Theatre Movement

In 1927 Tom Thomas saw an advertisement in the ILP Journal for a show by the Workers' Theatre Movement which had emerged from The Council of Proletarian Art. (The Council was formed in 1924 by members of the ILP and the Communist Party.) It was to be held at Caxton Hall, Westminster. He and several interested friends went along.

they were technically beneath contempt . . . ideologically completely muddled . . . they put on a play about a man and a woman who've got their last crust of bread and they . . . argue about who is to eat it, until suddenly there's a bit of a squabble and it falls . . . down a crack in the floor. . . . The last one . . . was called *Light the Candle* and it was simply stupid pornography. The candle was used as a phallic symbol and there were lots of candles all round the place. . . . I was furious when I left, I thought 'Good God, what do they think they're doing?'[22]

Nevertheless, the Hackney People's Players decided to affiliate to the Workers' Theatre Movement, only to learn that it had, in the meantime, disbanded. Tom Thomas concluded: '. . . if the Movement was to continue, the Hackney group would have to lead it. In this way our group became the nucleus of what was to be an entirely new Movement.'[23]

As the *New Red Stage* pointed out:

the group lost its identity as the People's Players, but gained a clearer class basis and the possibility of carrying out its work on a wider scale, although for several years after this it was the only consistently active group of the WTM.[24]

The Ragged Trousered Philanthropists was performed more than forty times that winter and the following year. In 1928 it was published by the Labour publishing company Plays for the People. But fresh material was soon needed and Tom Thomas wrote or adapted four new short plays which were performed for the first time at the Ladies' Tailors' Trade Union Hall, Whitechapel, December 17, 1928.

The Women of Kirbirsk, written partly because there was a majority of women in the group, attempted to tackle the problem which had arisen out of the Tressell play of showing how socialism is to be won. It dramatized the conflicts on a local committee of Russian peasant women whose men are fighting in the Great War. They must decide whether to defy the local landowner – they have cut wood for winter fuel on his estate without permission. Their solidarity in the face of the landowner's threats coincides with the news of the victory of the Bolsheviks.

The Fight Goes On dealt with the lockout of the miners in the aftermath of the General Strike. (To create the impression of a large demonstration Thomas put some singers in a back-stage lavatory and slowly opened the door as the 'marchers' drew near). Upton Sinclair's *Hell* became *Dawn*, a portrayal of fraternization and revolt by soldiers at the front, while the fourth piece was a Russian song-scene presented with the help of a Labour College choir and a 'communist' orchestra. There was an enthusiastic review of the latter in the *Daily Herald*:

> There were seven little scenes illustrating the Russian workers rise from slavery to freedom and each was accompanied by a song; they were most artistically produced and were a striking example of what brains and taste can do without any great expenditure except for time and trouble.[25]

But the programme as a whole required elaborate lighting and effects and as a result was only repeated three or four times. A retrospective article in the *New Red Stage* in 1932 concluded, 'This showed that elaboration and a multitude of properties reduced the usefulness of the plays very greatly, and was another important stage in the development towards a more flexible form.'[26]

A satire on the Labour Party followed in January 1929 entitled *Malice in Plunderland*.

> . . . The Knave of Hearts (MacDonald) is accused of organizing a party to expose capitalism, and successfully proves, by means of extracts from 'Labour and the Nation', that on the contrary, he and his party are one of capitalism's main supports.[27]

Then in May 1929, the group produced *Singing Jailbirds*, by Upton Sinclair. Tom Thomas describes how

> We booked a church hall for the performance – the hall of St Bartholomew's in Dalston Lane. When we gathered for the dress rehearsal, the Saturday before the show was due to open, we found the Vicar was there. I realized we had two alternatives, a dress rehearsal or a show. So I passed the word for a props, lights and movement run-through but no words spoken at all.
> The show went on to a packed house. But we realized that in spite of its powerful appeal, the effect . . . was profoundly pessimistic . . . the Wobblies are not released from their cells. They suffer as martyrs

in their cause. The play was . . . a glorification of martyrdom. . . .
After a discussion in the group it was decided there would be no repeat performance.[28]

By the autumn of 1929, the Hackney People's Players were on the threshold of a major breakthrough and as a consequence the WTM was about to become a genuine movement, in which the group found its place as Red Radio.

Hard work, experience and discussions had shown first, that there was a great amount of support for and an interest in working class dramatic art; secondly, that the forms we had been using were not really suitable for our purpose; and thirdly, that in some cases the effective message we had got across to our audiences was not what we had intended. In preparing our plans for the winter of 1929, two objectives stood out as being of the greatest importance: a more flexible and portable form, and greater political clarity in all our material. With these objectives in view, the next programme, the revue *Strike Up*, was prepared.[29]

9 · The old world's crashing . . .

What the drama was able to do for the Catholic Church, the Guilds and the ruling classes, it can be made to do for the working class. . . . No longer will it be confined to a professional clique, no longer will it be merely an entertainment.

(Ness Edwards, *The Workers' Theatre* 1930)[1]

The new Workers' Theatre Movement differed from the earlier theatrical efforts of the labour movement because of its sharp emphasis on class struggle. Like the young German revolutionary workers' theatre it decisively rejected:

the role of raising the cultural level of the workers through contact with great dramatic art which is the aim of the Labour Party and the ILP . . . the task of the WTM is the conduct of mass working class propaganda and agitation through the particular method of dramatic representation.[2]

This was in line with a critique by two of the Communist Party's leading intellectuals, Palme Dutt and Maurice Dobbs, of ILP and other socialist theatrical endeavours. It was also an important motive for the move towards a new type of theatre: short, improvisational agitprop sketches using music, song and cabaret.

Strike Up – the new revue form

In March 1928 a sketch called 'Still Talking' was produced by a group in Manchester. It was set in a political meeting addressed by three parliamentary parrots and had actors interrupting from various parts of the hall. Finally leaping onto the stage, they put the candidates to flight and offered the audience the alternative fighting policy of a 'real' party. (The show in Manchester also included a humorous sketch called 'Conscription' and a one-act expressionistic morality play called *The Judges of All the Earth* published by Labour Publishing Company. It was dedicated to the WTM secretary Christina Walsh whose cubistic stage setting appeared on the frontispiece). 'Still Talking' was possibly the first British example of the new dramatic form Tom Thomas was groping towards in London, but although it was performed successfully a number of times it was not followed up.

The Hackney People's Players, however, had grown in numbers, had begun to develop their own writers, and succeeded in reaching the so-called 'unconverted' working class, not just political activists. They had also periodically sat down and self-critically analysed their work, particularly the problem of building up a suitable repertoire. Their most important conclusion was that they must be able to take shows to people who would not be in agreement with the ideas they were putting over, rather than expecting workers to pay money to come and see them. This meant writing something that could be broken up, so that extracts could be inserted into meetings, and, as they eventually realized, even performed on the street.

In the autumn of 1929 an evening of songs, dances, sketches and monologues, by Tom Thomas, was presented at Conway Hall, Red Lion Square, London. It was called *Strike Up* because there were a number of strikes taking place at the time, and because the group was striking out in a new direction. Talking pictures were all the rage, as were American popular songs, and the show relied heavily on such musical comedy numbers as 'The Broadway Melody', which became:

> They're building up in Soviet Land,
> They're building socialism.
> The workers there are right on top,
> The parasites they've made to hop.
> The more they make the more they pay
> But here it's just the other way.
> In five years sped they'll be right ahead
> In the workers' Soviet Land.[3]

'The Wedding of the Painted Doll' was used as the opening for 'The Talking Shop', probably a scene about Parliament, and Al Jolson's hit song 'Sunny Boy' was parodied as 'Money Boy'. Jack Solomons who performed it had a big bag with '£5,000' written on it which he caressed as he sang:

> Cuddle up to me, Money Boy,
> Free from work and worry,
> I've no need to hurry.
> It's all done for me, Money Boy.
> Though there's unemployment

I get my enjoyment
While I've got you, Money Boy.[4]

The lyrics were certainly crude and used the same type of commercial and unreflective tunes to sing the praises of socialism as to make fun of the exploiting classes. Worst of all, the show 'opened with a "leg-show" or "Beauty Chorus" of six women whose balletic attainments were small but whose efforts were enthusiastically appreciated by the audience.'[5] But the gaiety of the show made people laugh, it didn't just rouse their indignation. And as in the earlier Manchester sketch they were breaking down the barriers between players and audience, a process which had started in *Ragged Trousered Philanthropists*.

In *Strike Up* there was a kind of antiphony between the group on stage and another group we sprinkled in the hall. At the appropriate moment they responded to what was happening on stage by saying 'Yes Strike!' so that it sounded as if the whole audience in the hall was calling for a strike. (Clifford Odets used the same device a few years later in *Waiting for Lefty*.)[6]

Malice in Plunderland had exposed the Labour Party, in *Strike Up* for the first time the satire was directed at a wide range of current political issues, using a variety of forms.

The growth of the movement

At this point the movement began to expand. Veterans of the WTM told us that other groups which had been experimenting with dramatic propaganda in a less consistent way either saw sketches being performed by the Hackney group at meetings, or heard that there was a WTM forming around the Hackney group. They sent representatives and got involved. Before long there were groups in Westminster, Islington, St Pancras, Lewisham and Central and East London, as well as northern England and Scotland.

Not all were entirely new. The Bowhill group from the Fife coalfield centred around Joe Corrie, 'may have provided the original nucleus for the Cowdenbeath WTM',[7] and the 'Salford Red Megaphones evolved from a group of Clarion Players.'[8] The Red Megaphones, founded in 1930, were named after the German group best known in Britain. In the same year another Lancashire group was formed, the Red Cops. Based in Rochdale, an area dominated by the textile industry, they took their name from spinning cops, conical balls of thread wound upon a spindle.

The northern groups were more strictly proletarian, miners, weavers etc., while the London groups, (reflecting perhaps the peculiar composition of the metropolitan Communist Party and Young Communist League) seem to have been drawn quite largely from clerks, school teachers, and out of work young people, together with a substantial complement of East End Jewish proletarians.[9]

Revolution round the corner

Most of those who joined the WTM were young, members of the Communist Party or close to it, and working class in origin. Many were unemployed, and all were enthusiastic about this 'new' inexpensive and accessible means of bringing socialist ideas to the masses.

Philip Poole, for example, the son of a fireman, had been influenced by a left-wing teacher and a parson. He left school at fourteen. Shortly after starting work as an office boy Poole joined the Labour Party. He was secretary of the propaganda committee of his local branch and in 1927 helped form the Stoke Newington Labour League of Youth. When this was disbanded and reformed, Poole was not asked to rejoin although he had been the League's first secretary. Disillusioned by the outcome of the General Strike he became a member of the Hackney Communist Party in 1928 at the age of 18. There he met Tom Thomas, now the National Organizer of the WTM, a young tailor called Mark Chaney, and Jack Solomons, all members of Red Radio as the Hackney People's Players were now called. He started working with Red Radio and became the secretary of the WTM in 1929.

Like the Blue Blouse, they began every show with a simple musical statement of their aims which had the function of a curtain-raiser:

> We are Red Radio,
> Workers' Radio,
> We show you how you're robbed and bled.
> The old world's crashing, let's help to smash it,
> And build a workers' world instead.[10]

The song expresses the idealism and the uncomplicated certainty of young people for whom socialism was a 'kind of fairyland' and the revolution 'just around the corner'. As Philip Poole remembers:

> If it didn't happen this year, it would definitely happen the following year. The possibility that capitalism would stagger out of the depression of 1929–33 just never occurred to us. Capitalism was bumping along the bottom, as one theoretician put it, and would inevitably collapse very quickly, it only needed one push from us and it would go . . . but it didn't quite work out that way, unfortunately . . .[11]

This confidence is all the more surprising in view of the fact that by November 1930, the Communist Party's membership was only 2,555, half what it had been in 1922, shortly after the Party had been founded. Philip Poole again:

> You've got to remember that the Communist Party probably didn't have more than 3,000 members all over the country. But the activity that it generated you'd have thought it was about 300,000. We used to have what we called individual reports at Party branch meetings where you'd be asked to say what you'd been doing during the week. . . . I remember once somebody was reading out his report and he left out Wednesday, and the Chairman said, 'And what did you do on Wednesday, Comrade?' He said 'I had a bath'. You were supposed to be politically active every day of the week. I remember once seeing a Party member coming out of what was then called the Hackney Empire. . . . Music Hall in Hackney, and I was absolutely horrified that this comrade should take an evening off and go to the music hall . . . terrible crime![12]

This hardline approach was to have a serious effect on the young WTM which was not considered a serious political activity by the Communist Party.

The Communist Party and cultural work

The British Communist Party as a whole has never been noted for its concern with theory. There has always been a strong anti-intellectual current among its members. Thus a Wigan member wrote in *The Communist* of December 1928:

> The continued exit of members from our party cannot be explained by a vague reference to 'objective conditions' or even to 'wrong approach'. . . . The main cause, in my opinion, lies in the political lifelessness in our Party locals. The average local Party committee does not function as the political leadership of the local. It is a purely organizational committee passing on instructions from higher organs and distributing routine tasks of a local character. . . . The relationship between comrades is not built on theoretical discussion and the mutual consciousness of the political aims of the tasks in hand. . . . When an attempt is made to raise a discussion on the politics of the task in hand this is discouraged on the grounds of lack of time, or that it is action we need, not talk. The 'practical' chairman . . . is intolerant of 'talkers'! It smacks of intellectualism.[13]

The attitude to culture was the same. All of the veterans interviewed, and all of them are, or were at one stage, Party members, agreed that the growth of the WTM took place in spite of, not because of, the Party.

Q: What was the Party's attitude to your work?

JACK LOVEMAN (Deptford Red Blouses and Streatham Red Front): It was something like the curate's egg. Good in parts. Sometimes it was thought that we were spending too much time on this kind of work. And there was always an attempt by some people to detach us from it and make us do what they considered real political work. . . .[14]

PHILIP POOLE (Red Radio, Hackney): There was no formal link and the Party as such took no interest whatever in the work of the WTM. . . . They probably regarded it as a bit of nonsense . . . as a way of dodging out of the political struggle. . . . I think the same goes for the other sort of semi-political activities like the British Sports Federation. . . . I was very active in the open-air movement. I started a club called the Progressive Rambling Club. We got a great deal of publicity because we used to agitate for opening the moors and creating national parks and objecting to fare increases, that sort of thing. We got quite a lot of support. But the Communist Party as such took no part in it. They regarded these cultural activities as a side issue. They didn't see it as a way in which one could build a bridge to the masses at all.[15]

BRAM BOOTMAN (Rebel Players, Hackney, and Unity): There wasn't a strong interest. . . . Most of these political organizations looked upon us as an adjunct to draw crowds in so that they could have a political harangue afterwards.[16]

CHARLES MANN (Lewisham Red Players): I was a Party member and they left me alone entirely. . . . I think their attitude was 'Here's the youngsters trying to do a bit of arty work. . . .' It was a sort of 'uncle' attitude rather than realizing that here was a weapon in the struggle. . . . They don't take theatre seriously in this country.[17]

PHILIP FIRESTEIN (Proltet): Party members were supposed to be not only Party members, but were also supposed to belong to one or two organizations to bring the influence of communist ideas into the organization, right? Now some people wanted to join a WTM branch. . . . Well, the top people frowned on this, because they thought they're wasting their time there, they're not going to get any great results out of this for the benefit of the communist movement or to win a lot of people into the . . . movement. A group might be made up of fifteen people and they would spend three weeks discussing and rehearsing, and when they had to report to the executive they'd have very little to say. They'd say 'Why not join something bigger?' say, the 'Friends of Spain', or 'Hands off the Soviet Union', or anything on a bigger scale to get bigger, quicker results.[18]

ANDRÉ VAN GYSEGHEM (Rebel Players, Unity): At first it didn't worry me at all, but I did feel as Unity Theatre grew and became more important politically and theatrically, because the two went quite well together, that it was not regarded with sufficient importance by the Party.[19]

The Lovemans and Charles Mann thought that Tom Thomas, as the WTM's National Organizer, had good contacts with the Party's Central Committee, but Thomas himself says that they were cold-shouldered by the Party, except locally.

It's one of the mysteries of life. Whether we hadn't achieved the technical level that would have struck them as being good. . . . I had several chats with Pollitt, not very long really, because it was usually at a meeting where he had spoken and we had performed, and he would say to me 'Jolly good stuff you're doing', or something, general approval, but the speakers, you see, didn't like the advent of a new force.[20]

This is corroborated by Jack Loveman, 'Strange to say, we were not too popular in some ways because we were so bloody successful that it aroused a certain resentment from some speakers.'[21]

Local activists and Party branches were often much more aware of the usefulness and effectiveness of the WTM and were happy to co-operate with them on specific issues. But the view that cultural activity was a deviation from the political struggle was all too common in the Party, as it had been in the KPD in Germany in the early 1920s. Not only was the development of the WTM held back, but an important means of making propaganda was ignored at a time when the worsening economic crisis, although weakening their industrial strength, was making workers receptive to communist ideas.

A measure of success

Despite having started out with only a few stable groups, with tentative experiments with dramatic forms, and without the help of theatre professionals, the WTM managed to build a genuine popular movement. The Party's indifference did not deter the dedicated young people who had stumbled onto an effective means of agitation and propaganda. They were convinced that they were getting results and this is borne out in the reports of the individual troupes to the *Red Stage*.

It was not just a question of large turnouts at meetings – 'An audience of anything under 1,000 is considered small for the Red Front Group of

Dundee . . .'[22] – or enthusiastic responses – 'Each sketch and song was greeted with thunderous applause. At the finish they called for three cheers for the Red Pioneers . . .'[23] – but of hard cash and recruitment figures. Jack Loveman and Charles Mann both remember that collections were usually taken immediately after their groups had performed, and, according to Loveman 'it would always be about 50% higher than if you waited to the end of the meeting. And in those days of financial stringency. . . .'[24]

As they usually performed as part and parcel of meetings it was difficult to determine the groups' role in recruitment, but they certainly made a contribution as this report from the Streatham Red Front Troupe testifies: 'Recruiting for Party at meetings where we showed: Greenwich 120; Wandsworth 22; Battersea (2 shows) 76; total 218'.[25]

In addition to their own first-hand experience, contact with movements in other countries confirmed in the minds of the young British workers the potential of theatre as a propaganda weapon. Tom Thomas represented Britain at the first congress of the International Workers' Theatre League, June 25–29, 1930. And in 1931, a delegation from the London groups was invited to Germany.

The German Tour: international inspiration and influences

We had written to German comrades in the *Arbeiter Theater-Bund Deutschlands* sending them some of our material and telling them what we were doing. They invited us to bring our group over and do a tour of the Rhineland at Easter. We started at Cologne where there was an enormous meeting in the Exhibition Hall. We were greeted with great enthusiasm up on the platform though there wasn't much we could put on – we had no material in German. We were able to take part in a special section written for *Die Engländer* and learned one or two songs. And then we toured the Rhineland up to Koblenz.[26]

The British delegates were impressed by the scale of the ATBD's organization. The awareness that they were part of an international movement which was regarded as 'A powerful factor in the workers' struggle',[27] even though their own Party did not recognize it, must have also boosted their confidence.

These international contacts also had an impact on the forms the British groups had begun to develop. The communist leadership of the ATBD was firmly opposed to naturalism, and in spite of considerable opposition the agitprop tendency was winning. Tom Thomas was struck by the flexibility of the shows: 'If there was any sort of interruption they would stop the play and say "Well, come on, we'll argue it out, that's what we want you to do." '[28] The actors, in basic dungarees, looked different in each scene, although they never changed costumes. The German cabaret tradition was evident in the effective use of music and song.

> I said to Pieck who was the organizer, 'You must have some wonderful people to write this music for you.' He replied to my astonishment, 'We do it ourselves', and convinced me that given some natural aptitude tunes for songs could be just as effectively written by amateurs as plays and sketches.[29]

(Apart from Rutland Boughton and Alan Bush who seem to have co-operated mainly on mass pageants and choral productions, the WTM had no assistance from British composers. Their own musical production was limited to writing new words to popular songs, not composed with the WTM's political objectives in mind and therefore of doubtful value except when used to parody the ruling class. International contacts enabled the WTM to translate or adapt militant workers' tunes, particularly German and Russian songs and marches. The publication of such rewrites became a regular feature on the back page of the *Red Stage*, although it seems unlikely that they ever achieved any mass popularity.)

Thomas returned convinced that the revue style would enable the WTM to achieve 'the freedom of the streets'.[30] He coined the slogan 'A propertyless theatre for the propertyless class' and juxtaposed the notion of a theatre of ideas to the bourgeois theatre of illusion.

'Naturalism (a mere photographic view of things as they appear on the surface)' was rejected and Tom Thomas's concept of 'dialectical realism – the X-ray picture of society and social forces'[31] put forward. To represent these forces the WTM abandoned individual characterization – 'the basis of the bourgeois stage'[32] and began to act types, representing a class rather than an individual. Costumes and props had to be functional – and minimal as they also had to be portable – and were not allowed to detract from the rhythm of speech and movement which became the chief means of expression.

In putting these new principles into practice they were assisted by their German contacts, who came to Britain to give the WTM advice and instruction. The first visitor spoke at a WTM weekend school in June 1930, on the 'brilliant work' of the Hamburg Riveters. He criticized the 'mistaken attempt' of the WTM to 'wed decadent and erotic jazz tunes to the revolutionary message'.[33] (The term 'jazz' was used here rather loosely. The German groups themselves used the forcefulness and synco-pation of jazz to great advantage. In this case, the music was called jazz because it was American, but it actually consisted primarily of Broadway tunes.)

None of the principles were fully developed yet, and their application varied from group to group, but they provided useful guidelines for the period in which WTM activity was to reach a peak.

10 · The heyday of the WTM

The WTM was most active at a time of heightened activity in the British working class, a time which called for intense agitation: the third National Hunger March, the largest mobilization of the unemployed, and the strikes against 'More Looms' in Lancashire. During this period the Movement grew in numbers and consolidated organizationally.

Material was duplicated and sent out to help new groups, which were springing up in Hammersmith, Poplar and in the provinces. A weekend holiday camp in Kent provided an opportunity for discussion of future activities, and talks by Rutland Boughton on music and Tom Thomas on theatre. An Easter weekend school in Derbyshire attracted eight members from London and twenty from other areas, including a contingent from Manchester. Just before Christmas 1930, a conference was called at which a mass speaking sketch with actions was collectively developed. An area committee was established and a central committee elected.

The Lewisham Red Players

One of the most effective and flexible groups in the WTM was the Red Players in Lewisham.

Forming a group

Forming a new group is quite a simple matter, if a few principles are adhered to. It is not necessary to obtain a large number of members; one London group has been working successfully for a long period with three only; but six or seven comrades form a better number. The first principle is proper organization. This means definite evenings for rehearsals (two or three a week), and at least one meeting a week to discuss new material, forthcoming shows and the general work of the group. A secretary should be elected who will keep in touch with other organizations, book the shows, obtain material, etc. Also a treasurer is necessary. A good group easily pays its own way. It is not usual to charge a fee to the NUWM (National Unemployed Workers' Movement – R.S. and K.M.) and such organizations, but co-op guilds, organizers of socials, etc. are usually willing to pay a small fee in addition to covering expenses. Local subscriptions are arranged according to local requirements, the only contribution to the national organization being one penny per month per member.

(C.B.M., 'How to Organize a New Group')[1]

'C.B.M.' was, of course, Charles B. Mann, and the group he referred to which had only three members was his own, the Red Players, which he formed in March 1931, in South London. From the amount they accomplished you would have thought they were thirty, not three, to paraphrase Phil Poole. When the British WTM entered into a contract of socialist competition with the North Caucasian Federation of TRAM in the USSR the Red Players undertook to do their share by establishing at least five new groups, and it wasn't long before they had succeeded in helping three get off the ground, in Croydon, Woolwich and Camberwell. Because of their own limited numbers it was decided that the Croydon group should temporarily amalgamate with the Red Players.

Mann was a frequently unemployed advertising agent, others in the group over the years included his wife, his cousin Philip Harper, an unemployed book-keeper, a teacher called Hawkins whom they had recruited from the Lewisham Labour Party dramatic group, Philip Beale, an engineer, Jack Larkin who was killed in the Spanish Civil War, and Sylvia Banks, later Mrs Atkins, who was elected secretary. (Charles Mann remembers working with the Lovemans, who were clerical workers, too, but they say they were members of the Greenwich Red Blouses and later the Streatham Red Front troupe, so it is possible either that there was sometimes collaboration between the groups, or that some confusion exists because of their contact in the YCL in pre-WTM days.)

Charles Mann was elected producer and he soon set about putting his mark on the Red Players.

My particular forte was to instil discipline, I was very harsh, a sergeant major if you like . . . punctuality, no talking during rehearsals, complete concentration, and when we were putting rhythm into a thing . . . they must adhere to the producer, which was me. . . .

Q: Did you perform at the same time as producing?

A: Yes. I wasn't satisfied . . . unless I was part of it as well. I used to dummy, used to put someone else in where I would have been and that way I could picture the whole thing. Discipline of movement, voices, rhythm, behaviour. We were probably the most disciplined of all. We had a sketch called 'Speed-Up'. If we hadn't had this discipline it might not have gone over. It did go over and always brought the audience in at the end, it had an hypnotic effect.[2]

The sketch Charles Mann referred to was, in fact, American and he had found it in a magazine published by the American League of Workers' Theatres. (The WTM adapted many American plays and sketches, which indicates that links must have existed between them and the American workers' theatres and progressive writers.) It was called 'Tempo, Tempo' originally, but this meant nothing in Britain so the title was changed to 'Speed-Up'.

'Speed-Up' and other sketches

The sketch as adapted by Tom Thomas deals with the Capitalist's attempts to maximize his profits by rationalizing and speeding up the work tempo, a highly topical subject in the early 1930s in Britain. ('Speed-Up' was very similar to another sketch in the WTM repertoire called 'Enter Rationalization', which was also performed by the Red Players.) It was written entirely in short rhythmical rhymes which lent themselves to simultaneous actions illustrating the work process. It required six or more actors, who all wore troupe uniforms, the actor playing the Capitalist and the Policeman adding a top hat and a helmet. It began with the Capitalist leading a group of workers on stage from left to right in a heavy march-like tread, while urging:

> Speed-up, Speed-up! Watch your step!
> Hold on tight, and show some pep.
> Move your hands and bend your body
> Without end and not so shoddy.
> Faster, faster, shake it up,
> No one idles in this shop.
> Time is money, money's power,
> Profits come in every hour.
> Can't stop profits for your sake,
> Speed-up, speed-up, keep awake.[3]

Workers who protest or can't keep up the pace are sacked, a young worker replaces them, the workers join in the Capitalist's refrain. The Capitalist turns into a Policeman who roughly pushes the workers along, while telling them:

> Streets are free for all to tread
> Except for unemployed and red . . .
> . . . In the name of law and order
> We will jail you for disorder . . .
> . . . You're not allowed to strike for bread
> Devil take you, goddam red.

The Policeman turns back into the Capitalist, one of the workers urges the others to 'stop this mad refrain', he is threatened with the sack, but the others support him and they advance on the Capitalist, turning his own rhythm against him:

> Speed-up, speed-up workers' power,
> Resist the bosses every hour.

And finally,

> Down with all the wealthy classes,
> All power to the toiling masses!

The workers, now armed with a red flag, call for a United Front. The Capitalist calls out the soldiers, but the workers counter with:

> Workers, Soldiers, We are brothers.
> Fight the Boss, not one another.

The soldiers join them and together they march on the Capitalist, shouting 'United Front!' The Capitalist flees, and the victorious workers and soldiers return to the centre of the stage, face the audience and present a tableau representing Workers' Control and Ownership of Industry with the Red Army on guard. Alternatively, say the stage directions, the sketch can be carried on to explain the workers' state under workers' control.

The sketch depicts the exploitation and oppression of workers by employers and police, but it does not explain the underlying causes. The workers and soldiers are won over by the militants with scarcely an argument: the third worker asks 'What's the use of your resistance? Without him there's no existence', but is quickly convinced by: 'There's a weapon he'll dislike, Workers' Power through Workers' Strike.' Private property, religion, government, are all dealt with in a few lines, the capitalist is easily vanquished and a static visual 'alternative' presented. (Charles Mann says that their sketches always ended positively, not necessarily with a victory by the workers, but encouraging the audience to take action, to join a union, to give money, to buy the *Daily Worker*, etc.) It is not a sketch likely to convert an unsympathetic audience. And yet Charles Mann maintains they performed such sketches successfully to non-socialists, outdoors:

> Our costumes, and disciplined presentation attracted a crowd. . . .
> They were just ordinary people. It doesn't apply today. There was
> a sort of working class loyalty against the powers that be, it wasn't
> exactly socialist, but there was a feeling of brotherhood among

working people which I don't find today. . . . We'd get 90% of the
people . . . well, let's be fair, we'd get more than 50% of the audience
with us, some just on-looking because it was something to watch,
and anything from one to ten per cent would be hostile, but these
were generally shouted down by the others. We always got an audience and we got respect from them. . . . And I think with the
simplicity of the material, the message went over.[4]

The sketches usually came from the bank of the WTM or were written
by one or two individuals in the Red Players.

I wrote a fair amount of material but it was all subject to adaptation
and then we'd take it to the Central Committee of the WTM and it
could be criticized and adapted and we'd hear other people's stuff,
there was an interchange all the time.[5]

Flexibility was undoubtedly one of the strengths of the Red Players.
In the beginning they tended to perform in Co-op Halls, but as they
became known they were often invited to take part in meetings, travelling
as far as Liverpool, Sheffield and Southampton for a single performance.
Sometimes the organizers would request a particular sketch, often they
would leave it up to the group to decide.

We'd ascertain the type of audience it was going to be . . . and
choose something suitable from our repertoire, sometimes we'd adapt
things. If there was a particular issue we might change the emphasis
or introduce a bit of additional material.
Q: How quickly could you do that?
A: Almost overnight.
Q: Did the other groups work in a similar way?
A: I think we were the most aggressive in this sort of thing. The
others were more localized, but then they started going out too,
and there was competition for bookings . . . not competition for a
particular booking, but to obtain more bookings, to be influential,
effective.[6]

The Red Players did not actually co-operate with workers in writing
sketches about their situation but they came close to it:

There was a place called Stone's, and there was a lot of unrest there
and we used to distribute leaflets outside. I enjoyed drawing hammer
and sickles on the pavement. But we had contacts there and we
learned what was going on inside and introduced part of that into
an existing sketch and adapted it.[7]

'Meerut' and production methods

The Red Players, in keeping with their attempts to win trade union bookings, focused on the oppression of workers in industry, attempting to provide a Marxist analysis of what was going on. They, like the other groups, also performed sketches on national and international subjects, in fact there was hardly an issue on which the WTM *didn't*-have a sketch.

One of the most popular was probably 'Meerut' about the jailing of twenty-nine Indian and three British militants in India for attempting to organize trade unions there. Charles Mann wrote an article called 'How to Produce "Meerut" ' in the *WTM Monthly Bulletin*, the organ that followed the *Red Stage*, and it gives additional insight into the Red Players' approach to production. The sketch was performed as part of the campaign for the prisoners' release and was usually followed by a collection for this purpose.

Mann warns that the sketch is not an easy one and should only be tackled by experienced troupes because the limitations on movement make greater demands on the voice and facial expression, and an unusually high degree of emotional intensity is necessary. The 'prison bars' consisting of six poles held by the six actors, three vertical and three horizontal, should be erected as quickly and efficiently as possible. (Tom Thomas said he thought Charles Mann brought this idea back from Germany where they saw a sketch in which rods were used to convey the idea of prison.)

And the bars must not be moved from position one inch until the time comes. Wobbling bars look like a prison that is as farcical as the trial. It doesn't matter about the space between the bars being large, as long as the effect is symmetrical. You are not portraying a jail, but symbolizing imprisonment.

Make an effective 'picture' by grouping properly – two kneeling, one half lying, perhaps two standing, but all close together and bursting to get the message through. The mass speaking where it occurs must be as perfect as possible. The sketch opens with the word 'Murder' repeated four times. Don't blare this raggedly. Let the leader count four in whispers, then all come in together – softly at first, then in crescendo until the last 'Murder' really sounds like it. Do this well and you will grip the audience from the beginning, and if this sketch is done properly, you won't hear a breath from the audience all through it.

Inflection of the voice is most important. Bitterness, oppression, resistance, triumph of class solidarity, and nearly every emotion is called for in the right place. This sketch offers most unusual opportunities for voice-acting. Take the first speech, for instance. Mere statement of fact is not enough. The voice must be pent up with repressed emotion so that the audience *feels* what is being described. And the bitter sarcasm of 'In India – the brightest jewel in Britain's crown' must be made the most of . . . but not overdone.

The tempo all through the sketch must be quick. As each player finishes his speech the next comes in at once – there is no time to waste – act – act – act – act is the message. Mass speaking, as nearly always, must be staccato and clear. Clip the syllables short and the aggregate effect will be words that can be understood . . .

When it comes to the mass-speaking line '. . . and thrown into Meerut Jail' the bars should actually tremble under the bitter emotion of the actors. But don't obviously shake them. Grip them hard and the very intensity of your feelings will do the trick. The same at the finish. 'Comrades – comrades – comrades – comrades – SMASH THE BARS!' As the word is repeated (half an appeal, half a demand) the bars sway ever so slightly from side to side till at the word 'Smash' they are flung down. (All the same way, please) . . . As the bars crash stand up in a straight line shoulder to shoulder for two or three seconds before going off. . . . All through the sketch, which is quite short, the main things are tempo and emotional intensity. . . . While one prisoner is speaking, the others must be acting all the time – reflecting the words. Tense, haggard, anxious, determined and other expressions suggest themselves as the lines progress. Feel the sketch, mean it, and you will convey the message of it in a way that will strike home to the class-consciousness that is latent in even the most reactionary member of your worker-audience.[8]

This vivid description indicates the extent to which the Red Players were able to overcome in performance deficiencies in the texts they had to work with. Charles Mann always liked ballet, and believes he was influenced by it, his emphasis on disciplined collective movement, clipped mass speaking and conviction made his group one of the most respected in the WTM.

Bookings – the elusive trade union audience

The group circulated a list of the sketches in their repertoire, and advertised in the *Daily Worker* and *Red Stage*. The bookings they liked best were from trade union branches. They put forward the idea of a break in a branch meeting with a theatre show, and this caught on: the workers were entertained, and a message put over. But the 'uncle' attitude Charles Mann described with respect to the Communist Party was also common in the unions:

I think the usual attitude at a trade union meeting was 'this is a bit of entertainment, the young folk are going to do a sketch' and they were surprised when it came over, because if our impact was sufficiently powerful, and often it was, the comeback from the audience was terrific – we hit 'em! And then a number of people would come and discuss what we were doing.[9]

But although the Red Players made more of an effort than most other groups to get trade union bookings, a list of their dates for January 1932, published in *Red Stage* included only three union bookings. Of those, two were for the National Minority Movement, a CP-led left opposition in the trade union movement, and the third was for the UCWU, a CP dominated breakaway from the Tailor and Garment Workers' Union.

Our show for the Tailors' Union (UCWU) at Aldgate, which included 'Enter Rationalization', proved particularly appropriate, as the workers were just entering on a fortnight's lock-out. Here is a list of our bookings for January, which does not include open-air shows, which we usually give at a moment's notice:

January 2nd – UCWU, Aldgate.
       "   4th – Tenants' Association, Barkingside.
       "   9th – Minority Movement, Cromer Street.
       "   15th – All-London Show, Greenwich.
       "   16th – Furnishing M.M., Cromer Street.
       "   18th – Croydon ILD (Probably a printing error – should read 'ILP' – R.S. and K.M.)
       "   20th – Action NUWM (National Unemployed Workers Movement – R.S. and K.M.)
       "   22nd – Croydon Show, Dennett's Hall.
       "   25th – Lewisham Show.
       "   30th – Croydon Co-op.[10]

A similar report in the April–May issue of 1932 listed performances for the Independent Labour Party, the ILO, the Communist Party, and Friends of the Soviet Union. Although the Red Players in particular also stressed open-air work in parks, on the streets, in market-places and housing estates, the evidence suggests that the bulk of their indoor work was for organizations created or dominated by the Communist Party and their sympathizers, such as the Minority Movement, National Unemployed Workers' Movement, Friends of the Soviet Union, etc., or for the ILP, the Co-op and so on. This comes as no surprise when one looks at the Communist Party's approach to the trade union movement at that time.

Left sectarianism and the spectator's consciousness

At its 1928 Congress the Comintern had proclaimed the 'third period' of capitalism (in which rationalization had brought about relative economic stability, but a sharpening of internal and international conflict and a consequent 'revolutionary upswing'). The CPGB moved swiftly and sharply to the left. In 1929 in *Labour Monthly* Harry Pollitt called for class-conscious workers not to vote Labour, stating, 'The fight now in every sphere of political activity, whether in elections, strikes, lock-outs, unemployed demonstrations, etc., is against the enemies, the capitalist class and the Labour Party and the TUC.'[11] Before the Tenth Congress they had supported the A. J. Cook–Jimmy Maxton 'socialist revival' campaign, even claiming credit for it. (The miners' leader and the ILP leader had issued a manifesto charging the Labour Party with 'a serious departure from the principles and policy which animated the founders'.)[12] The new ultra-left policy called for a strengthening of the revolutionary trade unions. Since none existed, this meant in practice attempting to create breakaway unions. Cook was alienated to the point where, after years of co-operating with the Party, indeed frequently defending it, he was forced to break with it. The CPGB bade 'farewell to him without regret and with the contempt he deserves'.[13] At the Tenth Plenum of the Executive Committee of the Comintern he was characterized as 'one of those who formed "an active and constituent part . . . of social fascism" '.[14] The ILP, too, was labelled an 'inseparable part of British social-fascism'.[15] (Party members were chastised for allowing a delegation to MacDonald in September 1931 from the NUWM, supposedly a non-Party organization, to 'get in the hands of Maxton and Kirkwood',[16] who were the leaders.) As Philip Poole pointed out:

> there's something to be said for it. The Social Democrats in Germany did pave the way for Fascism by telling the workers to vote for Hindenburg, who promptly installed Hitler as chancellor. But to antagonize the supporters of the Labour Party by calling them social fascists was the wrong way to go about it.[17]

These tirades against the Labour Party, the TUC leaders, the ILP and the trade union bureaucrats was intended to place the Communist Party – 'at the head of the rising wave of struggle'.[18] But the Party's attacks on anyone who didn't wear the CP label, as Cook put it, did not win over the masses of workers. Hugo Dewar points out what was needed:

> Mere denunciation of all reformist leaders, right, left and centre taught the workers nothing and served only to antagonize them. A campaign of patient, persistent, and consistent *explanation* was required; explanation that generalized the day-by-day defensive battles, bringing understanding of capitalism as a *system* and the utter

futility of the reformist method of attempting to prettify this or that 'ugly' face of it.[19]

It was not until the Twelfth Congress in November 1932 that the Party's sectarianism and isolation was criticized internally.

The Secretariat of the International Workers' Dramatic Union, in greeting the emergence of the *Red Stage*, reminded the British WTM that they had the task of 'exposing capitalism and its Labour lieutenants',[20] and in any case most of the WTM members were also good Party members. They would not have gone against the Party line, indeed their sketches reflected it. But instead of sectarian harangues, the WTM used a much more powerful weapon, humour. One of their most popular parodies was entitled 'Jimmy Maxton – And the ILP':

> The Labour Government, so they swear,
> Sold the workers' interest everywhere
> Jimmy Maxton, and all his men.
> > The reason why the Tories reign,
> > The Labour Party, it's quite plain –
> > Were out to serve their private gain –
> > So, fight to put the Labour Party back again!
> For inconsistency's no crime,
> We're bound to contradict ourselves some time!'
> > Jimmy Maxton and all his men.[21]

This song and others like it, were received with loud laughter by ILP audiences, and did not stop the WTM getting bookings with such organizations. With the trade unions, unfortunately this does not appear to have been the case. The reasons are probably two-fold:

1 'Ordinary' trade union members were not as politically conscious as rank and file ILP members, many of whom would have agreed with the WTM's criticisms of their leaders.

2 The WTM as a whole, in line with Party policy, made little effort to get trade union bookings. The Lovemans of Red Blouses and Philip Poole of Red Radio corroborated this in interviews. An article entitled 'Getting Down To It – Book Those Shows' in the *Red Stage* by 'Producer'[22] does suggest that troupe secretaries write to local trade union branches, among other organizations. This article, however, was almost certainly written by Charles Mann of the Red Players, but although they attempted to make inroads into the unions, it would have been difficult for one group to overcome the sectarianism and resultant hostility the Party had engendered. Neither could they expect to get industrial bookings from contacts their own members might have, since most were unemployed or in white collar jobs.

This relative lack of contact with the mass of organized workers may well have had important repercussions on their material. As they did not often perform for the broad masses in contexts where they could get proper feedback, this being very difficult outdoors, they would scarcely have been forced to take account of low levels of political consciousness and write their sketches accordingly. 'Speed-Up' is a good example of this. In theory, the Central Committee was aware of this problem, and they appointed a reading committee to decide which sketches should be performed and published.

> We first of all agreed that the question of the approach to the workers could be summarized in this fashion:
> '*From* what the workers understand or are familiar with, *To* what they do not yet understand,' i.e. the view point of the revolutionary workers.
> This may seem a very trite formulation, obvious, in fact. And yet sketches submitted have had to be turned down because the revolutionary point of view has been taken for granted at the very start of the sketch, instead of being one object to which the sketch has carefully worked up. This approach limits the value of any sketch to the relatively small number of people who are already convinced of this point of view – and it's unnecessary to play to them, anyhow.
> In a word, this approach is 'sectarian' and a technical mistake having big political importance.[23]

However, in practice, Tom Thomas, Charles Mann, and the others on the reading committee tended to be wary of discouraging prospective writers, and 'let most things pass, if they weren't just nonsense'.[24]

Agitation: its strengths and limitations

The WTM groups became very good at linking their sketches to particular issues and were able to respond to the events of the day with tremendous speed. The sketch 'Gas Masks', for instance, was performed as an introduction to anti-war meetings, and skits on the means test were presented to rallies of the unemployed. Sometimes the scenes were performed while local issues were still being fought out. Raphael Samuel has documented several examples of this:

> In Sheffield, the WTM was re-formed by a group of younger members who wanted to pursue a more activist course. Faced with a local strike of newspaper sellers they wrote a sketch about it and played it on the streets while the strike was proceeding, 'with very great success'. The 'Becontree Reds' at Dagenham, East London, wrote a sketch about an eviction and were able to perform it outside

the house where the actual eviction was threatening, 'thus contributing very effectively to the fight to defend the workers' homes.'[25]

Police assaults were on the increase at this time, and Jack and Alice
Loveman also remember a sketch on 'The Battle of Deptford Broadway'
which took place after a march to try to persuade dockers not to load
scrap metal for Japan, then invading China. Their troupe, the Red
Blouses, must have produced the sketch very quickly indeed, since they
recall Sandy Duncan, who had been hurt in the mêlée, watching it either
on the platform or in the audience with his head still in bandages.

But one of the most interesting contributions to local struggles was that
of the Salford Red Megaphones.

In 1932 the employers demanded that Lancashire weavers work eight
looms at a time. Some of the machines dated from the early nineteenth
century, and were very difficult to handle. The weavers were kept busy
operating four at once. Not only would conditions have become impossible in the mills but the work force would have been cut in half.

The craft nature of the industry meant that the decision to strike or
not had to be taken union by union which virtually meant town by town.
The Red Megaphone, many of whom had sisters, brothers, and other
relatives in the mills, made it their job to try and unify the fragmented
work force. Arriving just before a vote was to be taken, they would,
according to Ewan MacColl 'present the facts as clearly as we could . . .
so as to make them feel that they weren't alone, that there were other
workers throughout the area taking similar decisions.'[26]

Sketches were sometimes written in the bus on the way, rehearsed for
half an hour and performed at such venues as the marketplace in Wigan,
on the steps of the Public Baths, or outside factory gates. The police
would invariably arrive after ten minutes or so . . .

> occasionally we'd manage to get through a short play – certainly
> through a few satirical songs – outside the factory gate before the
> police moved us on. But as the strike became a big and burning
> issue throughout the country, and food was being raised on a
> mammoth scale for the whole of Lancashire, it became a question of
> going and performing on every single street of a town, putting on a
> show lasting about four minutes, collecting contributions and then
> moving on to the next street. You took a barrow with you, or a
> handcart, and collected food, bundles of clothing, and money and it
> all went into the strikers' relief fund. . . .
>
> One day in Burnley we played to a crowd of a hundred and fifty
> thousand strikers, many of whom had travelled for a couple of days
> over the moors, and perhaps had fights on the way with police. . . .
> And we played through megaphones on the tops of four giant lorries

to that great crowd – it really was a tremendous experience – with planks across to join the lorries into a huge stage.[27]

This combination of spreading the struggle, building solidarity and gaining material support is an example of very good agitational work and was only achieved by the best groups.

But even the best never got *beyond* agitation. Their sketches were moving, funny or informative, but as far as one can tell from the existing material, they didn't really help the audience to *understand* the complexities of the economic and political system. Although an alternative, the Soviet Union, was usually presented, in the more abstract sketches the cartoon bosses were thrown out in a totally unrealistic way by one-dimensional workers too easily convinced of the need for revolution.

The sketches based on real-life events were more down to earth and although more limited in their objectives, in some ways politically more successful. 'The Spirit of Invergordon', for example, made with the help of Len Wincott, one of the leaders of the 'Sailors' Strike', depicted the extraordinary mutiny of 'loyal' sailors against wage cuts imposed by the Labour Lord of the Admiralty, and called on all workers to follow their example. The action demanded was not the overthrow of the whole capitalist system, but a simple, but extremely important, and attainable strike when living standards were threatened. The sketch was frequently performed and had an 'excellent reception'.[28]

The West London Red Star Troupe was particularly concerned about more mundane but equally important local bread and butter issues, as well as reaching wider sections of the working class, as the following *Red Stage* report indicates.

A series of political discussions has shown us the necessity for dealing with the issues which are a life and death matter of every day. We have commenced work on a series of new sketches designed to answer the questions which are painfully unanswered – such questions as: 'How can we get the housewives into our meeting?' And 'Of what use is the Borough Council to the workers?' to mention only two of the important ones.[29]

However, a fairly complete description of another sketch, simply called 'Castleford', provides an excellent insight into how such a topical piece on a local event was written by:

a raw worker-player who knows nothing of the technicalities of dramatic writing, or even acting, but has had to learn what bit he does know from the hard school of experience and not in a nursery or school for dramatic writers.[30]

In the process he also exposed some of the weaknesses in the usual WTM formula for sketches, and made a few rough, but interesting innovations in response to the requirements of the real situation.

The sketch arose out of the events in Castleford in the summer of 1932 when a demonstration to present a petition to the local council was baton-charged by the police. The local WTM group had taken an active part in the demonstration, performing a number of sketches on local issues earlier in the day. One of them sent this report to *Red Stage*:

When the police charged with their usual ugly methods, the kiddies at the front got the first attack. The batons descended and one kiddy had to have three stitches in his head. Comrade Speight was knocked down and immediately died; our other comrades were knocked senseless, and beaten up while lying on the ground. Three WTM members were arrested among others – Comrades Humble, Lamb and Allington.[31]

The remainder of the group immediately began to prepare a sketch on the day's events. Later in the year the sketch was criticized, and in the February 1933 issue of the *Monthly Bulletin*, successor to the *Red Stage*, a reply to the criticism by the author, S.R., appeared. While admitting that the sketch may have been 'technically poor and negative in character'[32] he argued that the Central Committee should not have passed it for performance if this was the case, and then defended his work as follows:

It was based on many present WTM sketches, in theme, sequence, lines, action. . . . So if the 'Castleford' sketch was wrong, then many WTM sketches are likewise. In what way should it want to make one commit hari-kari? It was not intended as a sample of Shakespearian dramatic art, but an actual recital or restaging of a piece of working class history. (I am inclined to the theory that it has been badly produced, and instead of it being presented as a serious sketch it has been made the vehicle for a farce. I may be wrong in making this charge against the troupe concerned. If so, I apologize, but the reason I make this suggestion is the remark of another critic when he says that the second prisoner was dragged in grinning.)

In what way was this, and other sketches, negative? The actual history of the struggle has been based on months of organized work by the NUWM and Party, amongst them unemployed workers. . . .

There are 4,000 unemployed in this area, 1,000 more being dismissed on August Bank Holiday. The uniting of the two in common cause culminated in the mighty demonstration to the Trades Council. The brutal bashing by the police and still more brutal hustling away within twelve hours to six months hard labour apiece for six of our best fighters.

How else could this history have been portrayed than as it actually was? Why should it be portrayed other than it was? . . . The Town Council was thought best as a start because demonstrations of workers went there as a result of a Communist councillor hoping to get something done for them. . . . The lines were made up from press reports of council meetings, and being true show up the class character of each of the Councillors. We get the usual sort of dialogue with the Communist Councillor putting the workers' side, then the deputation presenting the petition, the dodging by the Councillors, and the insistence of the Communist . . . who warns them that the workers *will* demonstrate and fight.

Then we get the Communist Councillor . . . *drawing the audience of workers in to* the action by one simple line, then the militant leadership steps forward in the persons of the troupe members. They give a lead in the usual WTM slogan form. It is here that the important part of the sketch occurs . . . what else could the militant leadership, i.e., troupe members, do, but rally the workers to unite in common struggle . . . without having to make a long detailed statement which would result in the sketch becoming a play?

Then on from the slogans to the PAC (Public Assistance Commission – R.S. and K.M.) again, actual statements were used for lines . . . there doesn't seem to be enough guts in it, and it ends rather weakly, but I didn't want to again go into more slogans, so on to the Trades Council . . . made up from Press reports and actual incidents and statements. What . . . ought I to have done to be perfectly 'dramatic'? We get the usual hypocrisy of the Trade Union bureaucrats, and the militant deputation busting in and demanding of them that they fight instead of talk, and when they are forced to the wall they act just like capitalist lackeys. Then we get the street scene, the demonstration awaits the Labour-ites' answer. Here we again draw our audiences of workers into the action.

Here we get the cue to the police by the Labour-ites who do their duty like good citizens. Then the Court scene and the hustling away of the militants, and finally the conclusion of . . . continuing to struggle until this system is smashed. . . .

Why was it necessary for a comrade to go between scenes to explain what it was all about? . . . Posters, cards and properties should have been enough to explain the action. Its title should have been enough.

This spirited defence of the 'Castleford' sketch raises a number of interesting points. Perhaps the most important is the one about the sketch's negative character. The emphasis on positive endings had been a long-standing characteristic of the WTM since the days of *The Ragged Trousered Philanthropists*. On the one hand there was a real need at a time when the working class was on the defensive, to inject confidence into workers, to remind them of their strength and ability, and to point out that eventually the contradictions of capitalism would result in its abolition. On the other hand, this could lead to an idealized view of the working class and an underestimation of the very real difficulties standing in their way which had to be understood and confronted, as in 'Speed-Up'. It is unlikely that a working class audience during the Depression would take such a viewpoint at all seriously.

It is significant that a sketch about a real event gave rise to such questions. Here too were the beginnings of a living newspaper or documentary approach, attempts to try to draw the audience into the action, and awareness of the problem of too many slogans. At the same time the article clearly reveals the lack of models available, resulting in a tendency for worker-writers to go on reproducing a standard formula, with all its inadequacies as well as its virtues.

The Red Stage and All-London Shows

In spite of two enormous drawbacks, lack of support from the Communist Party and inadequate texts, the WTM flourished. In November of 1931, the first issue of the *Red Stage* was published. This was an important step in building a national movement and providing a forum for information and theoretical debate on such issues as 'Individualistic self-boosting' versus mass-speaking, initiated by the *Daily Worker* film critic after an All-London Show, or the use of American jazz. Charles Mann became the editor and his journalistic skills were evident in the professional layout and brisk style.

Another forum was provided by the All-London shows put on once or twice a year so that groups could see each other's work, learn from it and criticize it. Family, friends and supporters made up the bulk of the audience. According to Jack Loveman, 'We used to call them "demonstrations" because that got round the entertainment tax. We used to say "You couldn't call this entertainment, could you?" '[33] But although the audience was sympathetic, they were prepared to offer criticism too, which on at least one occasion was published in *Red Stage*. Lyall Watson who saw such a show at Greenwich, was critical of the blocking of several sketches, and suggested the use of a curtain, and of lighting: 'Surely people's lives are drab enough without taking . . . away the light.' Watson complained about the monotony of the choral scheme, and closed by saying that he had never seen such enthusiasm upon the stage but that it wasn't being used, and this could result in a falling-away.[34]

Touring Scotland and Wales

The 1931 election campaign and the WTM's contract with TRAM stimulated even more frantic activity than usual. In London Red Radio led by Mark Chaney made a lightning tour of ten constituencies in four nights performing on the back of a lorry. An open-air show near Whitechapel High Street attracted a crowd of 4,000. Traffic was halted, but the police couldn't intervene as the performance was part of a political meeting.

In October, a group of unemployed WTM members from London calling themselves the Red Pioneers toured Scotland in support of Willie Gallacher, the Communist candidate. The tour part of the TRAM contract was a huge success, and Ferguson, the Greenock candidate told them, 'If only you could stay till polling day, it would not be a question of getting in, but how big a majority we would have.'[35] At Port Brae, Kirkcaldy, they performed outdoors for the largest crowd since 1926; in Dundee, hundreds had to be turned away from the packed Forrester's Hall. In Edinburgh, they gave a show in front of the National Gallery to over 5,000 workers, after which an effigy of Graham the Labourite was burnt among cheers. They helped recruit sixty new members for the NUWM and several new members for the Women's Guild. Large collections were taken for the election funds, 2,500 WTM song sheets were sold, and in Dundee a new and vigorous WTM group was set up, and existing groups in Edinburgh, Greenock, Glasgow and Liverpool were spurred into action. (Douglas Allen, in his paper 'The Glasgow Workers' Theatre Group, 1937–1940', refers to the Glasgow WTM branch. It began in the late twenties and performed at 'meetings and socials organized by political groups like the Friends of the Soviet Union, but its repertoire of material [such as 'The Five Year Plan'] is remembered as rather crude sloganizing by those who saw it.')

The flexibility of the revue form was proven on the tour. The Pioneers had eight sketches and a number of songs in their repertoire which they varied to fit the occasion, trying them out under all sorts of conditions. Some of the performances were pre-arranged, others were set up at short notice by local Party members. (Local activists, particularly in areas like Scotland, were often much more appreciative of the WTM's efforts than Party officials.) On one occasion the group went around with a bell and a couple of megaphones and succeeded in drawing about 150 workers to the local Miners' Institute, on another, they rigged up a platform with trestles and boards at the bottom of a cul-de-sac outside the Greenock Labour Exchange and played to an audience of 1,000 workers. The most popular sketches, performed at almost every venue, were found to be 'Jimmy Maxton and the ILP' and the NUWM sketch 'The Crisis' in which typical capitalists smoking huge cigars and wearing box hats, and sinister-looking politicians armed with swords labelled 'cuts' and 'Tariff Reform', plot against the workers for the sheer joy of it. 'Meerut' would have been in the first four but it was found to be unsuitable for outdoor work.

In January 1932, with Charles Mann behind the wheel of the old Ford baker's van they had used in Scotland (they had to go up hills backward), the Red Pioneers toured South Wales. They had expected this tour to be even more successful than the Scottish one, because of the Welsh people's musical and dramatic tradition, but they found that their reception was mixed. The van broke down in Bristol, where they performed to a small but appreciative audience and helped start the nucleus of a Bristol WTM group. Finally on the road again, rehearsing en route, they arrived in Tonypandy only to find that the police had banned the show. 'This is Sunday in Wales. As CBM points out even the pubs are shut.'[36]

Monday evening after a gruelling rehearsal conducted by Tom Thomas they were only fairly well received by a non-political audience in Treherbert. But the show, which included 'Murder in the Coalfields', a short simple sketch inspired by a recent colliery disaster, was to have an unexpectedly dramatic ending. A miner burst in to announce a serious accident in a nearby pit. The Pioneers quickly packed their props and drove to the pit, where they witnessed scenes they had been enacting minutes before:

Anxious men and women at the Pithead. Rescue parties coming up gassed themselves. They've brought four dead up, and many injured. God knows what the death-roll will be. Home in the early hours, but not to sleep. The echo of a miner's clog breaks the stillness – then a voice: 'How is it now, Harry?' 'Six dead.' Later: 'Ten dead.' And in the morning twelve dead and more in hospital. An atmosphere of heavy gloom hangs over the whole valley. Groups of men and women with drawn faces, stand before house-doors everywhere.[37]

The next audience at Treorchi consisted of 60 per cent children, who jumped onto the stage, fought and played leap-frog throughout the sketches. It was useless going on so the curtain came down at half-time and didn't go up again.

At Trealaw, however, where the local miners were bitterly angry about safety conditions, the show was a triumph, the Judge's Hall was packed, and the group received an ovation. Equally important, the nucleus of a local troupe was set up. Next morning a short show outside some miners' houses in an isolated area fell flat. 'The workers are unable to comprehend us or conceive our purpose; our material is too advanced.'[38]

The last two shows were well received, and after some difficulties with the police who seemed determined to harass the group as much as possible, they set off for home. They had had a difficult tour, but they had learned an important lesson: much of their material was unsuitable for non-politicized audiences, and they resolved to adjust their work accordingly.

May Day

May Day 1932 provided the WTM with an opportunity to explore new forms and to take them to a wide public. The previous year had seen the biggest workers' demonstration since the General Strike, and the Central Committee saw this as a means to build the movement as well as a chance to add 'brightness, interest and meaning to the demonstrations in every town.'[39] They suggested that the troupes take part in uniform, lead the street-singing, and provide the bands with the music for their revolutionary songs.

Groups were encouraged to perform their topical sketches at the open-air meetings, and to link up and draw in other workers to perform the mass-sketch 'The First of May' by Tom Thomas, which required thirty to fifty performers. (It traced the development of May Day from the campaign for the eight hour day in 1889 to the crisis in Britain and the Soviet alternative in 1930. It was the only sketch the WTM had in which mass speech choirs were balanced against each other and a speaker, and was extremely sloganistic.) They could also help with tableaux on moving carts showing the work of the various organizations.

The troupes did indeed play an active part. The events of that May Day reveal clearly the extent to which they were in the forefront of mass work, and the growing police brutality:

There were twenty-one arrests made in Dundee on May Day. Four of the prisoners were members of the WTM – comrades Helen Whyte, Betty Clark, John Ragan and Frank Clark. As we started singing 'The Internationale' the police drew their batons and started smashing at the crowd. The two girl comrades made an attempt to rescue two other comrades: they succeeded in getting one away, then they were arrested. Our comrade carrying the banner was the next one, and was seen lying on the ground. While our four comrades were being marched up the road they started singing the rebel songs together and that inspired the people. The policeman said to comrade B. Clark, 'Ha! So you thought you would come out and fight us?' 'No', she said 'we came out to fight against the rotten conditions.' An inspector told the girls to put on their coats and not to have 'any bloody showman tricks here.' Owing to the arrests we were unable to put on the sketches because the four comrades had parts in them, but hearty cheers were given for our comrades when the reason was explained.[40]

In Bristol, too, the WTM troupe, founded during the Welsh tour of the Red Pioneers, was threatened with arrest if a sketch involving the Public Assistance Committee was given. In Preston

an enormous crowd gathered round the lorry, attracted chiefly by the WTM in glaring contrast to a small ILP meeting which was taking place opposite. Our rendering of 'Jimmy Maxton and the ILP', particularly appropriate, was well applauded.[41]

The Red Players performed three sketches from a lorry at the starting point of the march, and shouted mass slogans using megaphones en route. 'Meerut' and 'Do You Remember 1914', a sketch comparing the role of the war-mongering capitalist press in 1914 with its attempts to whip up anti-Soviet feeling in the early 1930s, were performed on the No. 1 platform at Hyde Park to a crowd of 3,000. The Castleford troupe affiliated to the local May Day Committee and played an active part with the help of a 'Means Test Coffin' which was carried on the march and set alight at the finish, as well as a huge red, gold and black WTM banner complete with hammer and sickle and Soviet Star, and megaphones draped in red and labelled 'WTM' through which slogans and advertisements of meetings were shouted. They duplicated mass slogans which were shouted en masse on a given signal, conducted a mass singing campaign, and sold Song Sheets, the *Red Stage*, and the *Daily Worker*.

The First National Conference

On 25 and 26 June 1932, thirty-six delegates from eight London troupes, the WTM choir and nine provincial groups, met in London. Their main tasks were:

To hammer out a common platform which will embody in a concise form the fundamental principles of the Workers' Theatre. To compare experiences during the past years. To see where·we are weak (that is not difficult) and from this to see why these weaknesses exist, and how we are going to remedy them.[42]

Low performance standards, fluctuations in group personnel, and in particular the question of street work and of providing specific material for particular factories and areas were all to be dealt with. To provide a basis for discussion the Central Committee published a statement on the nature, development and future activities of the Movement.[43]

Agitprop vs. naturalism

The document analysed the capitalist theatre and cinema which serves to 'blind the workers to the existence of the class struggle' while attempting to 'cover up their bankruptcy of ideas by means of extravagant and meaningless display.' Intellectuals rebelling against the triviality of the capitalist theatre give rise to the 'little' and repertory theatres and advanced sections of the amateur dramatic movement, but believing themselves to be 'above the battle' they become lost in 'ingenious but sterile technicalities and experiments.' Within the Labour Party, ILP and Co-op dramatic groups, one tendency seeks to bring the working class into contact with 'great' art (i.e. capitalist) while the other depicts the misery of the workers but shows no way out. Only the workers' theatre is a conscious weapon of the workers' revolution expressing their struggle in dramatic form.

The statement pointed to the importance of the workers' theatre abroad; here at home, the WTM must adapt itself to particular conditions, has a particular job to do, a unique role to play:

Every strike, every wage-cut, every attack on the workers' conditions must find its expression on the platform of the Workers' Theatre and no exclusive attention to general political events can be a substitute for this.

From 1926 to 1930 plays with progressive or even revolutionary content were produced in the traditional manner, experience had shown:

1 That the naturalistic form, namely that form which endeavours to show a picture on the stage as near to life as possible, is suitable for showing things as they appear on the surface, but does not lend itself to disclosing the reality which lies beneath . . .

2 That the unities of space and time, which are one of its main features, greatly hinder the portrayal of the class struggle in dramatic form (consider, for instance, the difficulty in bringing together in a reasonable, naturalistic way, an ordinary worker and an important capitalist.

3 That the audience reached by such plays which demanded a well-equipped stage were insignificant compared to the mass of workers who could not be brought to the theatre or hall to witness them.

In contrast, the agitprop style needs no elaborate stage, only an open platform, scenery which can be carried about by hand, no make-up, and a minimum of costume, enabling the players to go where the workers are waging the class struggle, at the factories, the Labour Exchanges, etc. Beside flexibility there are other advantages to the style:

2 Instead of emphasizing the ability to portray characters, a difficult job for workers with very little spare time, it used instead the class

experience of the worker-player, which convinces a worker audience much more than the studied effects of the professional actor.

3 The direct approach to the audience, together with the fact that the performance is surrounded by and part of the crowd, is of great value in making the worker audience feel that the players are part of them, share their problems and their difficulties, and are pointing a direct, reasonable way out.

The naturalistic method should not be ruled out and should be debated at the conference. At the same time:

It must be said that up to the present even the best performances have not touched a hundredth part of the possibilities of this new style, and the struggle for a higher level of technique (a higher level of effectiveness) is one that every group must undertake very seriously. To tolerate a low standard of performance is one of the worst forms of sabotage. Strict self-criticism from the audiences must be developed. Finally, the effectiveness with which our sketches are presented depends to a large extent upon the political consciousness and conviction of the players, which can only be heightened by systematically raising their political level.

The repertory problem: quantity, quality and collective playmaking

In discussing the question of repertoire, it was pointed out that over fifty items had been issued in the past two years and most had aroused great interest. But there were shortcomings, including

the narrowness of outlook, which assumes . . . that the audience is already familiar with the revolutionary point of view. This can only repel the majority of workers who are not yet convinced. The acid test of a sketch is whether it starts on a basis which is common to a non-political working class audience and leads them step by step to agreeing with its revolutionary conclusion. Without this all is merely preaching to the converted. . . . In choice of subject too, this sectarianism has often been apparent. . . . On the other hand, there has been an occasional tendency to revert to the plays of the 'Left' bourgeois theatre because of a desire to produce a naturalistic play.

The repertory problem can be solved through collective writing which will draw in new writers while still using the experienced ones:

As a regular activity, independently undertaken by each group, it can have great results, not only in the material produced, but by way of political and technical training. Every member of a group can help in some way. The most important method is to organize the collection of facts and information upon which the sketch can be based. First a theme is chosen, and then every member of the group endeavours to get information about it by talking to those workers it concerns. Then at a subsequent meeting, the information is collectively discussed, the line of the sketch determined, and if necessary, it can be left to one or two members to write it up. . . . A special report will be made to the conference embodying the experience of the past two years and of our brother organizations abroad.

Organizationally, the main task was to actively seek new working class members, both those who were already militant, and those who were attracted by the 'virility, originality and effectiveness of our performances'. A broad base in the working class was needed to withstand the inevitable attacks which would come as the Movement grew in numbers and effectiveness.

Trends towards the curtain stage

Only one group went against the line developed in the Central Committee's document, the Rebel Players from East London, to whom the well-known professional producer and actor, André Van Gyseghem became attached. The conference came down heavily in favour of agitprop and against naturalism and the curtain stage. But at least as important as the formal debates was the All-London Show staged on the Saturday evening. There the provincial groups and the new groups could see for themselves how the generally more advanced London troupes handled the common texts. In keeping with their position, the Rebel Players put on a realistic play set in a Russian peasant home. An old woman prayed to a new icon and some of her wishes were indeed granted. The climax of the play came when a priest arrived and asked, 'What are you doing with a photo of Lenin?' Tom Thomas remembered the play with horror when we interviewed him:

> The other people had been acting these other things for perhaps a year or two, and having all sorts of successes as you'll see in *Red Stage*, and felt they were doing an important political job . . . the idea of going back and doing a twenty minute play with an icon of Lenin's photograph seemed to me . . . contemptible, I couldn't say it at the time, but now I can whisper it to you.

The Rebel Players had lost the argument on this occasion, but the debate was to continue, and they were to gain some support from other groups.

The secretary of the Dundee Red Front troupe raised the issue in the *WTM Monthly Bulletin* in reply to an article on technique by the National

Organizer Tom Thomas. (The *Red Stage* had succumbed to mounting debts.) The Dundee group had begun to experiment with stage effects:

Take the 'Meerut' sketch as an example. The Red Front Troupe have played it both indoors and out, but on the last occasion . . . we used scenery consisting of the front of a prison with two cells; three comrades in each cell; the curtains . . . were closed, and the lights lowered. As soon as the curtains were opened everybody could be heard talking about the prison front. At the top we had in big letters 'MEERUT – 1929–1932 PRISON'. . . . We also brought in a few things we had never tried before; you could have heard a pin drop when one comrade started to sing the first verse of 'The Red Flag'. This in itself made us feel imbued with enthusiasm, in fact *we* were the Meerut prisoners, – and mind, this never happened any time we had played it before. . . . At the smashing of the bars, when the comrades came through the cell windows to the front of the platform, the applause was so great that we had to wait until it ended before we could finish the rest of the sketch. This was played on Meerut Sunday.

Quoting the MB, we read we must go on improving our present style until we reach the level of our *brother* organizations in other countries. You condemn the Hackney group (Rebel Players – R.S. and K.M.) for use of make-up etc. and say the open-platform style should be used. If you look up No. 1 Bulletin of the IWDU Page 15 we read about ARTEF, which has a regular studio in which political education is given and special theatrical technique, including diction, rhythmics, plastics, make-up etc. Then on Page 19 we see a photograph of a scene from a Documentary Play, with use of lighting effects, etc., and scenery. On Page 20 the same, so therefore we also should use these methods.

Of course, this can only be used indoors; we must use the open platform when the weather enables us to get outdoors.[44]

The Jewish Proltet troupe which had developed out of a progressive youth group based at the Workers' Circle in Alie Street were also criticized for their use of props. (Founded in 1911 the Workers' Circle was initially a friendly society for Jewish immigrants, but developed into a progressive Jewish social, cultural and political centre.) According to Philip Poole, a judge in one of their sketches wore a wig, which aroused heated controversy. Special meetings were held to discuss the matter and they were threatened with expulsion from the WTM. Rae Waterman, whose husband Alec was a founder member of Proltet, while she herself was a member of Red Radio, also recalls an argument 'over a sketch, collectively written, where the judge was given a wig, the prisoner a bloodied bandage, and the policeman a helmet.' Mrs Waterman believes that what had once been a 'useful, pithy slogan' had 'hardened into a dogmatic principle.'[45] Because Proltet performed in Yiddish, and only a fraction of a given street audience would have understood Yiddish, they were the only WTM group which performed exclusively indoors. This was no doubt one reason for their more naturalistic approach. (The use of Yiddish was criticized by the hardliners in the movement who believed it limited Proltet's audience, and expressed a narrow nationalistic outlook.)

The eighth All-London Show: a critique

The WTM went through a difficult patch in 1933. At the end of 1932 the National Organizer listed a number of achievements in the *Monthly Bulletin*: the writing of sketches dealing with real struggles in Castleford, Deptford, and Becontree, and in support of the London busmen and clothing workers, and a move towards collective writing. However, the Central Committee had failed to implement the demands made at the June conference for the holding of a special conference on production methods, and the issuing of instructional material on writing and production.

Some groups were still going strong, among them Castleford, which was able to split into two sections, one composed of young comrades, the other based on the three members recently released from jail. The WTM had at long last got its own premises at 94 Grays Inn Road, singing groups were started within existing troupes, and regional weekend schools were organized in Sheffield and Scotland. But as the Bureau of the Central Committee spelled out in its statement in the March *Bulletin*, there had been a falling off in the number of performances by the groups.

This time last year groups were reporting three or four shows a week – and no meeting was complete without a WTM group. They were advertised in the *Daily Worker* every day. This year hardly any such shows are being given although the meetings are taking place.[46]

There had also been in the opinion of the Bureau a deterioration in the level of the eighth All-London Show on December 18, 1932. A short criticism was issued of all the items produced and the show as a whole.[47]

First, there had been a lack of discipline at the performance. Some comrades had even refused to come onto the platform and take part in the mass singing, which was therefore extremely poor. Many groups behaved noisily offstage and in the hall. The groups were reminded that the audiences at the All-London Shows were composed of sympathizers and friends. This was why the request for written criticism asked for it to be made on the basis of 'effectiveness in the class struggle'.

The 'Castleford' sketch was criticized for unnecessary and distracting by-play from the policeman. 'The laughs got by presenting the police in a humorous way destroys the value of our propaganda. The comic policeman tradition of the music halls must have no place in the Workers' Theatre.'

'We Can Stop the War' received praise for excellent handling, but criticism for one or two mystifying gestures – 'gestures should always explain', and a 'tendency towards over-repetition of slogans' (themselves a weak part of the text).

'R.I.P.' (The 'Holy Three', Rent, Interest, and Profit) was also praised:

Excellent performance of sketch. Workers' plight forcibly contrasted with bosses' luxury, in a way that would be equally effective on the street corner. Religious parody should be deleted from opening, as liable to throw up in minds of some workers a barrier to the acceptance of the main message of the sketch.

The central idea of the sketch 'Law and Order' was excellent, but all the propaganda was contained in one long speech, and there was an over-emphasis on minor details of acting which distracted from the political message, while 'Rail Revolt' was marked by an absence of any production:

Sincerity of utterance does not make up for lack of movement and variety in emphasis, etc. Absence of positive policy of rank and file movement (except in slogans) as also in SPEED and PORT WORKERS. This must engage our serious attention. RECOMMEND: THAT CC ARRANGE FOR COMRADE TO ATTEND THIS GROUP FOR A PERIOD TO ASSIST THEM IN PRODUCTION.

Port Workers Unity' was much too long and too detailed:

Essentials only of a situation should be shown. Details of production and acting weak. *As a sketch written by comrades of the group in that industry about the actual struggles of the workers in industry it is one of the most important developments in the WTM.* (Our emphasis – R.S. and K.M.) RECOMMEND: THAT CC TAKES ALL POSSIBLE STEPS TO IMPROVE SKETCH BY DISCUSSIONS IN GROUP AND BY SENDING A COMRADE TO ASSIST IN PRODUCTION.

'Suppress' needed to be brought up to date, in 'Speed' there was a lack of attention to production detail – no busman's caps, bell or any other details. (This would appear to contradict those who maintained there was a completely dogmatic line on no props.) The end was weak, consisting of generalizations about the rank and file movement, a point made in a letter from a rank and file worker who had seen the show. 'Strike' was extremely effective, but:

slogans from crowd ragged and at times hysterical. Criticism of political line of sketch is overdue. Syndicalist in tendency; line is that 'strike' is the only necessity. Role of revolutionary party ignored, as well as all forms of mass-activity other than strikes (influence of IWW). Worship of the individual leader (petty-bourgeois ideology). Sketch reflects period of 'prosperity' in America when it was written; could be improved by making it deal with present-day realities in England (crisis, unemployment, dole-cuts, as well as wage cuts). RECOMMEND: THAT GROUP BE ASKED TO INITIATE POLITICAL DISCUSSION ON WEAKNESSES OF SKETCH AND COLLECTIVELY MAKE ITS CONTENT EQUAL TO THEIR PERFORMANCE.

This sketch was probably performed by the Proltet group. In reply to another criticism by a Comrade Woodward who said it was highly over-rated and should be banished from the WTM repertoire, they wrote:

Indeed, Comrade Woodward! This is the first we've heard of it! As a production it has been acclaimed by all, including the CC of WTM (see Dec. issue of MB). Its tremendous dramatic appeal, coupled with its attractive form (audience feeling itself part of play) make it (in our opinion) one of the most valuable of WTM sketches. We are all agreed that its political line needs altering, and this we are now engaged in doing.[48]

'Meerut' was effective as usual but new comrades were not made use of. 'The Theatre, Our Weapon', was vocally effective, but the accompanying movements were meaningless.

The Central Committee appeared to be making a genuine attempt to tighten up both artistically and politically. It is also clear that the criticisms they made were directed merely at improving the form, sketches and songs performed individually or in combination, which the WTM had been using for the past two years. No attempt was being made to develop new forms to solve the problem which the Welsh tour had highlighted of getting through to less conscious workers. There is no hint of outside pressures forcing them to analyse their approach in the light of a dynamic political climate. The upcoming visit to the Moscow Olympiad was about to provide these pressures, in an unexpected direction.

The Moscow Olympiad

In January of 1933 the contest for the International Olympiad began. Regional competitions were to be held in London and the South of England, Yorkshire, Lancashire and Scotland. A chart was to be prepared and the individual groups could claim points for performances, writing new sketches, sale of Red Song Books, founding new groups, contributions to the Olympiad fund, etc. The objective was to send a delegation representing the whole of Britain with a maximum of six from the winning troupe and one each from the five or six runners-up. A special fund-raising sketch had been written by Tom Thomas six months before entitled 'Their Theatre – And Ours'.[49] It is a cleverly constructed humorous piece which contrasts the ideological manipulation of the bourgeois media with the workers' theatre.

Written for six performers it begins with the Red Radio entrance song which could be adapted to whichever group was performing the sketch. The troupe then speaks directly to the audience, explaining in rapid-fire individual statements what the workers' theatre is, finally asking:

Why don't we workers unite and end this misery, this starvation, this mass-murder?

1ST: *Because* many workers are still satisfied with their rotten conditions.

2ND: *Because* others think that the workers always have been poor and oppressed and always *will* be.

4TH: *Because* thousands more think that the rich class are too powerful for us to overthrow.

the reason being that press, schools, theatres, cinemas are controlled by the capitalist class.

2ND: When things get bad, they sing to you at the pictures (the group gather round like a chorus on stage or film 'plugging' a 'cheer-up' song. A satirical picture of the way this stuff is put across. Faces ghastly with forced happiness. 2nd leads them in the song.)

The singing breaks off and we see a worker audience coming out of a show: 'Things have never been worse!' but 'There's a good time coming!'

Next comes a music hall star singing a patriotic song which helped send a million men to their deaths in World War I. Thomas was probably inspired by Noel Coward's *Cavalcade*. In a review he wrote for *Red Stage* he describes 'one splendid satirical scene':

To a background of soldiers marching up a gangway like cattle being driven to slaughter, three music hall stars perform with growing hysteria, their despicable role of luring men to their deaths with the actual songs of the period. ('We Don't Want to Lose You, But We Think You Ought To Go', etc.) The mind that could portray this, we venture to think, is not deceived by its own clap trap in the rest of the play.[50]

Another short scene follows, parodying a newsreel film of the 'royal parasites'. The prince is seen opening a bridge to raspberries from the 500 workers who spent two years building it, reviewing the police who recently baton-charged unemployed demonstrators protesting at the means test, and dancing at a ball in aid of unemployed opera singers. So while workers are encouraged to live vicariously through the aristocracy, 'poverty is shown as beautiful and noble – by actresses and actors getting up to £1,000 a week – more than an unemployed worker would get in 25 years.' A scene illustrating this, starring Miss Greater Garbage, is followed by a parody on a gangster film, which also serves to divert the workers.

The alternative, the Workers' Theatre, is then described, with excerpts from sketches on factories, housing, the 'Sailors' Strike', or the NUWM sketch performed to illustrate the point, depending on the individual group's repertoire and local requirements or issues. An appeal is then made to the audience to 'HELP THE FIGHT OF THE WORKING CLASS BY HELPING THE WORKERS' THEATRE!! SUPPORT THE OLYMPIAD FUND!'. The opening song is repeated and the slogan 'Workers' Theatre' shouted in unison.

This sketch is remarkable for the attempt to contrast the forms as well as the content of bourgeois and workers' theatre, to show how ideology is moulded in the first place, and the way in which speech choruses, songs, short scenes, parody and slogans are effectively interwoven. The sketch is, in fact, a montage, intercutting and juxtaposing a fairly complex content with a variety of forms. We have not come across another British WTM sketch which does this to the same degree, nor does there appear to have been any theoretical discussion of this question.

The complexity of the subject matter may have pushed Tom Thomas into going beyond the usual simple revue-type forms. His position on the International Presidium gave him additional opportunities to learn from his German and Russian counterparts. He was also one of the most experienced, thoughtful and qualified of the WTM writers. Another of his sketches 'Something for Nothing' is surprisingly modern in content and style. A sketch for six characters, it shows how a time-saving device invented by an ordinary worker enriches the company and leads to his getting the sack. The humour plus the imaginative but concise exploration of one aspect of the system rather than trying to handle the whole lot, help it to rise above the usual sloganistic ending.

In May a delegation of up to twenty worker-actors embarked for the Soviet Union. In the final contest the Red Players had been chosen the best troupe. They won the London contest with seventeen out of twenty points. In the activity section they achieved a grand total of forty-two points. Leeds was declared the winner of the Yorkshire contest. The Scottish and Lancashire contests did not take place. Dundee appears to have been the only active Scottish group at this time, and Dundee and Castleford were the only groups outside London to claim their activity points.

There are discrepancies between the memories of Charles Mann and Philip Firestein, and the official jury report, as to the size of the delegation, the numbers in each troupe, etc. What is clear, however, is that the Red Players were only able to send three or four of their own members. To their great disappointment their numbers had to be supplemented with delegates from Scotland and the provinces. The Red Front Troupe led by Mark Chaney was put together a few days before the trip, and included delegates from up to seven different groups who had never worked together before. Proltet sent their secretary Philip Firestein, a British-born Jew who had been drafted in to write their English letters and play in crowd scenes. Most of the members were recent immigrants who were afraid that if they went out of the country, they might not be let in again.

(According to Rae Waterman, although Firestein knew no Yiddish, he was a great success as a policeman in the sketch which aroused the props controversy: '. . . he had only to raise and lower his magnificent George Robey-like eyebrows for the audience to fall about helplessly.')[51]

Also on the boat was André Van Gyseghem, who watched Mann drilling his group with dismay:

I had the task of rehearsing these people who were very weak, no stage presence, never worked together, into the material we'd won the competition with. . . . I had my style, rhythm, forcefulness, conviction, and clarity so that the audience could not mistake the message we were putting over. . . . He said 'How can you get results with such methods? You're not training them, you're a sergeant major!' I said, 'I have to be, I've got to get results in three days!'[52]

This was not London chauvinism, Mann described an occasion in Southampton when the local group performed before the Red Players and recited the stage directions as though they were part of the text. Tom Thomas remembered another such incident:

I went up to Leeds to see some of the Yorkshire groups . . . to see which group could get the right to go to Moscow to represent us . . . there must have been four or five groups performing. . . . And I had written a declamation. . . . I had people in the hall who interrupted or rather participated, voices that came from the different directions as part of the declamations. And, of course, I had to say, 'In the Hall' and 'On the Stage' to interchange these one-liners, you see, but to my horror, in spite of the fact that in the texts we supplied them with these words were in brackets, as part of my declamation I heard 'ON THE STAGE AND IN THE HALL.'[53]

In the Soviet Union, a number of surprises, even shocks, were in store. Philip Firestein vividly describes the first, which occurred in Leningrad:

After tea they took us to a school and they improvised a stage and they got from somewhere a professional ballet group, and we all sat down . . . watching ballet for the first time. . . . I personally . . . didn't know what ballet was, and I don't think anybody practically did, and one chap amongst the twenty quietly said, 'What's this got to do with Workers' Revolution?' . . . And we all laughed, we couldn't stop laughing, it was so unexpected, there they were flying about like flowers or animals. . . . And the Russians, they loved it all.[54]

In Moscow the delegates were taken to a big theatre for an opening ceremony. There Firestein met Jews from Kiev in the Ukraine who took him to see Jewish professional and amateur theatres. Charles Mann remembers attending a number of large theatres, one or two workers' theatres, and an experimental theatre called Radek which had done away with the stage altogether. 'We sat on a bank of seats . . . another auditorium over there, and the action ran in galleries behind us, around us, in the middle, up and down. Nearly broke your bloody neck trying to follow it.'[55]

On another occasion the technical sophistication of the big Russian theatres gave Mann a 'turn' in a very real sense:

I was rehearsing this group on . . . a big revolving stage, which were not in our experience here, the English theatres were miles behind, and at one point I had to turn to the audience and harangue them and when I turned back they'd all gone round.[56]

In Moscow the British delegation had an opportunity to see groups from all over the world and to perform themselves. According to André Van Gyseghem:

it was the actual forms of presentation that were so new to us . . . how much could be done with so little in the way of groupings . . . mass movements, individual movements contrasted, a montage of effects which create a third thing . . . a synthesis . . . the use of the stage . . . it was made much more alive and . . . interesting and exciting and not so flat . . . you could do a great deal more than we had imagined . . . using the . . . shape of the body in space, and . . . levels, flags, poles, whatever props you had, using patterns, . . . every atom . . . to make the theatrical effect more potent.[57]

Compared with the more advanced groups from Scandinavia, Germany and the USSR, the ill-prepared British delegation did not score well, as Philip Firestein vividly remembers: 'the judges . . . made marks, came to the last day, the results were announced . . . Britain came last, they said we were amateurs, our plays were too raw, we kept shouting slogans all the time.'[58] For André Van Gyseghem this was, 'tremendously helpful to us, because it was really backing up what I had said to them, that our technique was bad.'[59]

But it was not just British technique which was under fire. The Russians were arguing by this time for a return to more realistic, traditional, longer plays. Charles Mann was very critical of this approach.

The Russians accused us of formalism and I think with some

justification. . . . I had a sketch and I had the actors standing in a line and at one moment they would become cops and they'd all put policemen's helmets on and sing,

And when the cops are on parade
With their armoured cars arrayed
Thousands of them riding horseback, thousands more on foot,
So why should they be dismayed? . . .
. . .
You can see them all arrayed,
Biff em, bang em, smash em,
See the corpses all a . . .

which we did with precision and they thought this was formalistic. They were in favour of using more legitimate techniques. . . . They used the word 'naturalism'. I didn't agree. They did not know the conditions under which we had to play, often on the street, in halls without a stage, the acoustics are terrible. . . . I was inspired but very critical of the ballet which I was surprised to see was some very bourgeois thing with pretty dresses. They were the formalistic ones. We said, 'We come here and we're using art as a weapon in the struggle, and you present us with bourgeois rubbish, why aren't you using ballet in the struggle?'[60]

There was undoubtedly truth in the Jury's critique:

Of primary importance is the absence of any definite character, type, image, which means that people and events reach the eye and ear of the audience only schematically and superficially . . . the same is true of the action. The plays are only sketches of real or invented happenings . . . political slogans relating to them are thrown directly into the audience. This is neither artistic nor convincing.[61]

As far as the performance was concerned the troupes were praised for their political seriousness but slated for their lack of technique. 'The actors make an impression of marionettes but without the exactness of good marionettes.'[62]

It was a sober British delegation which returned home from Moscow. The crack which had been apparent at the National Conference nearly a year earlier was widening. The Rebel Players and their supporters felt that their arguments for a return to realism and the curtain stage had been justified. The Workers' Theatre Movement had come to an important crossroads. Jack Loveman describes what happened:

Socialist Realism doesn't suit the kind of techniques that are applicable to street corner shows. The Soviet Union with its immense resources could go for subtlety. Whereas ours was a barbaric yob. I'm afraid we were out-argued. The Soviet Union had such immense prestige. And . . . strong arguments. Their argument was that agitprop wasn't near enough to life and lacked nuance and subtlety. True! Like some of Picasso's drawings, if I may say. Which weren't popular in the Soviet Union. You see, the general consensus of opinion in other parts of the world tended towards what the Soviet Union was standing for anyway, and I think we felt it was our duty to try and develop in that direction.[63]

11 · Return to the curtain stage: decline of the WTM

By 1934 Rebel Players were firmly set on their new course. They had been strengthened by an influx from Proltet. As its members learned English and became more integrated along with their audiences, the need for a Yiddish-speaking group seemed less pressing. Bram Bootman believes that Red Radio started to infiltrate or merge with Rebel Players too. (Mark Chaney, who had been with Red Radio according to Philip Poole, was a member of Rebel Players when Bootman joined.) And they had several professionals in their midst. Their producer was Shirley Wakeman, an actress trained at RADA whom Bootman believes was introduced by Van Gyseghem. John Allen, now principal of the Central School of Drama, was also a member.

A programme in Bootman's collection from May 26, 1934, illustrates the changes that were taking place. The Rebel Players were now affiliated to the British Drama League as well as to the Workers' Theatre Movement. They were no longer presenting just agitprop sketches but 'one-act plays'. One was called *Hunger Marchers* and was set in the kitchen of a farmworker's house. It depicted in naturalistic detail, with the aid of greasepaint, the effects of a hunger march on a small Midlands village. Another was entitled *Gas*:

> We used to carry a cart around with us with big black flats which were assembled like a box with the front open to the audience and it had a door to get in at the top, and, of course, being inadequately carpentered, very often you couldn't get in or . . . out. And my poor old friend Mark Chaney, he used to play the part of the worker who exposed all this to this group of people who'd rushed into this shelter. And the shelter was, of course, badly built, not merely from the stage point of view but by the capitalist contractors who'd made it, and they all got overwhelmed by gas. And Mark as the worker used to say with his last gasping, dying breath, 'This is what capitalism and war does for you,' or something like that. It was a dreadful thing, it had no humour at all.[1]

The mainstream of the WTM was still arguing strongly against the formal approach of the Rebel Players but some were no longer convinced. And by March 1935 the West Ham United Front troupe proudly announced that they had their own hall 'with a properly equipped stage, and an electric light outside'.[2] The Manchester Theatre of Action set up in a permanent home at about the same time, changing its name to Manchester Progressive Theatre in line with the popular front. Philip Poole, secretary of the WTM from about 1929, resigned in 1934 or 1935.

> I was disillusioned because the Central Committee refused to face up to this question of props and so on. Also, there were these professional people coming into the Movement with their new ideas and I just dropped out of it and took up other political activities, actually in the open-air movement.[3]

Poole, like Rae Waterman, believes that the 'propertyless theatre' slogan which Tom Thomas had brought from Germany was gradually developed into a rigid dogma.

> If you're going to show a judge in a sketch then the simplest thing to do is put a wig on his head. The suggestion that . . . you can convey the idea of a judge by some kind of facial expression is a bit far-fetched.

The rigidity of the slogan in practice is open to question as has already been mentioned with regard to the sketch 'Speed'. Published scripts often included suggestions for handprops. Tom Thomas himself, although he was certainly in favour of doing without props and costumes whenever the actor's face, voice, and body could do the job, remembered designing a huge prop:

> Lenin had said 'Socialism is . . . something plus electrification'. Of course, they had very little electricity over this vast area. And he laid down that they couldn't start building a socialist society without having mastered the techniques of distribution of electric power and the building of all the power stations. So I designed and then I got first of all a carpenter member, and then an electrician to have a map of the Soviet Union and Siberia which would show all the power stations that I'd noted were going to be built. I don't remember the sketch, but the idea was that this was the pièce de résistance that would be on the center of the stage. It came to grief, it grew so big and so heavy that we couldn't get it around. It was about 4' 6" long and about the same height and it had all this electrical wiring and had to be a fairly substantial piece of woodwork, it was going to light up with the dates.[4]

There was clearly a lot of controversy over this question, some of it possibly quite sterile.

The Popular Front

But the move towards 'socialist realism' was not the only change taking place which led to the demise of the WTM. A number of complex, often interrelated factors must be examined to explain the weakening of the Movement. One was so obvious that it could easily be overlooked: the pioneering youngsters who had been at the core of the Movement since the beginning were now adults with family responsibilities. They had lived through severe unemployment and when a job or a house was offered elsewhere they felt they had to take it. Charles Mann lost contact for this reason. The Lovemans had moved from Greenwich to Streatham where they worked with the Red Front troupe, then to Battersea where there was no group, so they remained attached to the Streatham group. Then they were offered a council house on the St Helier estate where again there was no WTM group. This time they were too far from Streatham, so they turned their attention to building the Party in that area.

With the partial stabilization of British capitalism in the mid-thirties the economy was beginning to improve. In late 1933 unemployment began slowly falling from its depression peak of 2,900,000. By July 1935, it finally fell below 2,000,000, and by the summer of 1937 it was under 1,500,000, helped by the growing market for military equipment. Even before the government began ordering arms, British industry was enthusiastically equipping the German Luftwaffe and Wehrmacht, a trade which continued until the country was on the brink of war.

The fact that jobs were more readily available had two ramifications. There were fewer unemployed WTM members with time to spare for the Movement. And one of the most important sections of their audience, the unemployed, for whom they wrote numerous sketches, were no longer so numerous. Nor were they so receptive to agitation which tended to simplify issues rather than revealing their full complexity.

In a period of recession the issues appear fairly clear-cut. With living standards on the rise, the official trade unions growing again, and war threatening, the basic class divisions can seem blurred. But an even bigger political problem was soon to arise for the WTM, which made it apparent that the controversies over formal questions were only symptoms of a much larger political issue.

The Communist International was preparing for yet another about-face, in view of the obvious failure of the 'social fascist' theory and the need to unite against the rise of Fascism in Germany. In August 1935, the policy of the People's Front was launched at the Seventh World Congress of the Communist International.

A year later, the *Daily Herald*, in an editorial on the CP's application to affiliate to the Labour Party (flatly rejected) sarcastically summed up what they termed 'the most phenomenal reversal of policy in the history of Parties in this country'.

Labour and Communism

Some time ago – we merely state the facts – the British Communist Party fell over backwards, ate all the words it had spoken and written for eighteen years and announced a new 'line'. It stopped dead its somewhat stupid campaign of slandering all loyal Labour leaders as 'traitors', 'capitalist lackeys' and (silliest of all) 'Social Fascists'. And it began with urgency to advocate co-operation with these men. . . .

It called off entirely the vendetta against the 'bourgeoisie' and the pillorying of 'class collaboration'. And it began to seek earnestly for middle-class supporters, actively collaborating with social elements for whom it used to reserve its choicest abuse.

Above all, it ceased to deride democracy and Parliamentary government, spurned as 'empty and useless' in its 1935 programme, called its members to 'defend democracy' and generally began to conduct itself in all outward appearances, as a constitutional Party.[5]

The confusion in the party was enormous, suddenly Communists were supposed to unite, not just with the 'social fascists', but with 'mass national liberation, religious-democratic and pacifist organizations and their adherents'.[6]

Tom Thomas resigns

Having loyally carried out Party and Comintern policy in their sketches the WTM was caught out. Tom Thomas, the founder of the Movement, was soon under fire:

The new Popular Front line didn't lend itself as easily to popular theatre. In theatre terms, it's much more difficult to present an argument for a constructive line, like building a united front against fascism, than to write . . . attacks on the class enemy.

I was very surprised when it was put to me in 1935 or 1936 that as the organizer of the WTM and as the author of so many lampoons upon the Labour Party my continued leadership might be considered in some quarters a minor obstacle to the development of the popular front. If my resignation would remove even a minor obstacle I would not allow my personal regret to stand in the way. So I resigned after nearly 10 years hard, but extremely interesting and enjoyable work. I then took up activities in the Communist Party in Welwyn Garden City. . . .

The WTM continued for some time, but it didn't really fit in with the Popular Front Campaign, and though it took a new name – the New Theatre – by 1938, it was, I believe, dead.[7]

The Rebel Players were almost certainly involved in removing Tom Thomas from the leadership. Bram Bootman, one of their members, remembers that Thomas was always regarded as 'redder than red' by the group. As National Organizer and the main theorist and writer for the WTM, he must have antagonized them on numerous occasions during the controversy over agitprop and realism.

There were also tensions over the centre's ability – or right – to 'guide' the individual groups. For example, at a meeting on 28 June, 1935, a Comrade Bliss, who had apparently been expelled from Rebel Players, defended himself on charges of having been unreliable. The Central Committee had allowed him to work in another group, and ill health was the only thing that kept him away. Maurice Abrahams retorted that the 'Central Committee does not guide this group'[8] and that although they were affiliated to the WTM they had a separate constitution. Comrade Bliss was asked if he would work as a serious and reliable member and given three months probation.

Things appear to have come to a head over *Waiting for Lefty* in October 1935. The Rebel Players had planned to stage Odets's play about the New York taxi-cab strike of February 1934 for the first time in Britain, but they had been unable to obtain permission from Odets himself or his agents. They went ahead with rehearsals, and booked the Fred Tallant Hall for Saturday, October 12, 1935. Tom Thomas did his best to help both them and the Manchester Theatre of Action, as the Red Megaphones were now called, who also wished to stage the play. There are letters and telegrams to him from the International Union of the Revolutionary Theatre in Moscow in Bram Bootman's collection which bear this out.

But by 8 October, 1935, permission was still not forthcoming and Tom Thomas wrote to the Secretary of the Rebel Players (on New Theatre League stationery) as follows:

Dear Comrade,

We discussed the possibility of *Waiting for Lefty* this evening, and we decided to convey the decision of this committee to you as follows: that in view of the definite refusal of Odets' agents it would be a great mistake and a violation of our principles for you to put on this play on Saturday . . . it would prejudice the whole of our relations with the playwrights of America, to whom we look for the greater part of our repertoire. We have to think of the future of the Movement, and not of one show only, and it is clear that no professional theatre person will continue to work with your group, or any other of our groups if you disregard professional etiquette in this way.

Morton is trying to arrange for the Singing Group to give half an hour's entertainment to fill up the blank made by *Lefty*; if you want them please write to Morton at the above address.

Yours fraternally,
Tom Thomas

This was hardly the letter of an ultra-leftist, but the Rebel Players were determined to go ahead. At a meeting the next day, just three days before the performance was to take place, Thomas' arguments were rejected. Pencilled notes in Bram Bootman's possession list the counter-arguments put forward.

1 Collapse of group if no performance.
  a Wide interest in transport circles
  b Sympathy of press and Labour organizations
  c No alternative programme possible
  d Financial question
  e Energy of group directed strenuously towards this play
  f Good influx of new membership
2 Legal aspect
  a Application made to Odets personally – no reply.
  b Cable and letter from MORT (Russian abbreviation for International Union of Revolutionary Theatres – R.S. and K.M.)
  c No heed to be taken of letter from agents – this appears to be a personal letter to Comrade Bolster.
3 'Professional etiquette' – question appears to be grossly exaggerated as far as prof. (professional – R.S. and K.M.) production is concerned in this country.
4 'Violation of principles' –
Delegate – organizer and Maurice (Abrahams – R.S. and K.M.)
Resolved (unanimously) that the committee recommends to the group that *Lefty* be produced on October 12.

Their only compromise was to agree not to use the name of the play or the author in their publicity. The programme was called 'An Evening of Social Drama'. It was a great success and the difficulties Tom Thomas had predicted did not in fact arise. What is clear is that this was no simple right-left conflict.

At subsequent meetings in the same month there were numerous indications that the Rebel Players were about to make an open split. On the 16th 'BB' (Bram Bootman – R.S. and K.M.) asked for a lead from the group as to how to deal with the centre with regard to disaffiliation. The following minuted conversation took place:

JH: Do we reapply for affiliation to NTL? (New Theatre League – R.S. and K.M.)
MA: We automatically reaffiliate.

AL: Has Centre done anything to our advantage?
MA: CC gave no help whatever, success due only to own work.
AL: Does T.T. (Tom Thomas – R.S. and K.M.) stand?
MA: No change in organizer.
MC: Reactionary when group started – even tried to stop group from forming – he is mainly responsible at the Centre.
Resolution Send letter of protest to IURT and explain fully what our position was in regard to W. for L. (*Waiting for Lefty* – R.S. and K.M.) Vote of censure to be passed against T.T.
Amendment JH – Failing resignation of T.T. suggests break with WTM.
MC – Only Workers TM leadership needs changing – Breaking would also mean breaking from IURT.
Resolution Carried
On October 28 a further resolution was agreed:
That this group expresses its dissatisfaction with the central organization and calls for a general meeting of the Movement for an exposition of the policy of the New Theatre League.
On October 29:
4 *Moved* (Van) (probably Van Gyseghem – R.S. and K.M.) formal notice that W.T.M. has ceased and officials retired and that individuals have constituted themselves as provisional committee to formulate New T.L. as per decision at meeting on 27 April.
Statement to this effect be circulated to all groups.
5 Publicity be given directly in variety of papers.
WTM non est – New Theatre organization being formulated.
6 Provisional Cttee – suggested names –

Rees	Bootman
Van	Abrahams
Marie Seton	Silk
Bolster	Loveman (not Jack or Alice – R.S. and K.M.)
Atkins	
Morton (Horrocks, from the Workers' Music Assoc. – R.S. and K.M.)	Shirley (S. Wakefield – R.S. and K.M.)
	Thorndike (Sybil – R.S. and K.M.)
Savory	Casson (Lewis – R.S. and K.M.)
	M. Webster

The League was to subsume the WTM in a larger umbrella organization linking all amateur dramatic groups with 'progressive ideas' and to enlist the co-operation of professional artists. The opening meeting included performances by the Dance Drama group, the Labour Choral Union, Theatre of Action – Manchester, and the Battersea Players. Among the speakers were Gillian Scaife of the Westminster Theatre, William Armstrong of British Actors' Equity, and the Earl of Kinoull, who spoke on 'Peace Plays'. No WTM names appeared among the speakers.

The professionals

The suspicion felt towards professional artists is clear in Philip Poole's account of André Van Gyseghem's introduction to the Movement:

> we received a short letter from André Van Gyseghem, a well-known theatre producer and actor. It simply said, 'I want to help the Workers' Theatre Movement', and was on notepaper from a theatre at Swiss Cottage. . . . He had recently visited the Soviet Union. There was a serious discussion as to whether we should even answer his letter. Eventually, it was decided that no harm would be done if we met this representative of the bourgeois theatre. I wrote to him and invited him to attend a meeting on a certain day at 8 pm. Needless to say the meeting didn't start till 9 pm and the first question André Van G. asked was 'Why didn't the meeting start at 8 pm as arranged?'
>
> After André Van G. left the meeting there was endless debate as to what we should do about him.
>
> At this time we had a troublesome, difficult group in East London called Rebel Players. It was decided that the best way to get rid of André Van G. would be to attach him to this group.[9]

According to Poole, professionals like Van Gyseghem literally had to force their way in. As the National Organizer Tom Thomas may have been a target for some of the hostility from the mainstream of the WTM towards the increasing involvement of professionals. He had, of course, written a number of perceptive articles, reviews and even a sketch in which he analysed the role of the bourgeois theatre, arguing that its content and form was inimical to the objectives of the WTM.

One of the most interesting is his review of Noel Coward's play *Cavalcade*, a series of brief scenes giving a 'historical' view of England from 1889 as reflected in the lives of a ruling class family and their servants. In it Thomas noted two leading characteristics of the bourgeois stage: 'This deliberate turn away from reality and the burning questions of the present, to find sweet consolation in the past', and 'An inability, or perhaps a determination to give no more than a surface picture of events, by refusing to penetrate beneath the appearance of things, to the causes'.[10] But the Lovemans remember that he sent a number of WTM manuscripts to W. H. Auden who wrote back saying he was very interested but he 'thought our stuff wasn't sufficiently picturesque'.[11]

And Charles Mann believes that Tom Thomas was definitely among those interested in attracting professionals to the WTM. This is borne out by an article Thomas wrote for the Bulletin of the Organizing Committee of the International Union of Revolutionary Theatres in 1934. He was frank in his analysis of the gap between the WTM's 'political achievements (resulting from unity of purpose and enthusiasm)' and 'the technical level of performance which is often very poor'. As well as regular criticism and training in the groups, attempts were to be made 'to win over groups and individuals hitherto associated with other dramatic organizations' and to utilize 'the services of professional theatre workers to the full extent that they are prepared to help'.

> To those individual actors, few in number as yet, who have been won to the workers' cause, we must set the task of trying to organize a group of unemployed actors who will travel about the country playing a repertoire of revolutionary material in the workers' clubs and institutes which exist in all areas, as well as at meetings. Such a group on the lines of some of the German professional 'collectives' would be a tremendous achievement. Anything on a more grandiose scale is foredoomed to failure. This plan would have the great advantage that it would also set before the ordinary WTM groups a very much higher standard of performance than that to which they are accustomed; would act as a shock brigade for the whole organization.[12]

How did this square with Tom Thomas' conflict with Rebel Players? This was Charles Mann's answer:

> Ah, now that was a different thing. What Tom Thomas was probably at loggerheads with was the attempt, and I believe there was an attempt, to legitimize the WTM, make it more as Unity Theatre developed, skilful actors presenting pictures to an audience for entertainment . . . and Tom Thomas would oppose that.[13]

In Germany and the Soviet Union the involvement of revolutionary professionals in the Movement was extremely important. In Britain few of the professionals gravitating towards the WTM – and by 1935 at least three other groups besides Rebel Players had professional directors – were, in fact, revolutionary.

The economic crisis, the rise of Fascism in Germany, and the Spanish Civil War had certainly pushed many of them leftward. Apart from Van Gyseghem's Embassy theatre, which was experimenting with the mass spectacle, and the Westminster theatre, which was putting on plays of social significance (among them two by W. H. Auden), there was the emergence of a West End left with the organization of Left Theatre.

Founded by Van Gyseghem and Barbara Nixon they put on Sunday performances at the Phoenix Theatre, and took shows to Labour, Co-operative and town halls. Their repertoire included Gorky's *Mother* and *They Shall Not Die*, a play about blacks in the American South.

At the same time one did not have to be a Communist or worker to hate Fascism and to see its dangers. Just as in Spain liberals of all classes and all parties rallied behind the Republican government, so in Britain they began to look for ways to do their bit in defence of democracy. According to DeWar,

> The communist policy of the 'people's front', eventually known as the popular front, blossomed in this atmosphere, which it helped to create and which it enhanced. The class struggle was suspended; now the forces in conflict were, on the one side, the fascists and warmongers, and on the other the anti-fascists and peace-lovers, classified under the category of 'all men of good will'. The occasional incantation of revolutionary catchwords, and assurance that the revolutionary aim had not been lost sight of, sufficed to keep the party faithful in line.[14]

But the interest of the professionals in the declining WTM was not just political. The stagnation of the bourgeois theatre was leading many of the younger and more adventurous among them to look elsewhere for artistic stimulation. André Van Gyseghem's approach was probably typical of many.

Q: How did you get involved with the WTM?

A: I was then directing at the Embassy theatre in Swiss Cottage and quite successfully from a bourgeois point of view. But I had already been to Russia on a visit, and I began to feel that I needed . . . a theatre which had . . . more important things to say in relation to the people as a whole, not just one small section of the bourgeois theatre-goer and their life.

Q: What made you feel that?

A: What makes any creative person look for another step forward? . . . I had to . . . get to know what other forms of theatre existed which were more closely related to society as one knew it, and particularly the emergence of the working class as a power in the world, through Russia and other places . . . I wanted to push the walls down, much as Meyerhold had done . . . to break away from old traditions and look for something new, and the WTM seemed to be a possibility. So I went down . . . to the East End where there was a group called Rebel Players . . . and I was fascinated . . . I thought they had something which was almost dead in the professional theatre . . . a guiding passion . . . an acknowledgement of the importance of what they were saying and standing for . . . the professional theatre was an entertainment, highly polished and extremely good and very sophisticated and often very witty, but passion, deeply felt, was not a paramount thing . . . it seemed to me I found it in these boys with their . . . political ideals. And their attempts to express these in theatrical forms seemed to me very naive and very simple. . . . As Lenin has said, 'Theatre is a weapon', the weapon could have been far better had they had more technical accomplishment. They asked me if I would work with them and I was delighted to do that . . . I would raise the quality of the technical side of the work with all their impulses and the ideals behind them. That was how we started.[15]

André Van Gyseghem gave of his time, energy and skills, not just to the Rebel Players, but to other WTM groups. Fegel Firestein said that he helped Proltet produce a Yiddish sketch, and Jack Loveman remembers going to 'a place near Biggin Hill where we assembled and he gave a short talk on production and gave one or two suggestions as to how things could be done more effectively'.[16]

Van Gyseghem never wrote for the Movement and said he never attempted to force his political ideas on it. At that point he was fairly new to politics and felt that his worker-actors knew more than he did about the class struggle although he did eventually join the Communist Party. In Moscow he worked under Piscator and Okhlopkov at the Realistic Theatre, he was a student at Meyerhold's Theatre School and attended lectures at the State Institute of Cinema by Eisenstein. But regrettably, considering the unique opportunities that were open to him and his undoubted talent as a director he never really developed the sort of fundamental theoretical conceptions that were needed to 'push the walls down'. His superficial approach to Brecht is very revealing:

I knew him in Russia, of course, because he was on the board of the organization that employed me, and he stayed with me when he came over. I didn't get on with him at all. I found him very cold, no heart. Eisler was marvellous. There was an emotional person . . . the truth of the heart and the other was the truth of the brain . . . I've never directed a Brecht play, I don't really want to . . . I haven't liked much that I have seen . . . I think the Germans can do it, and if there is poetry in that extraordinary prose the German language can do it. Plus the fact that the makeup of our two races is very different. I think it's very difficult to get inside Brecht.[17]

And again:

Alienation was the only thing that came out of his dramaturgy, I can't think of any other. I wanted to unify them, not to alienate them.[18]

Charles Mann:

> . . . he could not grasp, and he never did grasp, first the import of
> the WTM, the social import of it, and secondly the techniques we
> had to use . . . he couldn't have done, his background wouldn't let
> him. . . . We had many a discussion on this, and we never actually
> agreed on anything, but I liked him, he was a nice chap.[19]

For Van Gyseghem 'the exciting thing, of course, was to go and play
for audiences which weren't used to going to the theatre at all, it might
be outside a factory gate or at a demonstration'. But the underlying
purpose of the WTM was not quite the same for him as for the people
who had built it.

> I think basically it was to create a working class theatre. Whether
> that meant a theatre with the actors drawn from the working class
> or a theatre which went and played to the working class I wouldn't
> like to say. . . . To me, it didn't really matter which it was, because
> both are very valuable.[20]

Compare this with Philip Poole's answer to the same question: 'I think
our aim was to put across political ideas in a simple form that workers
could understand.'[21]

Fegel Firestein's all-embracing approach was based on her own experience
in Poland and in the East End of London.

> A workers' theatre should stand for that – wherever a group of
> housewives who haven't got a lot of time or anything – there should
> always be a workers' theatre for them at any time, at any hour . . .
> and they should always have their own life in front of them, a mother
> should have in front of her in action how to bring up her children,
> a child should be breast-fed or not, everyday problems. . . . I thought
> the theatre is like a looking-glass, I never looked in a looking-glass
> at the time, but I looked at the theatre and I learned a lot. From the
> looking-class I could only learn about my face, but from the theatre
> and from culture I could learn how to build a better future. . . .
> Whatever we done, they saw their own life, they just woke up and
> saw what they've gone through in this country and why we are calling
> out 'Strike!' Before it never occurred to them that a strike is a kind
> of weapon for better conditions. They just opened their eyes and
> realized. . . . You didn't see Russia when I saw it in 1918 when cows
> and dogs and chickens lived together with people. . . .
> Philip – You saw that in Poland.
> It was part of White Russia. What they've done first thing, the
> revolutionaries, they started to cultivate the peasants, they told
> women to pick up the dirt from the floors. . . . Because the revol-
> ution was started already, and they wanted the people to get culti-

vated . . . to look after the revolution, and that's why you need workers' theatres and workers' movements.[22]

There is an obvious gap between 'creating a working class theatre', and 'putting over political ideas' or 'looking after the revolution'. During the period of the popular front, the former became the dominant trend, due in part to the influence of the professionals, but also, more fundamentally, to the changing political and economic climate described earlier. For all these reasons the process of 'legitimization' that Tom Thomas had fought against had begun.

Unity Theatre

You may ask 'What is Unity Theatre?' It began on the street corners and at meetings in 1936 with sketches, mass declamations and one-act plays. Collections and the small fees charged at trade union meetings helped the group to acquire its first permanent home in Britannia Street. . . . Its audience was, and has always been, drawn from the ranks of the Trade Unions, Co-operatives and the whole of the Labour Movement.   ('Outline History of Unity')[23]

The first meeting of Unity Theatre Club was held at the beginning of January, 1936, at the Workers' Circle in Alie Street. The Rebel Players' great success with *Waiting for Lefty* had provided the impetus for establishing an indoor theatre. The name Unity was chosen so as not to limit either the audience or the people who might wish to join the Club. This was in the true spirit of the Popular Front, just as the name Workers' Theatre Movement had given way to New Theatre League, since the former was considered too sectarian. But although these changes indicated the new direction, it was to be some time before their full effects were felt.

The early Unity repertoire included mass recitations like Ernst Toller's 'Requiem' for Luxemburg and Liebknecht and Jack Lindsay's 'On Guard for Spain', satirical sketches like 'The Fall of the House of Slusher', and of course, *Waiting for Lefty*. Agitprop had certainly not been abandoned, and for a time links with the organized working class even seemed to be strengthening. According to Bram Bootman:

We got rather involved with the Transport and General Workers Union . . . because when we did *Waiting for Lefty* the cab . . . section . . . got very interested. Two blokes who wrote for their journal reviewed the play and got very enthusiastic, and then one, Herbert Hodge, went on, together with his other writer friend, to write us a play *Where's That Bomb?*, which was satirical almost in the agitprop style . . . Then he went on to write another one for us called *Cannibal Carnival* . . . in which he satirized colonial imperialism . . . We had the upstairs hall (at Britannia Street – R.S. and K.M.) and managed to take control of the downstairs hall as well, and they used to hold their meetings there which was a useful addition to help us pay the rent.[24]

By the middle of 1937 there were three groups operating out of Britannia Street with eighty actors. Two of the three groups carried on the mobile tradition, performing at meetings, rallies and socials for trade unions and Co-op Guilds, Spanish Medical Aid, and the Labour and Communist Parties.

The producer of *Lefty*, John Allen wrote, 'Such performances serve the fourfold purpose of training the actors, spreading socialist ideas and opinions, taking plays to people who would never dream of buying a ticket for a theatre, and enlivening political meetings.'[25]

Under the auspices of the Left Book Club, tours to the Midlands and County Durham were organized, the eighteen actors travelling appropriately enough in three old London taxi cabs. In April 1937, a Left Book Club Theatre Guild was formed with an office at Unity, to deal with the enquiries which had begun to flood in on how to start a similar theatre in other localities. Speakers and producers were provided and lists of recommended plays issued, and a few short scripts published.

'The first workers' drama school in England'[26] was started at Summerhill, and a monthly penny paper, *New Theatre*, came out in the autumn of 1937. By 1938 there were 250 groups all over Britain.

The Glasgow Workers' Theatre Group, formed in 1937, is an interesting example. London Unity's strong influence could be seen in a repertoire which included *Waiting for Lefty*, *Plant in the Sun*, *Where's That Bomb?* and *On Guard for Spain*, but they also devised original living newspapers for Indian students and Irish immigrants, as well as a boldly experimental investigation of unemployment called *U.A.B. Scotland*. Although the group had their own premises they devoted a lot of energy to going out to Miners' Social Clubs, town halls, street corners, May Day parades, pageants, and to events in support of Scottish hunger marchers and Spanish food ships. They also encouraged other workers to use theatre, such as the striking Clydeside apprentices who staged a variety show in the summer of 1939 with the help of GWTG. In 1941 they helped found Glasgow Unity Theatre.

With such a tremendous growth larger premises were needed and in September 1937, Unity moved to Goldington Street. An appeal was issued in trade union branches, political organizations and in the *Daily Worker* to help renovate the old Methodist Church they had leased, and the response was overwhelming. One hundred and fifteen carpenters, forty-one electricians, thirty-three painters and decorators, thirty-four artists and signwriters, twenty-two plumbers and domestic heating engineers and many others in specialized trades volunteered to work without pay, and finished a job that would normally have taken six months in two. William Holmes, writing in the *Daily Worker*, compared the exhilaration he experienced upon visiting the Unity project to that aroused by the heroic achievements of the First Five Year Plan in the Soviet Union. However, 'the opening ceremony was performed not by an agitprop troupe, but by Dr Edith Summerskill, the victorious peace candidate in the Fulham East bye-election, and in later years a well-known cabinet minister.'[27]

Paul Robeson, who had sung at the opening, came back to perform in the American play *Plant in the Sun*. According to the programme, it dealt with the 'important question of trade union recruiting and recognition', and the struggle for better working conditions. The workers in a sweet factory fight a dismissal and triumph over internal feuds with a sit-down strike and working class solidarity: 'Gee, it's growing fellas, like a plant in the sun', exclaims one of the characters.[28]

In 1938 Unity produced their first living newspaper, *Busmen*, about the bus strike of 1937 during the coronation of King George VI which led to the court martial of seven leaders of the rank and file movement. The strike committee were asked to oversee the details, and according to the programme, 'Help of bus drivers and conductors was elicited to ensure naturalness of dialogue; anecdotes made by passengers are incorporated in a scene inside a bus.' Bram Bootman believes this was the closest collaboration Unity ever had with the unions.

'Which side are you on, Masters of Culture?'
. . . people at . . . Unity . . . had a theory that you merely had to change the class of your heroes and villains, and that would do it . . . even when they were successful, they weren't successful in our terms – in changing the nature of the *audience*. They were still playing to that 5 per cent.   (Ewan MacColl)

All through the early years people got us mixed up with Unity Theatre, but the whole point was that Joan (Littlewood – R.S. and K.M.) and all of us working with her were very much opposed to Unity – not on political grounds, but because Unity seemed to believe that if your political message was right, that was good enough. We felt it wasn't sufficient just to say the right thing: you'd got to say it in the right way.

(Howard Goorney, Theatre of Action, Manchester)[29]

On the surface it might appear that Unity was carrying on the WTM tradition, but on a bigger and better scale. However, it was not just the name which had changed. Because of Robeson, noted *Everybody's Magazine*, 'the West-Enders were just falling over themselves to get inside'.[30] The fourteen-man General Council included Tyrone Guthrie, Michel St Denis, and Sir Stafford Cripps. H. G. Wells was the first life member. The theatre had begun to write in its publicity of the advantage of a theatre built to suit the needs of the plays, enabling them to reach a higher standard of production than if they had to perform outside. Less and less emphasis was put on touring. During the war, while many of the old guard were in the services, the decision was taken to have the actors' names in the programmes. For Bram Bootman this meant the end of an era. Gradually, the East End stalwarts from the Rebel Players were edged out.

> We were doing plays of the calibre of *The Star Turns Red* . . . which wanted depth of characterization and technical acting skills which our . . . people . . . from . . . Rebel Players days couldn't aspire to, because they never would go to classes to learn how to project their voices or . . . anything. I think basically they weren't really actors, they enjoyed shouting political truths at a captive audience . . . so there was always this gap, it was sufficient for them to go on being themselves. They were all right in *Waiting for Lefty* and *Plant in the Sun* with American accents, but when you wanted a more in-depth characterization it was awfully difficult, so naturally you looked at the amateur stage. A continuous flow of people came in and out of the movement, some using it as a stepping stone to the more professional stages . . . with that type of person coming in you created further difficulties . . . it was inevitable . . . the more experienced actors from the amateur field, some of them almost semi-pro . . . gradually swept the others to one side.[31]

But perhaps the most important single change which had taken place was both a cause and result of the other changes. Unity Theatre was not a weapon of the class struggle, as the WTM had been, it was increasingly becoming a showcase for progressive drama on the one hand, and a place to go for a provocative, entertaining night out on the other. True, many of its active members were still working class, true, it still numbered many working class people among its audiences, true, some of its plays still dealt with important political and social questions. But the intention had changed fundamentally. Its job was no longer to 'kindle in the audiences the flame of revolt against the system which means to them unending poverty and want' as the *Red Stage* had put it.[32] In the Annual Report for 1945–46 the basic aims and objects of Unity were listed as follows:

a To foster and further the art of drama in accordance with the principle that true art, by effectively presenting and truthfully interpreting life as experienced by the majority of the people can move the people to work for the betterment of society.

b to train and encourage actors, producers and playwrights in accordance with the above ideals.

c to devise, import and experiment with new forms of dramatic art.[33]

A certain schizophrenia continued to exist in Unity for some time as can be seen in an undated copy of the *Active Member*, published for members and friends of Unity. On p. 1 the editorial board slated a *Daily Worker* critic and a writer in the same issue for failing to understand the integral part played by the 'brilliant' forms used in West End theatres in stunting the faculties of the audience. The board quoted Gorky who twenty years before had asked 'Which side are you on, Masters of Culture?' On pp. 6 and 7, H. Hancock described a talk given by Herb Tank on production and acting in which Tank pointed out that 'We have no body of writings to guide us apart from Stanislavsky'. (Brecht was not even mentioned.) Hancock concluded as follows:

The discussion which followed was not very fruitful. More than one speaker could not see what was 'bourgeois' about the West End stage, and at least one thought that no distinction could be made between the period of bourgeois realism and the decadent theatre of the imperialist epoch, but it soon became clear that they regarded everything, even movement and speech on stage, as inventions of the bourgeois theatre! Clearly, this discussion has hardly begun and there is a great need for a group, similar to the writers' group, which will discuss the problems of actors and producers.

Why had serving the theatre become more important than serving the class? There can be no doubt that the influx of professionals had a lot to do with it. Philip Firestein remembers an American advising the British delegation on the way back from the Moscow Olympiad never to go professional.

He said, 'Well, you'll get people who'll want to join to get ability to write . . . others to be stage managers, to be directors, and once they think they've got enough ability, they'll approach the professional theatre, you'll lose them, and you've got to start all over again, teaching others, training others.' And this is what did actually happen, we all thought 'Well, we'll somehow be different'. . . Soon as we got back a load of people were keen to start something professional, out of which came the Unity Theatre. And then we saw all kinds of people came and volunteered to do work and then after six months or nine months or a year or two years they drifted away into the profession.[34]

Fegel Firestein is particularly severe in her condemnation of the professionals, blaming them for 'killing' Unity. (David Kossoff, Lionel Bart, Bill Owen, Maxine Audley, Alfie Bass and John Slater all got their start at Unity.)

> Ted Willis and a chap named Bennett, they were more of the intellectual Young Communist Leaguers, and I think they wanted to make capital out of this WTM. . . . Suddenly, if you had a member's card you could go in, if you didn't have a member's card you couldn't go in. It lost all the connections with the people. Then they had . . . people they used to . . . train as writers. There was no checkup of the knowledge of these people, what are they going to discuss, a lot of time was wasted. It's forgotten all the work what a workers' theatre should stand for. . . . I can tell Alfie Bass in his face, he started to help the working class theatre movement but he finished it. Ted Willis is a writer, he finished it. . . . When Alfie Bass was in *Fiddler On the Roof* in the West End, I refused to go and see him.[35]

But for André Van Gyseghem, himself a professional, the underlying causes were political. His answer to the question of why there were no longer mobile groups based at Unity is very perceptive:

> I would say that it stopped with the War . . . one moment we were against it, the next moment we were for it when Russia came into it. All this tended to . . . disintegrate the . . . political unity. . . . Theatre always does reflect what's going on. . . . The emergence of the Labour Party and the necessity for putting the Communist Party behind the Labour Party . . . blunted a great many people's weapons . . . the theatre itself became blunted, and it became very difficult to find the right things to say.[36]

Unity's inability to come to grips with the complex new political situation was partly due to the fact that the movement had been watered down by the new open-door policy. But to lay the blame at the feet of the middle class intellectuals or would-be professionals would be too simplistic. This policy was partly a result of the Communist Party's own attempt to build a popular front and to change its image from that of a sectarian party of revolution to one of a democratic, reasonable, even respectable party, eager to co-operate with the social democrats it had once reviled.

The ramifications of the difficulties of finding the right things to say which Van Gyseghem referred to, and of the growing number of theatrically motivated rather than politically orientated members, were soon to be seen in the repertoire of the Unity branches. The movement had come full circle. Nearly twenty years after Tom Thomas and the other young pioneers had abandoned Shaw, Unity groups were presenting *Candida* and *Widowers' Houses*. Ibsen, O'Neill, Priestley, O'Casey, Steinbeck, Lope de Vega, even Shakespeare's *A Midsummer Night's Dream* were included in the list of plays put on in 1945–46, as well as several by the up-and-coming Ted Willis. He formed a short-lived professional company at Unity in 1946 which toured the country with such plays as *Black Magic*, sponsored by the Ministry of Fuel. Unfortunately, they piled up debts which, according to Bram Bootman, were left to the amateurs to pay.

Bootman stayed on until 1956. In hindsight he is critical of the return to the curtain stage, of the move to Goldington Street before Unity's foothold in the labour movement had been consolidated, and of the neglect of touring, which he still felt was Unity's real function. There were too many committees, and the theatre had become a 'white elephant'. With the change in repertory came a change in the composition of the audience. By 1956,

> Audiences had been . . . dropping off, although they'd picked up because the first three months of that year we had *Nekrassoff* by Jean Paul Sartre. But the audience we got was the audience I had expected to get . . . middle class . . . I remember one occasion when . . . a liveried chauffeur came in, took his cap off and stood in the office there and said, 'Sir Tiddlypuss so and so would like some tickets for the performance of *Nekrassoff*' . . . so we gave him a membership card, and forty-eight hours had to elapse before you could accept members, and back he came and bought tickets. And that was the sort of audience.[37]

Not surprisingly, Sartre did not appeal to working class members of the audience. Neither did most of the other Socialist Realist plays presented at Unity. In 1956 Bootman convened a conference of trade unionists only to be told by the workers themselves:

> We do not want plays that deal with working class lives and the struggle of the working people. Our wives won't come. They say, 'We know that already.' Put on old-time music hall, and we will bring you block bookings galore.[38]

Having struggled for twenty odd years to put on plays which would develop the 'consciousness of trade unionists and Labour Party people'[39] Bootman was understandably chagrined. He came to the conclusion that the answer was to go back to the work that had made Unity famous in the late 1930s, the living newspapers, the musical revues:

> The best work we ever did at Unity looking back, was the satirical revues, which were on the ball, had poison darts in them, the songs, the wit . . . used to have all types of audience with us then. This sharpened their outlook . . . if you're playing to the converted, the converted has got its nose to the grindstone, agendas, meetings, what not, they can't quite see what's happening on either side, but if you put a few darts into them, they could see . . . equally important, it

would encourage them to bring non-converted people with them. . . .
The idea I had when I left there, and I tried to get a group around
me, but then again the lack of writers is your stumbling block, I
wanted to do . . . what subsequently became *That Was The Week
That Was* . . . I wanted to put on that stage an almost political,
satirical cabaret . . . explore the headlines, if something required
depth, get somebody to write a one-act play around the situation
. . . but nobody ever came forward . . . what I wanted was no setting
at all, I wanted hat racks or a row of pegs, take bits of costumes off
and say, 'Right – '.

Q: In other words, going right back to where you started?

A: Yes, and the thing could be taken anywhere . . .[40]

12 · Achievements and weaknesses

I am convinced that 'agit-prop' – for want of a better term – is a far more effective method of conducting propaganda and the workers' struggle than the closed theatre selling tickets to members and friends . . . it can speak to people's own experience of life, dramatize their troubles, present them with ideas. It is mobile – it can be taken to the people, instead of waiting for them to come to you. And it is a theatre of attack. 'Naturalistic' theatre gives you the appearance of reality, but it does not show what lies beneath it.

(Tom Thomas, July 1977)[1]

For nearly ten years, the WTM which Tom Thomas had founded, played its part in the struggles of the British working class. It was a decade which began with the disillusionment engendered by the betrayal of the General Strike and the first Labour government under Ramsay MacDonald. Then came the economic crisis, and the rise of Fascism abroad and at home.

Throughout this time the WTM helped to raise money, sell literature, recruit for the Communist Party, campaign for Communist candidates and other related movements, and boost morale. But most important of all they tried to show what lay beneath the 'reality' around them and with inspired optimism to point the way forward to a socialist Britain. As Jack Loveman said:

We expressed the resentments and struggles of our time. The titles of some of our sketches show this – 'Blood on the Coal' (miners), 'The Sailors' Strike' (Invergordon), 'Meerut' (India), etc. Our repertoire was a mirror of contemporary history – war, speed-up, unemployment, the means test, labour camps (to prevent the labour force from 'deteriorating' during unemployment) and fascism.[2]

This ability to respond to the events of the day and put them into a wider political framework was probably the greatest strength of the WTM. It was partly due to the fact that many of the young worker-players had their roots in the very class struggle they were portraying. But it would not have been possible if they had not developed forms which were so flexible and mobile.

Unfortunately, they were never able as a movement to go beyond the agitational revue sketches which they first used in 1929. There were a few exceptions to this: Tom Thomas, for example, had begun to write sketches involving montage. Charles Mann attended a conference on film in Moscow and came back full of ideas about its potential.

> We started a Workers' Film Movement from the WTM. Later on this became an organization called Kino, but first of all, we had cameramen out taking demonstrations . . . and I started a technique, I think it was at Shoreditch Town Hall, and to my knowledge it was the first time it had ever been done, I may be silly about this, but I feel it was. I had a projector up in the gallery and a scene playing on a screen behind the actors which was relevant. (Documentary film had been used as a specific 'argument' and to provide a general background by Piscator almost ten years earlier – R.S. and K.M.) It was a hunger march and the characters were showing the distress caused by the means test, and here were the marchers behind them, and I had voices in the audience, which other people had done before, differently placed, coming up, and I had the three things going together, and I'd liked to have developed that a lot more. . . . That was 1933 or 34. . . . I still think this multi-media technique had a tremendous potential that has not been exploited.[3]

Just before the war Mann, who had lost contact with the WTM, started another group in Beckenham. It was organized along the same lines as the Red Players, but produced mostly new material. He managed to attract amateur actors with radical leanings from a local dramatic group dissatisfied with doing *Lady Windermere's Fan*. They began to put on anti-fascist sketches at trade union meetings using the montage form. They were ten or twenty minutes long, with a dominant theme or a continuous thread running through, constant changes of time, place and character, the use of voices offstage and so on. Regrettably, the group only lasted a year before the outbreak of war finished it.

After the war Mann tried again. He started a group in Uxbridge called Progress Theatre, and a film society which succeeded in producing films on topical issues, such as 'Two Thousand Houses for Uxbridge.' The theatre group did not develop, but the film society showed more potential, until 'we got a silly crowd in that wanted to make detective films.'[4]

Charles Mann says he had begun to work on the idea of montage with the Red Players before he left. But the WTM as a whole was stuck with the revue, a form that did not lend itself to the increasingly complex political and economic situation the working class and the revolutionary organizations were facing.

The WTM too had to contend with formidable problems. The movement in Britain was much smaller than in Germany and the USSR, with the result that there were too few dedicated people trying to do too much with too little. The lack of writers bedevilled the groups from beginning to end. Short revue sketches were easier to churn out than complex montage sequences, and certainly more suited to collective writing.

After the formative years from 1926 to 1929 the movement had little time to evaluate its work. Sporadic attempts were made in the pages of *Red Stage* and the *Monthly Bulletin*, and at the National Conference, but the analysis was limited and did not substantially affect the practice of the member groups.

The pragmatic British Communist Party failed to recognize the potential of agitprop theatre. It did not provide even the barest material resources, the organizational support and follow up, or the personnel which might have helped the WTM to overcome some of its practical difficulties so that more time could have been given to political and artistic development.

Had the Party thrown its weight behind the WTM there could have been more and better organized performances as part of campaigns and struggles. Political follow-up would have helped the troupes make a deeper and longer-lasting impact. And if the CP had not been so blind to the dangers of sectarianism, it would have been easier for both WTM and Party to get to the less militant workers they seldom reached except through street work. Objective conditions would have then *forced* the groups to develop new and better forms capable of educating, persuading and mobilizing the majority of working people, not just confirming and reinforcing what their more conscious audiences already largely knew.

What they learned in working with such audiences should also, of course, have been fed back into the Party and would have enriched the Party's own agitprop work. In the realm of theory a serious on-going debate on these questions with constructive criticism, regular in-depth reviews and articles in Party organs, etc. could only have helped the WTM, and would certainly have helped to counter the narrowness and economism of the British Communist Party.

The political shortcomings of the Communist Party also had a negative effect on the artistic development of the WTM. The mistaken assessment of the economic situation led to a belief that this capitalist crisis was the final one and would precipitate a revolutionary upsurge. Such an analysis favoured agitation – for one last quick effort to overturn the tottering system – instead of the huge job of propaganda which was necessary in the long-term struggle with a recovering capitalist class. The simplistic 'social fascist' theory and the tendency to sectarianism also favoured the use of the agitational revue with its power to attack and ridicule, rather than the complex propaganda forms required by a thorough analysis and critique of Social Democracy. Consequently, the spectator's political learning process was limited.

Unfortunately, the Party's own belated self-criticism of the sectarian period led to a complete about-face. For the WTM, this had serious consequences, in particular the influx of professionals, those who had professional aspirations, or amateurs interested primarily in theatre, not politics. Obviously, it would be wrong to imply that the Party was *directly* responsible for this influx, and for the eventual weakening of the politics of working class theatre. But the uncritical assimilation of such people was certainly in line with the prevailing policy of building a popular front, which was in turn linked to the virtual abandonment of revolutionary politics in favour of an attempt to improve the Party's image. If the Party had tried to correct its past mistakes in a more principled and less superficial fashion, this would certainly have been reflected in the agitprop and cultural field. The surrender which seems to have taken place both politically and artistically need not have happened.

This is not to imply that professionals had no role to play. Charles Mann considers today that the movement's unwillingness to learn from and adapt 'legitimate' stage techniques, the tendency to dismiss all bourgeois culture instead of critically absorbing those aspects which would have been useful, was one of the WTM's greatest drawbacks. But as there were no professionals in this country with the revolutionary experience, understanding and creativity of men like Piscator, Eisler and Wolf, Meyerhold, Eisenstein, Mayakovsky and Tretyakov, it was even more important that the criteria for deciding what was to be utilized and what discarded be based on a Marxist analysis of culture and the needs of the working class and the revolutionary party.

Finally, in trying to understand the artistic stagnation that occurred, and the WTM's demise, one has to look at the international movement's effect on Britain. The British WTM visited Germany when the revue form was dominant there, which confirmed them in their new approach. They went to the Soviet Union when the arguments for 'socialist realism' and for long traditional plays had begun. There they were severely criticized for their inability to present a more complex portrayal of political and social questions, as well as their lack of technique. They were unaware of the newer and more appropriate forms of agitational and propagandist theatre which could have provided an alternative to 'socialist realism'. (Because of financial difficulties, no British delegate attended the second IWDU conference in November 1932 when the movement moved away from making agitprop an absolute.) They were, as Jack Loveman put it, 'over-argued'.

In the end the choice was not between two equally developed formal vehicles, it was between one which was scarcely ten years old, whose potential had scarcely been tapped; and one which had had many years to mature, all the resources of the bourgeois and commercial theatres, Stanislavsky for a theoretician, and now the tremendous prestige of the Soviet Union to back it up. The result was – at this stage – a foregone conclusion. The WTM was not able to adapt fast enough to the sudden changes taking place around it, and was 'overtaken by history'. The disruption caused by the war was the last nail in the coffin. As Jack Loveman said,

> Gradually, agitprop died out in this country. A pity, since we do not have the theatrical and other resources of socialism to back us up; and we *do* have an ever-present need of agitation and propaganda.[5]

THE
RED STAGE

Price 1d

"Art is a weapon of the Revolution."

ORGAN OF THE
WORKERS' THEATRE MOVEMENT.

Vol. 1   NOVEMBER, 1931   No. 1

First Worker:
Do not play the bosses' game,
That is how we slaves became.
There's a weapon he'll dislike—
Workers' power through workers' strike.

Second: Strike!
Third: Strike!   *This very quickly, all down the line.*
Fourth: Strike!   *As each shouts "Strike," fold arms.*
Fifth: Strike!   *They all march quickly off the stage*
Sixth: Strike!   *at left.*

36 Insignia of the Workers' Theatre Movement . . .

REBEL PLAYERS

AFFTD. WORKERS THEATRE MOVEMENT
BRITISH DRAMA LEAGUE

ALL COMMUNICATIONS TO :-
SECRETARY :
52, LAMBS CONDUIT ST.,
THEOBALDS ROAD,
W.C.1.

NEW RED STAGE

No. 7   SEPTEMBER, 1932   2d.

ORGAN OF
THE
WORKERS'
THEATRE

"RED FRONT"

No. 3   FEBRUARY, 1932   One Penny

36 contd Insignia of the Workers' Theatre Movement

37 Tom Thomas as shown in *The International Theatre* in 1934. Founder of the Hackney People's Players, later Red Radio, and of the WTM, he became its national organiser and member of the presidium of the International Revolutionary Theatre Union

38 Philip Poole, London 1983; member of Red Radio and WTM secretary

39 Bram Bootman, London 1983. Joined Rebel Players in 1934, founder-member of Unity Theatre, London

40 Charles Mann, Somerset 1977; producer
of the Lewisham Red Players and editor
of *The Red Stage* and *New Red Stage*,
looking at Broadside Theatre's publicity
material

41 Fegel Firestein, London 1930; member
of the Yiddish group Proltet

42 and 43 Alice and Jack Loveman, London
1983; both members of Deptford Red
Blouse and Streatham Red Front

44 *left* 'Meerut', performed by the Lewisham Red Players in 1932. (Standing on the right is 'producer' C. B. Mann.)

45 *below* The Salford Red Megaphones during their 1932 May Day Performances

46 *above 'Waiting* for
Lefty' – exposure of
the 'rat': 'He is my
own lousy brother.'
Unity Theatre, 1935

47 *left* The *Lefty* Finale:
'Hello, America,
Hello! We're storm-
birds of the working
class and when we
die, they'll know
what we did to create
a new world.' The
final words: 'Strike,
strike, strike!'

48 From *Babes in the Wood*, Unity Theatre, 1938

49 and 50 *Crisis*, Unity Theatre living newspaper about the invasion of Czechoslovakia by Nazi Germany, 1938

Part Four

Conclusion

13 · Three movements

In the Soviet Union the workers' theatre began to develop after the Revolution. Its general aims were in accord with those of the working class, the state and the Party. The degree of mass mobilization was, at least initially and in the industrial centres, very high. The workers' theatre became an integral part of the revolutionary process. For those Blue Blouse troupes which worked in the less politicized areas, however, the situation was closer to that of the groups working in capitalist countries. Their audiences still needed a lot of convincing of the correctness of the aims of the Revolution.

In Germany after the defeated November Revolution a number of workers' insurrections established local soviets, but all these revolutionary attempts were crushed. Nevertheless, the German working class had become aware of its own strength. This taste of power kept it militant throughout the temporary stabilization of capitalism during the Weimar Republic. The struggle began to escalate again in response to the employers' attack during the crisis of the late twenties and early thirties. But the movement was not strong enough to prevent the Fascists from sowing confusion in the ranks of the workers, and finally destroying their organizations.

The German workers' theatre was carried along on a wave of working class confidence and enthusiasm, but in almost constant conflict with the state, a conflict which intensified as the crisis deepened and increasingly repressive legislation was passed.

In contrast, the British workers' theatre developed after the bitter defeat of the General Strike and during a period of high unemployment. Although there were huge mobilizations by the unemployed, those workers fortunate enough to have jobs were reluctant to jeopardize them by taking action, and most strikes were defensive. The lack of any real revolutionary tradition or leadership, the disillusionment in the wake of 1926, and the Communist Party's inability to win the masses away from their allegiance to the parliamentary system and the Labour Party, together with the objective economic conditions, meant that the British WTM could count on much less support than the Germans and Russians.

The role of the revolutionary party which attempts to lead the class struggle is obviously crucial, particularly if the workers' theatre is attached to this party. It is the party's assessment of the political situation and the strategy and tactics resulting from this assessment which the workers' theatre dramatizes in its repertoire. The extent to which the Party is based in the working class, expresses the progressive aspirations of this class, or is sectarian, also has a great influence on the workers' theatre. Its party links help to determine the type of audiences it will perform for and the context in which the performances will take place, as well as the organizational preparation and follow-up. And of course the party's attitude to cultural activity and the cultural heritage, and to the actual forms employed by the agitprop theatre can have important consequences.

In all three countries the relationship was a problematic one. In the Soviet Union there was agreement on the general direction of the Revolution. Although many on the theatrical left may initially have seen the introduction of NEP as a betrayal, in time they began to accept it as a necessary intermediate measure. The Bolsheviks were in control of the state organs because they had become the leading revolutionary party in the soviets. The Blue Blouse enjoyed a tremendously broad base in factory and co-operative clubs throughout the country, without becoming the official agitprop arm of the Party, although they supported many of its campaigns.

The major clash was over the government's emphasis on the maintenance of the cultural heritage, and its financial support for the State Theatres which took up most of the resources allocated to the theatre. The Blue Blouse movement and the theatrical left had to operate in an environment which was sometimes quite hostile. However, the government tried to encourage the transition from agitation to propaganda as early as 1923 and the workers' theatre was slow to comply, although it was in full agreement with the need for this transition. But this lack of progress was itself partly due to the Party's hostility to experimentation with unconventional forms which finally expressed itself in the codification of Socialist Realism, virtually putting an end to the exploration of episodic and fragmentary montage forms.

The German Communist Party changed its leadership and direction frequently after the defeat of the November Revolution. Its strategy and tactics veered between what it termed itself (with hindsight) left and right opportunism. In the early stages of the workers' theatre the Party maintained a strategy for a revolutionary situation, even when German capitalism was already re-stabilized. Its mass base only began to grow along with rising unemployment. The KPD was also quite sectarian at times and pursued splitting tactics in the German labour movement, particularly during the period in which the Social Fascist policy prevailed.

In its early days the Party rejected all cultural activity as a deviation from the class struggle and was therefore hostile to the efforts of the proletarian theatres. It later reversed this position and supported the agitprop movement fully. However, it clung to its belief in a short-lived capitalist recovery and a revolutionary resurgence. Partly for this reason the German agitprop movement held onto agitational forms. The fact that it was the arm of an often isolated and sectarian political movement meant that in its early stages it performed mainly to Party audiences or sympathizers, which also prolonged the use of agitational forms. This problem was overcome from the late 1920s onward, when it became a broad-based movement performing in factories, on housing estates and in the countryside. To reach these new audiences it had to develop propaganda forms, which were mainly based on theatrical montage.

Throughout the 1920s and 30s the British Communist Party too was extremely sectarian and believed in the early collapse of capitalism. Its base in the working class was very small as it recruited most heavily among the unemployed, who had no power to confront capital where it counted, at the point of production. The British Workers' Theatre Movement faithfully reflected the Party's analysis and strategy in spite of the fact that the Party gave the WTM little real support. The WTM's audiences too often consisted of Party members and sympathizers, which contributed to the fact that the movement was not forced to develop beyond agitational sketches projecting an easy victory for the working class.

When the Party finally changed course during the Popular Front years, it also began to take an interest in political culture, but in such a superficial way that it often capitulated to bourgeois concepts of art and culture.

The political struggle had given rise to the revolutionary workers' theatres, and it was also largely political events that brought them to a halt. In the Soviet Union the Revolution had sparked off a 'theatre epidemic' – mass spectacles, agitational street performances, experimentation in the professional and workers' theatres with forms which had revolutionary potential. But the growing domination of a bureaucratic state, which controlled the workers rather than being controlled by them, increasingly restricted the development of a critical theatre.

In Germany the November Revolution and the subsequent insurrections gave the working class the confidence to build a strong cultural front with the agitprop movement as its spearhead, which was able to challenge the bourgeoisie politically and culturally. But the tottering capitalist system turned to Fascism for its salvation, which destroyed the workers' political and cultural organizations.

In Britain the emergence of the workers' theatre was accompanied by less momentous events. However, the experience of the General Strike and of the hungry 1920s and 30s radicalized a good number of people. This was expressed in a militant and attacking theatre which supported the fightback whenever it took place. It yielded fewer formal innovations than the other movements and it declined largely because of the adoption of the Popular Front policy, an indication of the limited base of its member troupes.

In all three countries the Communist Party had a good share of responsibility for the demise of the workers' theatre or for the political events that brought it to a halt. This should not be an argument for keeping the political theatre aloof from direct involvement in the agitational and propagandist activities of revolutionary organizations. Rather it is an argument for the need to develop Marxist aesthetic, cultural, and ideological theory so that revolutionary organizations have a better understanding of the importance and implications of agitprop, and so that the political theatre has a better theoretical basis. This would enable the political organizations to give more appropriate and adequate support to their groups. The groups would be able to hold their ground more firmly on their artistic and political objectives, rather than becoming a pawn in the parties' tactical considerations.

Despite the tortuous and problematic relationship between art, theatre, cultural politics and revolutionary organizations, experience has shown the necessity of uniting these fronts if workers are to challenge the dominance of the bourgeoisie. Without its own class-orientated cultural activity the working class can remain or become the prisoner of bourgeois ideology in spite of having made economic or even political gains. And these gains are more difficult to achieve, maintain or to extend without an on-going process of politicization of those who achieve them and reap their benefits.

This brings us to the attitude the members of the workers' theatres had to their own medium, its traditions, and to professionals. Their motives were mainly political, but equal consideration must be given to the dramatic forms they employed. Without artistic achievement the effect of political theatre is negligible or even negative.

'Achievement' here is more than the theatrical equivalent of the political content. A dramatic presentation is in most cases a simplification of the political analysis on which it is based. It is this very ability to simplify which can concretize abstractions, bringing them to life in a social form. Such a live demonstration makes theories more accessible, enabling the audience to relate them directly to their own lives and conditions, and to generalize from them. It also gives the political content more immediate impact.

To facilitate a learning process the revolutionary theatre had to develop forms which expressed the dialectic between those aspects of theory based on concrete experience, and those which involve generalizations. When these two elements are successfully interwoven, the political content is not reduced but expanded on a different level. Forms capable of expressing the contradictions in the content enrich the subject matter of political plays in the same sense that an undialectical form would detract from it. The forms themselves, therefore, have political content. In such a theatre the audience is 'educated' in an enjoyable way, they are helped to think dialectically and given mental tools which can be applied to many more subjects than those in the play.

In our view this was the main task which objective conditions demanded of the agitprop groups. Not many fulfilled it. Particularly in the Soviet Union and in Britain, most never got beyond agitational revues based on simple juxtaposition. Only a few of the leading German groups began to develop structures that would enable a more complex portrayal of the subject on a number of levels and from a number of perspectives.

One reason for this was the lack of a militant workers' dramatic tradition. In Russia no such tradition existed, partly due to the heavy censorship, partly due to the belated emergence of an industrial proletariat. In Germany the tradition declined along with the SPD's reformist deterioration. This broken and reformist heritage was then rejected by the radical workers' movement after 1918. In Britain working-class theatrical activity was mainly based on Shaw, utopian or pacifist idealism, or plays depicting workers' misery without explaining what caused it or how to overcome it. There was also a rich workers' musical tradition of folk song, critical broadside and instrumental music which had great potential for popular, political music, but it was completely ignored by the WTM.

When they started, the workers' theatres in all three countries saw culture as the ideological tool of the ruling class used to keep workers in their place. They rejected most of it as bourgeois and juxtaposed to it the building of a workers' or proletarian culture.

This break might have been temporarily advantageous or even necessary. It meant that one did not feel compelled to use the same aesthetic measuring stick which one would have applied to the highly developed bourgeois culture. Such a comparison might easily have led to a dismissal of the often clumsy and primitive early attempts at self-expression of a deprived class. The workers' theatre was given a chance to develop its own approach and its own forms of artistic expression on its own terms. Besides, the existing dramatic forms simply did not lend themselves to forging a direct link with the workers' struggle.

However, a number of qualifications must be made here. Firstly, the most ardent supporters of the break with all previous culture were mainly the intellectual theoreticians or leaders of these movements. They had already had an opportunity to critically assimilate the culture of the past and its dramatic traditions; for them it might have been quite correct to concentrate mainly on the creation of new dramatic forms, uninhibited by theatrical conventions. But for the majority of workers, who had not had the advantage of the intellectuals' education this attitude could lead to actual cultural impoverishment and therefore to a brake on their own creativity.

It was seldom actually argued that the previous culture should be completely ignored, but it did mean that very little emphasis was put on its critical assimilation. (The British Proltet group was a notable exception. As immigrants one of their concerns was to preserve the rich Jewish culture they brought with them from Eastern Europe.) This can have other serious implications. If one attempts to start from scratch, without linking up with an already existing radical tradition, and one has not critically assimilated the dramatic forms of the past and present, then one can easily begin to copy them unconsciously. This happened with some of the German mass spectacles.

In Britain the original hostility to the theatre of the past and to the work of the professional stage remained virtually unchanged. It is significant that those individuals who did not adhere to this policy in a dogmatic way and did try to come to terms with the contemporary theatre in a critical fashion would appear to have been the most inventive writers and directors. However, they too succumbed to or were unable to resist the general trend. The plays and sketches reflected the class struggle and were often performed in struggle situations, but they were unable to dramatize a complex political argument or analysis.

It was not only the repertoire, audience and performance context of the established theatre which was dismissed, justifiable for a workers' theatre, but also its techniques of staging and acting. The British WTM therefore did not acquire even the rudiments of play production and acting, nor did it make any serious attempts to adapt them for its own purpose. (Obviously there were exceptions to this: André Van Gyseghem, for example, certainly did attempt to raise the technical level of Rebel Players and the other groups he came in contact with.)

Thus the crude sketches were staged and acted in an extremely unrefined way. Political opponents were portrayed in a cartoon-like or caricatured manner while working-class characters were either acted 'realistically' which meant the worker-actors behaved 'naturally' on stage rather than 'acting', or were presented as stylized 'heroes'. Again there were exceptions where the class commitment of the players was channelled into a heightened collective expression of working class anger or revolutionary enthusiasm. But the overriding hostility to the professional stage and all its attributes meant that they were few and far between.

In the Soviet Union and in Germany this trend, which was seen as one of the main tenets of the Proletkult, was gradually reversed, although it continued in both countries up to the late 1920s. By then it was no longer identified with Proletkult, which had been heavily routed in the early 1920s.

In the Soviet Union the prolongation of this hostility could have been disastrous, mainly because of the cultural backwardness of the broad masses. However, the state instigated a thorough campaign to abolish illiteracy, in which Proletkult and the Blue Blouse movement participated. Secondly, the professional revolutionary theatre had a number of outstanding directors, in particular Meyerhold, and writers like Mayakovsky and Tretyakov, who provided the workers' theatre with an arsenal of theatrical techniques and literary models. They had assimilated the cultural tradition critically and thoroughly and had distilled from it what they considered useful for the revolutionary theatre. They had also rediscovered and adapted popular forms of entertainment and had begun to combine them in episodic play structures.

Through them the workers' theatre had a link with the theatrical past and that helped tremendously in the early stages of its development. However, even the forms that the professionals who joined the Bolsheviks had pioneered were predominantly agitational. They were hardly ever complex enough to portray a thorough political argument and counter-argument. The breakthrough in acting, again pioneered mainly by Meyer-hold who combined the techniques of the fairground booth, travelling players, the circus and commedia dell'arte with the eccentric and biomechanics, gave their sketches tremendous liveliness and often startling virtu-osity. But it also helped perpetuate the emphasis on the agitational at a time when the transition to or complementary use of propaganda forms was long overdue.

Of course, the NEP man and his attitudes needed attacking, and this the Blue Blouse could do brilliantly with revue sketches. But the ideo-logical confusion sowed by NEP, and the slow process of revolutionizing the backward areas of the Soviet Union required a more differentiated treatment.

In these areas the lack of writers, a reflection of cultural backwardness, made itself felt particularly strongly. The encouragement of worker and factory correspondents who reported events from local and industrial life to trade union journals, local papers and the *Blue Blouse* journal was a positive step. But the evolution of their writing skills was slow. They produced reports which were useful for the Blue Blouse's living news-paper but which would have needed a lot of adaptation if they had been worked into a more complex montage.

The German working class was more developed culturally and had a long tradition of activity in amateur theatre. Again the revolutionary professionals, above all Piscator, provided theatrical models and techniques. And again they were based on popular traditions, as well as on the conclusions revolutionary artists like Piscator, Heartfield and Grosz drew from their involvement in the anti-art and Dadaist movement. It was partly from this experience that their conceptions of montage or collage in photography and design derived. These were explored and developed for the theatre during their co-operation with Piscator's Proletarian Theatre and his subsequent work in more conventional theatre buildings, which did not stay conventional under his directorship.

There is a strong parallel here between the experiments of the Russian Futurists and Symbolists, and Dada in Germany. Fiebach characterized the montages of the Surrealists, Dadaists and Futurists which used simultaneous and parallel scenes in his essay about Piscator:

> The montage arises in late bourgeois art as an artistic form of a disintegrating order of things and human relations, of a world that has become incomprehensible, senseless and untransparent, of the alienation of people from each other and from things. The montage essentially reflects the consciousness of this lack of cohesion and sense of life, expresses the unreality of reality, representing the world as a chaos, deformed and absurd. Whilst the individual 'montage elements' show one aspect of reality very precisely, clearly and in realistic detail, the whole montage, its structure expresses in a poem, picture or performance, unreality, lack of cohesion, incomprehensibility and even complete absurdity, non-sense.[1]

The artists who participated in these movements and became revolutionaries had been through a process of analysing artistic forms in their social context. They reorganized and restructured these 'montage elements' to portray the disintegrating capitalist society and its chaos. But they structured this portrayal in a way that facilitated an understanding of the causes of this chaos and of the emerging forces that could, after a revolution, create a coherent, non-exploitative society.

Piscator's experiments in the early 1920s with the episodic and fragmentary forms of the revue were already concerned with the dramatization of very concrete topical political subjects. This gave the German workers' theatre a head start over the other movements. Meyerhold's experiments with the eccentric were based mainly on adaptations of only vaguely political plays, and Eisenstein's montage of attractions was extremely abstract. The professionals who co-operated with the British WTM had no such tradition to learn from even if, like André Van Gyseghem, they were interested in experimental forms. As far as we know they never consciously applied themselves to the problem of developing political forms for political content.

This helps explain why the German revues developed so rapidly and became, even in the agitational stage, more complex and coherent than the revues of the Russian or British workers' theatre. But although the German agitprop movement slowly began to develop a new approach to acting, it did not have the spectacular qualities of the Blue Blouse who owed a debt of thanks to Meyerhold. Piscator did not emphasize acting techniques to the same extent, possibly because he was never an actor himself, while Meyerhold certainly was. However, when the German workers saw the need for propaganda forms, with complex montages and more differentiated character portrayals, their acting developed more in the direction of the heightened selective realism associated with the Brechtian theatre.

The transition to montage was, however, delayed in Germany too. Although Piscator continued the development of theatrical montage, and achieved great flexibility with the use of projections of slides and films, as did Meyerhold with his more complex montages, they required modern theatre equipment. This ruled out such forms for a mobile theatre. The German workers' theatre had to develop a montage of the 'small' dramatic forms, and for that it lacked literary models. It also lacked qualified writers, already a problem in the agitational phase.

The scarcity of writers producing political plays made to measure for the workers' theatre bedevilled the movements in all three countries and became a serious obstacle to their development. They tried to find a solution by extending the collective principle governing the political aspects of their work to the artistic ones, and in particular, to the production of texts. This was a temporary answer as long as the main theatrical vehicle was the revue where different styles of presentation and writing did not jar.

The collective evolution of a political and artistic approach gave the groups cohesion. The actors who participated in the writing process understood in detail the political and scenic intentions of each sequence of scenes or sketches.

But as was often the case in the history of the workers' theatre methods that have proven themselves as solutions to a particular task or problem, became enshrined as almost inviolable working principles. The transition to more complex plays required a more detailed, coherent and thorough literary method, which is much more easily achieved by an individual. The principle of collective text production then became an obstacle.

This problem was only really tackled in Germany. In Britain the workers' theatre never had a differentiated enough approach to the learning process of its audiences to make the transition to propagandist dramatic forms appear a necessity. In the Soviet Union the development of the Blue Blouse and TRAM was brought to a halt by the change of their leadership and the promotion of an unsympathetic if not hostile cultural policy, Socialist Realism, before they could fully explore the montage technique.

In Germany the most advanced troupes, above all the Red Megaphone and Performance Troupe South-West, began to evolve a working procedure where a single qualified writer would produce a text in closest consultation with the group, or would use and synthesise collectively written and often improvised material. The idea was to evolve a writer specialist who was fully integrated into the group's work and accountable to the collective.

Many groups were opposed to this on the grounds that it was against the concept and principles of an artistic and political collective. They either made the transition to propagandist dramatic material extremely slowly or never even attempted it. They confined themselves to the simple revue, and the learning process of the spectator was limited as a result.

But those troupes flexible enough to adapt their working methods in response to the new objective requirements of the political situation, and which produced their own writers as integral members of the group, began to evolve the necessary dramatic forms. They were able to take the spectators through a differentiated but enjoyable development of understanding. Not only were specific policies dealt with in their plays, but also the economic, political and ideological sources of the growth of Fascism and its effect on German society. The historical alternative socialism offered was also included.

It is this ability to make links between the wider political and historical trends and alternatives without losing touch with the concrete reality from which they emanate, which constitutes the strength of the dialectical montage.

Fiebach described the montage as:

the essential principle of composition, as the form of expression that flows from the portrayal of great historic subjects almost like a law. . . . The completely independent emergence of the great Soviet montage films and of course the German montage theatre, beginning with *In Spite of Everything* in 1925 and traceable in its manifold forms up to the productions of Troupe 31, was not mere chance.[2]

He defined the revue as:

a form of the Epic Theatre. It is based on the principle of pointing up, of the gestic. It demonstrates to the spectator outside social or factual phenomena and human attitudes which could not be expressed by exclusively interhuman relationships. . . . In contrast to the epic 'dramaturgy of historical events', which portrays processes and developments, the revue gives in a sequence of scenes or numbers which are not or are only loosely linked – an overview on phenomena which exist spatially next to each other or timewise after each other without having to be related to a plot or to interhuman relationships. . . . The revue can portray human attitudes or social phenomena only in a static way and in their specific factual framework . . . which often consists only of their thematic relevance to each other.[3]

The revue lends itself to the agitational portrayal of the daily events of the class struggle, to the stating of facts and policies rather than to a process of convincing, of explaining long-term policies.

In the dialectical montage on the other hand, the individual sections, scenes and songs are interrelated and cannot be arbitrarily exchanged. The combination of the different scenic elements needs careful attention, for as Eisenstein says: 'When two pieces are placed next to each other they unavoidably form a new impression which arises as a new quality from this juxtaposition.'[4]

The montage makes it possible to portray in a dialectical dramatic form laws of social development which are not visible or tangible in reality. As Fiebach says: 'Unlike the revue . . . the montage is able to make a process, a development visible.'[5]

At the same time continuous jumps and dislocation of the 'plot' expose the actual dramatic means with which the performers attempt to affect the consciousness of the spectators. The spectators are given an active role by the montage: it provides them with Marxist tools to assess the political situation they find themselves in as well as its historical context. The intercutting and juxtaposing of scenic elements and episodes demands constant alertness and associative thinking in order to make links and associations. The episodic and fragmentary structures distance the audience so that they can critically assess the content as well as the form of the dramatic argument to which they are exposed.

The fact that very few groups lived up to such a tall order does not mean that the rest were failures. Their use of the agitational, mobilizing revue complemented the propagandist montage. It was a necessary stage in the political and theatrical development of the workers' movement.

This uneven and contradictory development which reached its peak in the montages of the best German agitprop troupes contradicted a number of beliefs and dogmas, some held by its own members, some advocated by those who thought that the very existence of a workers' theatre and culture was impossible.

1 The workers' theatre movements proved that art can become an effective tool in the class struggle, that theatre can become a dynamic part of a revolutionary cultural arm of the workers' movement and its organizations, that workers can create a 'proletarian culture', a culture that serves the workers. Trotsky, among others, disputed this.

2 They did not achieve this by linking up with the 'great' forms of the bourgeois drama as Mehring and Zetkin argued, but with a whole variety of small, flexible and adaptable forms; many of which derived from the time when the bourgeoisie itself was using them in its struggle against feudalism.

3 In order to explore these forms and to adapt them for its own purpose the workers' theatre had to abandon the stated aim, which was never truly implemented, of breaking with all previous culture. It had to begin to assimilate this culture critically in order to pinpoint and develop those artistic trends which had played a popular and dynamic role in the past.

4 To assist them in this analysis and in the development of new forms, the workers needed revolutionary intellectuals. They had to overcome their own separatism and forge a link with progressive directors, writers, actors, musicians and professional collectives of these artists.

5 In order to mobilize their audiences while raising their consciousness, they had to develop new forms, on the basis of a new historic draft plan as Brik put it. New wine put in old bottles usually turns sour, as Brecht reminded Lukàcs, a firm supporter of nineteenth century realism.

6 This development could take place against so many odds only because it was linked to the class struggle and attempted to respond to its needs, and because it tested its theories in practice in the course of this struggle.

In this way the workers' theatre began to hammer out the 'new draft plan' for a dynamic political theatre. Brecht, who inherited and developed this draft drew on their experience when he defined what is popular and realistic, with a 'fighting people in mind':

Popular means: intelligible to the broad masses, adopting and enriching their forms of expression / assuming their standpoint, confirming and correcting it / representing the most progressive section of the people so that it can acquire leadership, and therefore comprehensible to other sections of the people as well / relating to traditions and developing them / communicating to that portion of the people which strives for leadership the achievements of the present section that rules the nation.

Realistic means: discovering the causal complexes of society / unmasking the prevailing view of things as the view of those who rule it / writing from the standpoint of the class which offers the broadest solutions for the pressing difficulties in which human society is caught / emphasizing the element of development / making possible the concrete, and making possible abstraction from it.[6]

Appendix · 1

USSR: The repertoire of the Blue Blouse Movement

By 1927 the ranks of the Blue Blouse included up to 7,000 workers' circles as well as four or five professional groups with names like 'Model', 'Shock', 'Fundamental' and 'Variety Vaudeville'. These professionals served workers' clubs in Moscow, but they were also responsible for providing the workers' circles with up-to-date material on the questions of the day – via the bi-weekly journal *Blue Blouse*.

The following index covers the repertoire of the first thirty issues from 1924–1926. The journal was published until September 1928, eighty issues altogether. The repertoire is discussed in Part 1, Chapter 3.

INDEX OF THE BLUE BLOUSE REPERTOIRE AND METHODOLOGICAL ESSAYS 1924–1926[1]

The Blue Blouse repertoire, the fruit of almost three years' work, is a great example of the tortuous road of mistakes and achievements in the field of agitational and artistic work. It is a valuable heritage and the richest inheritors will be all those who work critically over this material. The index can serve as a reference work for the everyday effort of the Blue Blouse member who wants to combine different texts, to insert them into various scenes in productions, and will make it easier for him to find the items he needs in the mass of published material

	Issue	Page
I Entrée (march)		
We Have Come to Tell You	1	10
With the Brisk Step of the Blue Blouse	4	3
Before You Appears the Blue Blouse Journalists' Brotherhood	5	5
Prepare for Galleys	11	5
Link to Link	16	7
March-Parade	25	3
End-pieces		
Shine Everywhere, Shine Always	1	62
When the Paper Is Finished	5	60
Our Courage Is in Cheerfulness	11	50
End-Piece	25	57

IX Co-operation/Co-operative

X Soviet Construction and the Economy

XV Miscellaneous (24 items, most of which are also incorporated in the other 15 sections of this index)

XVI Method, Theory and Practice

Appendix · 2

Germany: Statistics and repertoire of the Agitprop Movement

STATISTICAL ANALYSIS OF THE COMPOSITION AND WORK OF THE ATBD[2]

At its Eleventh Congress the ATBD had about three hundred local groups, but about five hundred agitprop groups existed in the country. The Congress report gives a statistical break-down of the groups' nature and activities in 1929. However, the figures are based on only 41.5 per cent of the questionnaires sent out to all the groups. As one must assume that it was the most active groups who answered and returned these questionnaires, the accuracy of the estimated total figures, arrived at in the report by doubling the results of the details received, appears questionable. But if one makes allowances for exaggerations the figures are still highly revealing:

Performance details
    In *1929* the groups of the ATBD performed:
    For organisations: 1986 times = 77.5 per cent of all performances
    Own performances: 574 times = 22.5 per cent
    In or for factories: 90 times = 3.5 per cent
    In the countryside: 600 times = 33.5 per cent
    To a total audience of: 2,000,000
    Maximum performances by one group: 120
    Less than ten performances a year: 47 groups

The social structure of the ATBD
    The membership of the ATBD consists of:
    82.3 per cent factory workers (this break-down is based on the questionnaires actually received – R.S.)
    3.2 per cent farm workers
    5.0 per cent office workers
    0.6 per cent civil servants
    8.9 per cent professional people

    60 per cent are organised in political organisations,
    75 per cent in trade unions.
During 1931 60,000 new members were recruited for the agitprop movement.

STATISTICAL ANALYSIS OF THE COMPOSITION AND WORK OF KJVD TROUPES[3]

At the Third National Conference of KJVD Troupes in 1930 a survey of the Party's agitprop troupes was undertaken. The following breakdown is based on the details of 70 of the Party's 150 troupes which returned the questionnaires:

Organisational links

Groups of the KPD	35
Groups of the KJVD	27
Groups of sympathising organisations:	3
Groups emerging from the ATBD	3
Groups organised in the ATBD	35
Groups without firm links to organisations:	2
Groups not organised politically 100%	23

Age of the groups

Groups existing since 1925	1
Groups existing since 1927	5
Groups existing since 1928	10
Groups existing since 1929	17
Groups existing since 1930	30

The social structure of the groups

100% workers	39
Workers and office workers	12
Workers, office workers and professional people	12
Farm workers	1

Numbers of performances of groups per year

Less than 10 performances	1
Between 1–50 performances	14
Between 50–100 performances	10
100 and more performances	6

Numbers of groups prohibited, arrested or prosecuted: 18

Performance context

Number of groups that performed for works meetings:	15
less than 5 times	8
more than 5 times	7
Maximum of performances for works meetings of one group:	40
Number of groups agitating in the country	47

Text production

Number of groups producing their own texts	50
Groups working with writers	17
of those writers, the number of professionals	8
Groups using texts from *Red Megaphone*	45

Effectiveness: KPD-Election campaign of Berlin agitprop groups – June 1930[4]

19 groups gave 349 performances in 25 days

Nature of performances: in the countryside	86
at housing estates	61
at public places	14
for factories	31
in halls	157
Total audience	(180,000)

Members recruited:

300 for KPD by 11 groups
120 for KJVD by 7 groups
375 for Red Aid by 5 groups
260 for International Workers Aid by 5 groups
  66 for Revolutionary Trade Union Opposition by 2.

THE REPERTOIRE OF THE WORKERS' THEATRE – A REFLECTION OF POLITICAL EVENTS

Events	Repertoire
1919 The murder of Luxemburg and Liebknecht	*Spartakus*
1920 War of intervention against the Soviet Union by the Entente	*Russia's Day (Russlands Tag)*
1921 KPD attempts to unite town and country	*Worker, Peasant and Spartacus (Arbeiter, Bauer und Spartacus)*
1923 Collaboration of SPD with Capital under the pretence of 'socialisation' The Weimar Republic maintains the old anti-abortion law	*Chorus of Labour (Chor der Arbeit)* *Paragraph 218*
1924 7,000 political prisoners; the aftermath of the suppression of the Hamburg uprising. The Dawes Plan: American monopolies gain control under the guise of helping Germany pay war reparations. KPD election campaign.	*7,000* *German National Theatre (Deutsches Nationaltheatre)* *Red Revels of the KJVD (Rote Rummel des KJVD)* *Red Revel Revue – RRR (Revue Roter Rummel)*

Events	Repertoire
1925 Tenth Congress of the KPD. Draft into involuntary 'Labour-Schools'.	*In Spite of Everything! (Trotz alledem!)* *That's How Young Workers Will be* *Drilled in the Involuntary Labour* *School (So sollen junge Arbeiter in der* *Arbeitsdienst-pflichtschule gedrillt* *werden)*
1926 Referendum on the compensation of expropriated aristocrats.	*Take from the Kaiser – What Belongs* *to the People (Nehmt dem Kaiser was* *des Volkes ist!)*
1927 Germany supports war of intervention against revolutionary China. German arms build-up against the Soviet Union. Ten Year Celebration of the Russian Revolution.	*Hands Off China! (Hände weg von* *China!)* *Gas War Against Soviet Russia* *(Giftgaskrieg gegën Sowjetrussland)* *Five week tour of the Moscow Blue* *Blouse through Germany.*
1928 The 'Great Coalition': its arms expenditure and suppression of revolutionary organisations. Fascist and reactionary youth organisations are gaining influence. Cultural reaction is on the increase in the mass media.	*Knock Out; The Wonder Horse Called* *'Great Coalition' (K.o.-ein Boxkampf;* *der Wundergaul-genannt "Die grosse* *Koalition)* *Hello. Young Worker! (Hallo, Kollege* *Jungarbeiter)* *Film; This Way or That Way (Film: So* *– oder So?)* *The World of Wonders of the German* *Philistine (Des deutschen Spiessers* *Wunderwelt)*
1929 Ten Year Comintern Bloody May: police fire on and kill 30 marchers in a banned May Day demonstration of 200,000. Banks begin to expropriate peasants unable to pay back their credits.	*Third International (Dritte* *Internationale)* *'Red Wedding' – Song (Roter Wedding* *– a workers' district in Berlin)* *Landed Property (Grundeigentum), and* *North West Forward's countryside* *agitation*

Events	Repertoire
1930	
In the aftermath to Bloody May the 'Law in Defence of the Republic' leads to arrests, convictions and bans of agitprop activity.	*'We Sound the Alarm' – Song (Wir schlagen Alarm!); How Does the Proletarian Defend Himself in a Political Case (Wie verteidigt sich der Prolet in einem politischem Straffall?); The Drum of the RFL (Die RFB – Pauke); Hallo! – State Power! (Hallo! – Die Staatsgewalt!).*
Mass activity of revolutionary organisations at work places and in working class communities.	*Leuna!; Agfa – Revue; Black Plague (Schwarze Pest), and performances in support of revolutionary factory councils and cells and in housing estates by Red Megaphone, Red Wedding, North West Forward and Red Forge.*
Fascist dictatorship imminent, NSDAP with 6,000,000 votes the 2nd strongest faction in the Reichstag.	*Nazis Among Themselves (Nazis unter sich).*
Deepening of the economic crisis. Need for an alternative to National Socialism, war against the Soviet Union a probability.	*Surplus Value (Der Mehrwert); For Soviet Power (Für die Sowjetmacht).*
1931	
Emergency laws require a united front in action and in the ideological battle.	*Song of the Red United Front (Lied der Roten Einheitsfront); Mass-Strike (Massenstreik); Freethinkers' Revue (Freidenker-Revue); The Mother (Die Mutter).*
1932	
Preparations for fascist takeover Peak of crisis: 6,000,000 unemployed, pauperisation of industrial proletariat and of peasantry is severely worsening.	*In Spite of Everything! (Trotz alledem!); Where are the Frontlines? (Wie stehen die Fronten?); Mousetrap (Die Mausefalle); Kuhle Wampe; Peasant Baetz (Bauer Baetz).*
German monopolies support Japanese intentions to invade China.	*From New York to Shanghai (Von New York bis Shanghai).*

1933

Some of the troupes continued performing some of these plays, sketches and songs. They did this in most cases covertly and on a 'hit and run' basis – often disguised as 'light entertainment' of rambling and social clubs. Mass arrests, imprisonment, torture and murder of many troupe members forced the still remaining troupes to combine their dwindling numbers until the cultural fight against fascism from within Germany became impossible. Those who escaped jailings or death continued to fight with artistic and other weapons from abroad.

Appendix · 3

Britain: The groups of the WTM and its repertoire

THE MEMBER GROUPS OF THE WTM

The number of groups affiliated to the WTM fluctuated considerably and only a few of those listed below were active at the same time. However, as this is such an under-researched and undocumented area, we will provide a survey that is as complete as existing sources will allow.[5] Groups existed in:

London and Southern England
Battersea Players
Becontree Reds
Bermondsey
Bethnal Green
Brighton
Camberwell
Chelmsford
Croydon
Hammer and Sickle Players (former Charter Players – St Pancras)
Lewisham Red Players
Poplar
Proltet (Yiddish Group – East End)
Reading
Rebel Players (Hackney)
Red Blouse Troupe (Greenwich and Deptford)
Red Dawn (Southampton)
Red Flag Troupe (Islington)
Red Front Troupe (Streatham)
Red Magnets (Woolwich)
Red Pilots
Red Pioneers (touring Scotland and South Wales, made up of members of several
    London groups)
Red Radio (formerly Peoples' Players, earlier the Hackney Labour Dramatic Group,
    the first to establish the WTM)
Red Star Troupe (Hammersmith)
Walthamstow
West Ham United Front Troupe
Westminster

Lancashire and N.W. England

Barrow-in-Furness
Bolton
Burnley
Drama Section of Liverpool Young Teachers' Association (instrumental in founding the Merseyside Left Theatre, after 1945 the Merseyside Unity Theatre)
Krasny Textile Group (Rochdale, Krasny is Russian for 'red')
Pendlebury
Preston
Red Anchor Troupe (former Soviet Star Troupe – Liverpool)
Red Anvil (Manchester)
Red Cops (Rochdale)
Salford Red Megaphone (later the Manchester Theatre of Action)
Wigan
Warrington

Midlands

Birmingham
Burslem
Nottingham

Yorkshire and N.E. England

Castleford
Leeds
Red Magnets (Sunderland)
Sheffield
Todmorden
Wakefield

Scotland

Aberdeen
Cowdenbeath
Edinburgh
Glasgow (later the Glasgow Workers' Theatre Group, 1937–1940)
Greenock
Red Front Troupe (Dundee)

Wales and W. England

Porth
Rhondda
Scarlet Banner (Bristol)
Trealaw

This total of almost 60 groups is deceptive. In London a number of groups collaborated, merged at times when they were too weak to sustain independent action, and covered several boroughs; particularly south of the Thames it is difficult to differentiate between some South London groups and the boroughs in which group activities have been mentioned.

In the country at large, some groups existed only sporadically, became active only at particular events or occasions or, as Tom Thomas observed:

Cases are continually occurring of groups which have achieved extraordinary results collapsing as soon as the necessity for exerting all their strength disappears.[6]

THE REPERTOIRE OF THE WTM AND EARLY UNITY

We can by no means claim that this is a complete list of all sketches and plays performed by the WTM; we have attempted to give an insight into the scope of the movement's activities by analysing all available source material.[7] Tracing the authors of the various pieces was particularly difficult, as often only the titles are referred to, and then sometimes in variations or abbreviations. One can assume, therefore, that the same sketch may have appeared under a slightly different name. However, to avoid omitting an item we thought it worth risking possible duplication.

Title	Author
A Man and a Woman	Ernst Toller
Adding Machine, The	Elmer Rice
Archbishop's Prayer, The	?
August 1st, 1931	?
Babes in the Wood, (Unity production)	Robert Mitchell/G. Parsons
Battle of Deptford Broadway, The	?
BBC, The	?
Bessie Burton's Father	Tom Thomas
Big Parade, The	?
Blood on the Coal	?
Busmen (Unity production, a Living Newspaper)	?
Call, The	?
Cannibal Carnival (Unity production)	Herbert Hodge
Castleford	?
Class Against Class	?
Clothing Workers	?
Conscription	?
Co-operate Against the Boss	?
Crisis (Crisis at No. 10)	?
Crisis (Unity-production, a Living Newspaper)	?
Crisis, Cuts and War	?
Dawn (originally *Hell* but adapted by Tom Thomas)	Upton Sinclair
Death of Lenin, The	?
Doctor Mac	Tom Thomas
Do You Remember 1914?	P. Adams
Dubb's Reduction	Jack Loveman
Economy in the Docks	?
English and Russian Children	A. Laundy (age 11)
Enter Rationalisation	?
Ever-Ready	?
Fate or-	?
Fifteen Years	?
Fight Goes On, The	Tom Thomas
Finest Child in the World, The	?
First of May, The	Tom Thomas
Five Year Plan, The	?
Frame-up, The	P. Adams
Gas and Gas Masks	?

Title	Author
Get on with the Funeral	?
Great Deception, The (Yiddish)	?
Hunger March (Hunger Marchers)	?
In Time of Strife	Joe Corrie
It's a Free Country	H. Baron
It's Your Country – Fight for It!	?
Judges of All the Earth	?
Lady Houston	?
Lady Betty's Husband	Bernard Woolf
Law & Order (Yiddish)	?
Lenin, Liebknecht and Luxemburg	?
Light the Candle	?
Love in Industry	?
Malice in Plunderland	Tom Thomas
Mammonart	?
Manchuria	?
Means Test Murder	?
Meerut	?
Mock Democracy	?
Mrs Warren's Profession	G. B. Shaw
Murder in the Coalfields	?
New Saint, The	?
Next Great War, The	?
1914–1931	?
Nobility of Women	?
N.U.W.M. (National Unemployed Workers' Movement)	?
On Guard for Spain (Unity production)	Jack Lindsay
Our Leaders, Preachers and Teachers	?
P.A.C. (Public Assistance Committee)	?
Passaic	John Dos Passos
Peace in Industry	R. Woddis
Stanley Baldwin's Pipe Dream	?
Plant in the Sun (Unity production)	Ben Bengal
Port Workers' Unity	?
Ragged Trousered Philanthropists, The	Robert Tressell/T. Thomas
Rail Revolt, The	W.S.
Ramsay Mac	?
Red Cavalry	?
Requiem for Liebknecht and Luxemburg (Unity production)	Ernst Toller
R.I.P. (Rent, Interest and Profit)	?
R.U.R. (Revolt of the Robots/Workers)	Čapek
Russian Timber 'Dumping'	?
Sailors' Strike, The (Invergordon)	?
Señora Carrar's Rifles (Unity production)	Bertolt Brecht
Singing Jailbirds	Upton Sinclair
Slave Labour Bill, The	?
Slickers, Ltd.	?
Social Service	?

Title	Author
Something for Nothing	Tom Thomas
Speed	?
Speed-up! Speed-up!	Tom Thomas
Star Turns Red, The (Unity production)	Sean O'Casey
Still Talking	?
Strike Sketch, The	?
Strike Up	Tom Thomas
Suppress, Oppress and Depress	M. Chaney/T. Thomas
That Foreign Competition	?
Theatre – Our Weapon, The	?
Their Theatre – and Ours	Tom Thomas
Trial of Private Enterprise	?
Two Paths, The	?
Two Pictures and Three Frames	?
UAB Scotland	?
Waiting for Lefty (Unity production)	Clifford Odets
War (the second author seems to be WTM-Secretary Philip J. Poole	J.L./P.J.P.
War in the East	?
We Can Stop the War	?
Where's that Bomb? (Unity production)	Buckley Roberts/Herbert Hodge
Women of Kirbirsk, The	Tom Thomas
Youth Unity Sketch	Philip J. Poole

The many questions marks do not necessarily mean that the names of so many authors are still unknown. Many sketches were written collectively. They were then sent to the organ of the WTM by the groups that had produced them without claiming them. Indeed it was an expression of the high degree of collectivity that many groups performed the material produced by the others.

In addition to the over 100 sketches and plays listed above, the repertoire of the WTM included a great many songs. Some were borrowed from its Russian and German sister organisations but many were written by its own members. They reflect the high degree of satirical wit and humour with which the movement intervened in the daily struggle of its class – a humour born in this stuggle.

Notes and references

Introduction

1 F. Wolf, *Ausgewählte Werke*, Vol. XIII, Berlin 1957, pp. 20–1.
2 McCreery/Stourac, Interview with Fegel and Philip Firestein, London 1977.

Chapter 1   The roar of the dynamo

1 *Sinyaya Bluza*, Moscow 1925, No. 23/24, p. 5.
2 *Album Blue Blouse* (Russian), Moscow 1928.
3 *Sinyaya Bluza*, 1925, No. 23/24, p. 3.
4 *Ibid.*, 1927, No. 69/70, p. 50.
5 *Ibid.*, 1928, Five Year Edition, pp. 6–7.

Chapter 2   From the reformers to the revolutionaries

1 *Sinyaya Bluza*, 1927, No. 69/70, p. 53.
2 R. Lorenz, *Proletarische Kulturrevolution in Sowjetrussland*, Munich 1969, p. 9.
3 *Ibid.*, p. 10.
4 P. A. Markov, *The Soviet Theatre*, London 1934, p. 9.
5 F. Deak, 'Blue Blouse', in *The Drama Review*, New York, March 1973, vol. 17, No. 1, p. 43.
6 C. V. James, *Soviet Socialist Realism*, London 1973, pp. 22–3.
7 *Ibid.*, p. 29.
8 *Ibid.*
9 N. A. Gorchakov, *The Theatre in Soviet Russia*, New York-London 1957, pp. 47–8.
10 C. Stanislavsky, *My Life in Art*, New York 1948, p. 353.

11 I. Saville, 'Theatre in Revolution', unpublished thesis, London 1976, pp. 8–10.
12 *Sinyaya Bluza*, 1925, No. 23/24, pp. 27–8.
13 E. Braun, *Meyerhold on Theatre*, London 1969, pp. 63–4.
14 *Ibid.*, p. 137.
15 *Ibid.*, p. 43.
16 *Ibid.*, p. 48.
17 *Ibid.*, pp. 138–9.
18 *Ibid.*, p. 124.
19 *Ibid.*, pp. 54–5.
20 *Ibid.*, p. 141.
21 V. I. Lenin, *Collected Works*, Moscow 1966, Vol. 33, pp. 469–70.
22 *Sinyaya Bluza*, 1928, Five Year Edition, pp. 56–8.
23 G. Browning, 'Agitprop', unpublished thesis, p. 18.
24 *Sinyaya Bluza*, 1925, No. 23/24, pp. 8–9.
25 Browning, *op. cit.*, p. 15.
26 *Ibid.*, p. 16.
27 *Der Kämpfer*, 12 October 1927.
28 P. M. Kerzhentsev, *Tvorcesky teatr*, Moscow 1920, chapter XI.
29 *Ibid.*, chapter XV.
30 F. Deak, 'Russian Mass Spectacles', in: *The Drama Review*, June 1975, vol. 19. No. 2, p. 1.
31 R. Rolland, *Le Theatre du peuple; Essai d'esthetique d'un theatre nouveau*, Paris 1926, pp. 124–6.
32 *Sinyaya Bluza*, 1925, No. 23/24, pp. 8–9.
33 W. E. Meyerhold, in: *Teatr i iskusstvo*, Petrograd 1917, No. 18, p. 297.
34 Braun, *op. cit.*, pp. 165–6.
35 *Ibid.*, p. 163.
36 *Ibid.*
37 *Ibid.*, p. 166.
38 *Ibid.*, p. 188.
39 *Ibid.*, pp. 190–2.
40 A. W. Fevralsky, *Zapiski rovesnika veka*, Moscow 1976, pp. 270–1.
41 *Sinyaya Bluza*, 1925, No. 23/24, pp. 8–9.
42 *The Soviet Small Encyclopedia of Circus.*
43 Y. Barna, *Eisenstein*, London 1973, pp. 50–1.
44 Browning, *op. cit.*, p. 22.
45 A. V. Lunacharsky, 'To my opponents' in: *Vestnik teatra*, 14 December, 1920, No. 76–77, p. 4.
46 B. Arvatov, *Kunst und Produktion*, Munich 1972, pp. 80–4.

Chapter 3 Born of the press

1 *Sinyaya Bluza*, 1925, No. 23/24, pp. 10–14.
2 *Ibid.*, 1925, No. 18, pp. 3–5.
3 *Ibid.*
4 *Ibid.*, 1924, No. 1, p. 9.
5 *Ibid.*, 1925, No. 23/24, pp. 56–8.
6 *Ibid.*, 1925, No. 18, pp. 37–42.
7 *Ibid.*, 1924, No. 2, pp. 24–9.
8 *Ibid.*, 1926, No. 33, pp. 53–61.
9 *Ibid.*, 1924, No. 2, pp. 84–5.
10 *Ibid.*, p. 91.
11 *Ibid.*, 1924, No. 1, p. 59.
12 *Ibid.*, 1925, No. 23/24, p. 11.
13 *Ibid.*, 1924, No. 2, p. 51.
14 *Ibid.*, 1925, No. 23/24, p. 14.
15 *Ibid.*, pp. 58–9.
16 *Ibid.*, pp. 84–7.
17 *Ibid.*
18 O. Brik, *Estrada pered stolikami*, Moscow-Leningrad 1927.
19 *Ibid.*
20 *Sinyaya Bluza*, 1925, No. 23/24, p. 11.
21 *Ibid.*, pp. 11–12.
22 *Ibid.*, p. 4.
23 *Ibid.*, p. 84.
24 *Ibid.*, pp. 11–12.
25 *Istoriya Sovetskogo Dramaticheskogo Teatra*, Moscow 1967, vol. 3, p. 176.
26 *Sinyaya Bluza*, 1927, No. 69/70, p. 53.
27 *Album Blue Blouse, op. cit.*
28 *Sinyaya Bluza*, 1925, No. 23/24, p. 5.
29 *Ibid.*, pp. 6–7.
30 *Ibid.*
31 *Ibid.*
32 *Ibid.*
33 *Ibid.*, 1927, No. 69/70, p. 53.
34 *Ibid.*, 1925, No. 23/24, pp. 28–9.
35 *Ibid.*, 1928, Five Year Edition, p. 14.
36 *Ibid.*, 1925, No. 23/24, pp. 27–8.
37 *Ibid.*
38 *Ibid.*, 1928, Five Year Edition, p. 6.
39 *Ibid.*, 1925, No. 23/24, pp. 84–7.
40 *Ibid.*, p. 52.
41 *Ibid.*, p. 26.
42 *Ibid.*, pp. 20–3.
43 *Ibid.*, pp. 28–9.
44 *Ibid.*, pp. 61–2.

45 *Ibid.*
46 *Ibid.*, p. 63.
47 *Ibid.*, p. 65.
48 *Ibid.*, pp. 29–31.
49 *Ibid.*
50 *Ibid.*, 1925, No. 13, pp. 59–61.
51 *Ibid.*, 1928, Five Year Edition, p. 9.
52 *Istoriya Sovetskogo Dramaticheskogo Teatra, op. cit.*, p. 177.
53 Brik, *op. cit.*
54 *Sinyaya Bluza*, 1925, No. 23/24, pp. 66–82.
55 *Ibid.*, 1925, No. 18, pp. 3–5.
56 Brik, *op. cit.*
57 *Sinyaya Bluza*, 1925, No. 23/24, pp. 15–16.
58 *Ibid.*, pp. 20–23.
59 *Ibid.*
60 *Ibid.*, pp. 15–16.
61 *Ibid.*
62 *Ibid.*, pp. 20–3.
63 *Ibid.*, pp. 17–20.
64 *Ibid.*
65 *Ibid.*
66 *Ibid.*, 1925, No. 18, pp. 3–5.
67 *Ibid.*, 1925, No. 13, pp. 59–61.
68 *Ibid.*, 1925, No. 23/24, pp. 10–14.
69 *Ibid.*
70 *Ibid.*, pp. 24–5.
71 *Ibid.*, 1927, No. 67/68, p. 58.
72 *Ibid.*, 1925, No. 23/24, p. 9.
73 *The Christian Science Monitor*, March 3, 1928.
74 *Sinyaya Bluza*, 1927, No. 69/70, pp. 46–9.
75 *Ibid.*
76 *Ibid.*
77 *Ibid.*, pp. 50–5.
78 *Ibid.*, pp. 46–9.
79 *Pravda*, 16 October 1928.
80 *Sinyaya Bluza*, 1927, No. 69/70, pp. 50–5.
81 *Ibid.*
82 *Ibid.*
83 *Ibid.*
84 K. L. Rudnitsky, *Rezhisser Meierkhold*, Moscow 1969, p. 241.
85 James, *op. cit.*, p. 1.
86 *Sinyaya Bluza*, 1925, No. 18, pp. 3–5.
87 *Ibid.*, 1927, No. 69/70, pp. 50–5.
88 Brik, *op. cit.*
89 *Sinyaya Bluza*, 1927, No. 69/70, pp. 50–5.
90 *Ibid.*

91 *Russkaya Sovetskaya Estrada 1917–1929*, Moscow 1976, p. 344.
92 *Istoriya Sovetskogo Dramaticheskogo Teatra*, op. cit., pp. 177–8.
93 *Teatralnaya Entsiklopediya*, Moscow 1965, Vol. 4, column 949.
94 *Russkaya Sovetskaya Estrada 1917–1929*, *op. cit.*, p. 344.
95 *Istoriya Sovetskogo Dramaticheskogo Teatra*, op. cit., pp. 177–82.
96 *Ibid.*, pp. 182–3.
97 *Ibid.*
98 *Ibid.*
99 E. Braun, *The Theatre of Meyerhold*, London 1979, p. 238.
100 *Ibid.*
101 *Sinyaya Bluza*, 1927, No. 69/70, pp. 50–5.
102 Browning, *op. cit.*, p. 52.
103 O. Brik, 'Die Schriftsteller ausbilden' (1928), in H. C. Buch, *Parteilichkeit der Literatur oder Parteiliteratur*, Hamburg 1972, pp. 144–8.
104 *Ibid.*
105 *Mahnruf*, No. 11, 1927.
106 *Der Rote Stern*, No. 21, 1927.
107 *Der Kämpfer*, 21 December 1927.
108 *Ibid.*, 12 October 1927.
109 *Rote Fahne*, 18 December 1928.

Chapter 4   The origins of German agitprop

1 *Die Volksbühne*, February 1909, p. 20.
2 F. Knilli und U. Münchow, *Frühes Deutsches Arbeitertheater 1847–1918*, Munich 1970, p. 338.
3 F. Knellessen, *Agitation auf der Bühne*, Emsdetten 1970, p. 254.
4 *Der Gegner*, October 1920, No. 4, p. 109.
5 Knellessen, *op. cit.*, p. 43.
6 E. Piscator, *Schriften*, Berlin 1968, vol. 1, p. 41.
7 *Ibid.*, pp. 40–1.
8 *Ibid.*, pp. 39–40.
9 Letter from Piscator to Friedrich Wolf, 9 October 1930; F. Wolf-Archive.
10 *Rote Tribüne*, November 1924, No. 2.
11 *Ibid.*
12 *Ibid.*
13 *Rote Fahne*, 19. June 1924.
14 L. Hoffmann und D. Hoffmann Ostwald, *Deutsches Arbeitertheater 1918–1933*, Berlin 1972, vol. 1, p. 136.
15 *Rote Tribüne*, 1924, No. 1.

Chapter 5 Agitate! A movement evolves

1 Piscator, *op. cit.*, p. 60.
2 *Ibid.*, p. 62.
3 *Rote Fahne*, 26 November 1924.
4 Piscator, *op. cit.*, pp. 61–2.
5 *Der junge Bolschewik*, 1927/28, No. 12.
6 Deutsches Arbeitertheater, *op. cit.*, vol. I, p. 204.
7 Archiv des Instituts für Marxismus-Leninismus, Akte 12/71.
8 *Der junge Bolschewik*, October 1925, No. 2.
9 *Ibid.*
10 *Ibid.*
11 *Ibid.*, 1927/28, No. 12.
12 Deutsches Arbeitertheater, *op. cit.*, vol. II, p. 428.
13 *Der junge Bolschewik*, 1927/28, No. 12.
14 *Arbeiter Illustrierte Zeitung*, 1928, No. 36.
15 *Rote Raketen*, Textbuch der Berliner Spieltruppe des RFB, p. 3.
16 Deutsches Zentralarchiv, Merseburg, Rep. 77, Tit. 4043, No. 244.
17 *Ibid.*, No. 353a.
18 *Die Rote Front*, 1928, No. 40.
19 *Arbeiter-Bühne*, 1930, No. 3.
20 *Die Rote Fahne*, 11 January and 16 September 1930.
21 *Das Rote Sprachrohr*, 1929, No. 12.
22 *Ibid.*, 1930, No. 4.
23 Programmheft der Sturmtruppe Alarm, Deutsche Akademie der Künste.
24 *Die Rote Fahne*, 5 August 1922.
25 *Ibid.*, 9 December 1919.
26 H. Scherer, 'Die Volksbühnenbewegung und ihre interne Opposition in der Weimarer Republik', in *Archiv für Sozialgeschichte*, Bonn-Bad Godesberg, 1974, vol. XIV, p. 223.
27 *Ibid.*
28 *Ibid.*, p. 224.
29 Knellessen, *op. cit.*, p. 44.
30 Piscator, *op. cit.*, pp. 36–7.
31 C. Zetkin, 'Kunst und Proletariat', in: *Ausgewählte Reden und Schriften*, Berlin 1957, vol. I, pp. 490–505.
32 *Die Rote Fahne*, 17 October 1920..
33 *Ibid.*, 26 October 1920.
34 Zetkin, *op. cit.*
35 Piscator, *op. cit.*, p. 120.
36 *Die Arbeit*, 1921/22, No. 5.
37 *Die Rote Fahne*, 2 August 1922.
38 *Die Arbeit*, *op. cit.*
39 Landeshauptarchiv Potsdam, Akte 3813.
40 *Taschenkalender für Arbeiter-Schauspieler*, Berlin 1929.
41 *Der junge Bolschewik*, 1928/9, No. 1.

42 *Ibid.*
43 Deutsches Arbeitertheater, *op. cit.*, vol. I, pp. 295–6.
44 *Arbeiterbühne und Film*, 1931, No. 5.
45 *Das Arbeiter-Theater*, Neue Wege und Aufgaben proletarischer Bühnenpropaganda, 1928.
46 *Ibid.*
47 *Ibid.*
48 *Ibid.*
49 *Ibid.*
50 *Der junge Bolschewik*, 1927/28, No. 12.
51 *Ibid.*
52 *Die Rote Fahne*, 15 April 1928.
53 *Ibid.*
54 *Arbeiterbühne und Film*, March 1929, p. 1.

Chapter 6   Propaganda – coping with the crisis

1 *Arbeiterbühne und Film*, 1930, No. 7.
2 Knellessen, *op. cit.*, p. 249.
3 *Das Rote Sprachrohr*, October 1930.
4 *Ibid.*, 1930, No. 5.
5 *Die Rote Fahne*, 5 December 1928.
6 H. Weber, *Der Deutsche Kommunismus*, Köln-Berlin 1964, pp. 183–184.
7 *Das Rote Sprachrohr*, November 1929.
8 *Ibid.*
9 *Die Rote Fahne*, 15 December 1929.
10 *Das Rote Sprachrohr*, June 1930.
11 *Die Rote Fahne*, 22 April 1931.
12 *Ibid.*, 26 May 1932.
13 *Ibid.*, 7 March 1930.
14 *Ibid.*
15 *Ibid.*, 3 December 1929.
16 *Ibid.*, 1 August 1930.
17 A. Lacis, *Revolutionär im Beruf*, Munich 1971, pp. 107–8.
18 *Die Rote Fahne*, 29 May 1931.
19 Deutsches Arbeitertheater, *op. cit.*, vol. II, p. 93.
20 Archiv des Instituts für Marxismus-Leninismus, Akte 10/339.
21 *Arbeiterbühne und Film*, 1931, No. 5.
22 Deutsches Arbeitertheater, *op. cit.*, vol. II, pp. 60–1.
23 *Das Rote Sprachrohr*, April 1930.
24 *Arbeiterbühne und Film*, November 1930.
25 *Ibid.*
26 *Ibid.*, 1931, No. 4.
27 *Die Rote Fahne*, 21 October 1930.

28 *Arbeiterbühne und Film*, 1931, No. 5.
29 *Ibid.*
30 *Ibid.*
31 *Das Rote Sprachrohr*, January 1931.
32 Deutsches Arbeitertheater, *op. cit.*, vol. 11, p. 428.
33 H. Eisler, *Reden und Aufsätze*, Leipzig 1961, p. 46.
34 *Das Rote Sprachrohr*, 1929, No. 10/11.
35 *Ibid.*, 1930, No. 2/3.
36 Knellessen, *op. cit.*, p. 280.
37 *Arbeiterbühne und Film*, January 1931, referring also to the next quotation.
38 *Freund der Sowjets*, 1930, No. 8/9, pp. 139–40.
39 *Das Rote Sprachrohr*, Special Edition, Oct. 1930.
40 M. Kolzov, *Das Internationale Theater*, Moscow 1933, Bulletin No. 3.
41 *Arbeiterbühne und Film*, January 1931, p. 11.
42 *Illustrierte Rote Post*, 1932, No. 23.
43 *Arbeiterbühne und Film*, 1931, No. 3.
44 *Das Rote Sprachrohr*, June 1931 and April 1932, Special Edition No. 2.
45 F. Wolf, *Ausgewählte Werke*, Berlin 1957, Vol. XIII, pp. 205–6.
46 *Die Rote Fahne*, 17 April 1930.
47 *Arbeiterbühne und Film*, 1931, No. 4.
48 *Das Rote Sprachrohr*, 1932, Special Edition 'Massenstreik'.
49 Wolf, *op. cit.*, p. 23.

Chapter 7 Towards a popular theatre

1 *Thesen und Resolutionen des erweiterten Präsidiums des IATB*, Moscow 1932, p. 12.
2 Lacis, *op. cit.*, pp. 115–16.
3 B. Brecht, *Schriften zum Theater*, vol. VI, Berlin and Weimer 1964.
4 Wolf, *op. cit.*, p. 54.
5 Knellessen, *op. cit.*, p. 192.
6 B. Brecht, 'Anmerkungen zur Mutter', *Stücke*, vol. V, Berlin 1957.

Chapter 8 From Luddite melodrama to the Workers' Theatre Movement

1 W. S. Hilton, *Foes to Tyranny*, London 1936, p. 82.
2 McCreery/Stourac, Interview with Bram Bootman, London 1977.
3 R. Estill, '*The Factory Lad*: Melodrama as Propaganda', in *Theatre Quarterly*, London, October/December 1971, vol. 1, No. 4, p. 24.

4 *Ibid.*, p. 22.
5 R. Stewart, Foreword to *When Dreams Come True*, by F. Simpson, Perth 1920, p. 5.
6 *The Young Socialist*, 1907, p. 65.
7 McCreery/Stourac, Interview with Jack and Alice Loveman, London 1977.
8 *Ibid.*
9 *Ibid.*
10 T. Thomas, 'A Propertyless Theatre for the Propertyless Class', in *History Workshop Journal*, November 1977, No. 4, p. 113.
11 McCreery/Stourac, Interview with Tom Thomas, Welwyn Garden City 1977.
12 *The Sunday Worker*, 20 March 1927.
13 Thomas, *op. cit.*, p. 117.
14 *Ibid.*
15 'A History of the Workers' Theatre Movement', Part 2, in *New Red Stage*, September 1932, No. 7, p. 8.
16 Thomas, *op. cit.*, p. 117.
17 'A History of the WTM', Part 2, *op. cit.*, pp. 8–9.
18 Thomas, *op. cit.*, p. 117.
19 'A History of the WTM', Part 2, *op. cit.*, p. 8.
20 Interview with Tom Thomas, *op. cit.*
21 'A History of the WTM', Part 2, *op. cit.*, pp. 8–9.
22 Interview with Tom Thomas, *op. cit.*
23 Thomas, *op. cit.*, p. 119.
24 'A History of the WTM', Part I, *New Red Stage*, June/July 1932, No. 6, p. 8.
25 Thomas, *op. cit.*, p. 119.
26 'A History of the WTM', Part 2, *op. cit.*, p. 9.
27 *Ibid.*
28 Thomas *op. cit.*, p. 119.
29 'A History of the WTM', Part 2, *op. cit.*, p. 9.

Chapter 9   The old world's crashing . . .

1 N. Edwards, *The Workers' Theatre*, Cardiff 1930.
2 T. Thomas's papers, memorandum of resolutions, dated July 1930, in 'Documents and Texts from the Workers' Theatre Movement, 1928–1936', *History Workshop Journal*, November 1977, No. 4, p. 106.
3 McCreery/Stourac, Interview with Philip Poole, London 1977.
4 Interview with Tom Thomas, *op. cit.*
5 L. A. Jones, The British Workers' Theatre, 1917–1935; Ph.D. thesis, Karl-Marx Universität, Leipzig 1964.
6 Thomas, *op. cit.*, p. 120.

7 'Documents and Texts from the WTM', *op. cit.*, p. 105.
8 *Ibid.*
9 *Ibid.*, p. 106.
10 Interview with Philip Poole, *op. cit.*
11 *Ibid.*
12 Interview with Philip Poole, *op. cit.*
13 *The Communist*, December 1928.
14 Interview with Jack and Alice Loveman, *op. cit.*
15 Interview with Philip Poole, *op. cit.*
16 Interview with Bram Bootman, *op. cit.*
17 McCreery/Stourac, Interview with Charles B. Mann, Somerset 1977.
18 McCreery/Stourac, Interview with Fegel and Philip Firestein, London 1977.
19 McCreery/Stourac, Interview with Andre van Gyseghem, London 1977.
20 Interview with Tom Thomas, *op. cit.*
21 Interview with Jack and Alice Loveman, *op. cit.*
22 'What the Groups Are Doing', *Red Stage*, January 1932, No. 2, p. 5.
23 'The Scottish Tour', *Red Stage*, Nov. 1931, No. 1, p. 3.
24 Interview with Jack and Alice Loveman, *op. cit.*
25 'News from Everywhere', *Red Stage*, January 1932, No. 2, p. 4.
26 Thomas, *op. cit.*, p. 120.
27 'The Basis and Development of the WTM', Statement from the Central Committee, First National Conference, WTM, London 1932, June 1925/26, p. 2.
28 Thomas, *op. cit.*, pp. 120–1.
29 *Ibid.*
30 *Ibid.*
31 *Daily Worker*, 8 February 1930, p. 11.
32 *Ibid.*, 3 January 1931, p. 4.
33 *Ibid.*, 11 June 1930, p. 5.

Chapter 10   The heyday of the WTM

1 C. B. Mann, 'How to Organise a New Group', *Red Stage*, January 1932, No. 2, p. 2.
2 Interview with C. B. Mann, *op. cit.*
3 The complete text of *Speed-Up, Speed-Up* is reproduced in *New Red Stage*, September 1932, No. 7, pp. 7–8, and 10.
4 R. Samuel, Interview with C. B. Mann, 30 June 1977.
5 McCreery/Stourac, Interview with C. B. Mann, *op. cit.*
6 *Ibid.*
7 *Ibid.*

8 C. B. Mann, 'How to Produce Meerut', *WTM Monthly Bulletin*, February 1933, No. 3, pp. 14–16.
9 Interview with C. B. Mann, *op. cit.*
10 'News From Everywhere', *Red Stage*, February 1932, No. 3, p. 4.
11 H. Dewar, *Communist Politics in Britain*, London 1976, p. 91.
12 *Ibid.*, p. 94.
13 *Ibid.*, p. 96.
14 *Ibid.*, p. 94.
15 *Ibid.*, p. 100.
16 *Ibid.*
17 Interview with Philip Poole, *op. cit.*
18 Dewar, *op. cit.*, p. 91.
19 *Ibid.*, p. 93.
20 Secretariat, I.W.D.U., 'Greetings', *Red Stage*, September 1931, No. 1, p. 1.
21 *Red Stage*, March 1932, No. 4, p. 5.
22 *Ibid.*, February 1932, No. 3, p. 2.
23 'The Work of the Readers' Committee', *ibid.*
24 Interview with Tom Thomas, *op. cit.*
25 'Documents and Texts from the WTM', *op. cit.*, p. 106.
26 E. MacColl, 'Grass Roots of Theatre Workshop', in *Theatre Quarterly*, London January–March 1973, p. 58.
27 *Ibid.*
28 P. Poole, 'Reviews of Current Material: *The Spirit of Invergordon*', *Red Stage*, February 1932, No. 3, p. 6.
29 *Red Stage*, January 1932, No. 2, p. 4.
30 'The Castleford Sketch', *WTM Monthly Bulletin*, *op. cit.*, p. 17.
31 'Dramatising the Class Struggle', *New Red Stage*, September 1932, No. 7, p. 10.
32 'The Castleford Sketch', *op. cit.*, pp. 17–18.
33 Interview with Jack and Alice Loveman, *op. cit.*
34 'What Readers Say', *Red Stage*, March 1932, No. 4, p. 7.
35 'The Scottish Tour', *op. cit.*, pp. 2–3.
36 'We Tour Wales', *Red Stage*, March 1932, No. 4, p. 3.
37 *Ibid.*
38 *Ibid.*
39 'May Day', *Red Stage*, April/May 1932, No. 5, p. 2.
40 'How We Played Our Part on May Day', *New Red Stage*, June/July 1932, No. 6, p. 6.
41 *Ibid.*
42 'Our National Conference', *New Red Stage*, June/July 1932, No. 6, p. 9.
43 'The Basis and Development of the WTM', *op. cit.*, pp. 1–4. This document provides the source for the quotations in the following section 'Agitprop vs. Naturalism'.

44 'What Is the Line of Our Development?', *WTM Monthly Bulletin*, *op. cit.*, pp. 13–14.

45 R. Waterman, 'Proltet: The Yiddish-speaking Group of the WTM', in *History Workshop Journal*, Spring 1978, No. 5, p. 176.

46 'The Bureau's Manifesto', *WTM Monthly Bulletin*, *op. cit.*, p. 4.

47 *Ibid.*, pp. 2–4; this provides the source for the following quotations concerning the critique of sketches produced at the eighth All-London Show on 18 December 1932.

48 Proltet's Letter on B. Woodward's Criticism, *ibid.*, p. 6.

49 T. Thomas, 'Their Theatre and Ours', *History Workshop Journal*, November 1977, No. 4, pp. 137–42.

50 T. Thomas, 'Cavalcade – A Review', *Red Stage*, March 1932, No. 4, p. 2.

51 Waterman, *op. cit.*

52 Interview with C. B. Mann, *op. cit.*

53 Interview with Tom Thomas, *op. cit.*

54 Interview with Fegel and Philip Firestein, *op. cit.*

55 Interview with C. B. Mann, *op. cit.*

56 *Ibid.*

57 Interview with André van Gyseghem, *op. cit.*

58 Interview with Fegel and Philp Firestein, *op. cit.*

59 Interview with André van Gyseghem, *op. cit.*

60 Interview with C. B. Mann, *op. cit.*

61 Jones, *op. cit.*, p. 174.

62 *Ibid.*

63 Interview with Jack and Alice Loveman, *op. cit.*

Chapter 11   Return to the curtain stage – decline of the WTM

1 Interview with Bram Bootman, *op. cit.*

2 'Documents and Texts from the WTM', *op. cit.*, pp. 108–9.

3 Interview with Philip Poole, *op. cit.*

4 Interview with Tom Thomas, *op. cit.*

5 *Daily Herald*, 16 July 1936.

6 Dewar, *op. cit.*, p. 45.

7 T. Thomas, 'A Propertyless Theatre for the Propertyless Class', *op. cit.*, pp. 124–5.

8 This quotation and the following ones, documenting the resignation of Tom Thomas and the subsequent split in the WTM derive from documents, letters and minutes of meetings in the Bram Bootman Collection.

9 Philip Poole's letter to McCreery/Stourac, London, 13 March 1977.

10 Thomas, 'Cavalcade – A Review', *op. cit.*

11 Interview with Jack and Alice Loveman, *op. cit.*

12 *The International Theatre*, 1934, No. 1, p. 24.

13 Interview with C. B. Mann, *op. cit.*
14 Dewar, *op. cit.*, p. 109.
15 Interview with André van Gyseghem, *op. cit.*
16 Interview with Jack and Alice Loveman, *op. cit.*
17 Interview with André van Gyseghem, *op. cit.*
18 *Ibid.*
19 Samuel, Interview with C. B. Mann, *op. cit.*
20 Interview with André van Gyseghem, *op. cit.*
21 Interview with Philip Poole, *op. cit.*
22 Interview with Fegel and Philip Firestein, *op. cit.*
23 'Outline History of Unity', Bram Bootman Collection.
24 Interview with Bram Bootman, *op. cit.*
25 M. Page, 'The Early Years at Unity', *Theatre Quarterly*, London, October/December 1971, vol. 1, No. 4, p. 61.
26 *Ibid.*, p. 62.
27 'Documents and Texts from the WTM', *op. cit.*, p. 109.
28 Page, *op. cit.*, p. 63.
29 MacColl, *op. cit.*, p. 63.
30 Page, *op. cit.*, p. 63.
31 Interview with Bram Bootman, *op. cit.*
32 'Our Theatre Awakens the Masses', *Red Stage*, January 1932, No. 2, p. 8.
33 Bram Bootman Collection.
34 Interview with Fegel and Philip Firestein, *op. cit.*
35 *Ibid.*
36 Interview with André van Gyseghem, *op. cit.*
37 Interview with Bram Bootman, *op. cit.*
38 *Ibid.*
39 *Ibid.*
40 *Ibid.*

Chapter 12 Achievements and weaknesses

1 Thomas, 'A Propertyless Theatre for the Propertyless', *op. cit.*, p. 12.
2 J. Loveman, Letter to Dr. Wilfried van der Will, 3 April 1975.
3 McCreery/Stourac, Interview with C. B. Mann, *op. cit.*
4 *Ibid.*
5 Loveman, *op. cit.*

Chapter 13 Three movements

1 J. Fiebach, 'Die Herausbildung von E. Piscators Politischem Theater 1924/25', in: *Weimarer Beiträge*, 1967, No. 2, p. 216.
2 *Ibid.*, p. 220.
3 *Ibid.*, p. 202.
4 S. Eisenstein, *Ausgewählte Aufsätze*, Berlin 1960, p. 326.
5 Fiebach, *op. cit.*, p. 219.
6 B. Brecht, 'Against Georg Lukács', in *New Left Review*, March–April 1974, No. 84, p. 50.

Appendices

1 *Sinyaya Bluza*, 1926, No. 33, pp. 53–61.
2 *Kampfkongress der Arbeiterschauspieler*, ATBD, Berlin 1931.
3 *Das Rote Sprachrohr*, June and October 1930.
4 A. Lacis, *op. cit.*, p. 107.
5 *The Red Stage, New Red Stage, WTM Bulletin* and L. A. Jones, *op. cit.*, pp. 236–7.
6 T. Thomas, *Das Internationale Theater*, No. 1, 1934, p. 28.
7 *Red Stage, New Red Stage, Report of the First National Conference*, June 25/26, 1932, *WTM Bulletin* and L. A. Jones, *op. cit.*, Appendix B, and the private collection of Bram Bootman.

Select bibliography

(In addition to publications already listed in the Notes and references)

Althusser, L., *For Marx*, London 1969.

Althusser, L., *Lenin and Philosophy and other essays*, London 1971.

'Arbeitertheater in der Weimarer Republik', in *Wem gehört die Welt*, Catalogue for the exhibition 'Kunst und Gesellschaft in der Weimarer Republik', published by Neue Gesellschaft für Bildende Kunst, Berlin 1977.

Art in Revolution, Soviet Art and Design since 1917, Arts Council Catalogue, London 1971.

Barker, C., 'The Chartists, Theatre, Reform and Research', in *Theatre Quarterly*, vol. 1, No. 4, London 1971.

Barth, H., *Zum Kulturprogramm des deutschen Proletariats im 19. Jahrhundert*, Dresden 1978.

Benjamin, W., 'The Work of Art in the Age of Mechanical Reproduction', in *Illuminations*, London 1973.

Bogdanov, A., *Die Kunst und das Proletariat*, Berlin 1920.

Bogdanov, A., *Was ist proletarische Dichtung*, Berlin 1920.

Bradby, D., and McCormick, J., *People's Theatre*, London 1978.

Bradby, D. et al., *Performance and Politics in Popular Drama*, 1980.

Bucharin, N., *Proletarische Revolution und Kultur*, Hamburg 1932.

Carter, H., *The New Spirit in the Russian Theatre 1917–28*, New York 1929.

Damerius, H., *Über zehn Meere zum Mittelpunkt der Welt*, Erinnerungen an die 'Kolonne Links', Berlin 1977.

Davies, C., 'The Volksbühne: a Descriptive Chronology', in *Theatre Quarterly*, vol. 2, No. 5, London 1972.

Deak, F., 'The Agitprop and Circus Plays of Vladimir Mayakovsky', in *The Drama Review*, vol. 17, No. 1, New York 1973.

Dennett, T., and Spence, J., *Photography/Politics: One*, The International Worker Photography Movement, London 1979.

Diezel, P., *Exiltheater in der Sowjetunion 1932–1937*, Berlin 1978.

Fähnders, W., and Rector, M., Literatur im Klassenkampf, Munich 1971.

Farner, K., *Der Aufstand der Abstrakt-Konkreten*, Neuwied and Berlin 1910.

Fischer, E., *The Necessity of Art*, London 1963.

Fitzpatrick, S., *The Commissariat of Enlightenment*, New York 1970.

Fülöp-Miller, *The Mind and Face of Bolshevism*, London 1927.

Gallas, H., *Marxistische Literaturtheorie*, Kontroversen im Bund proletarisch-revolutionärer Schriftsteller, Neuwied und Berlin 1971.

Geras, N., 'Essence and Appearance', in: *New Left Review*, No. 65, London 1971.

Gerould, D., 'Eisenstein's Wiseman', in *The Drama Review*, vol. 18, No. 1, New York 1974.

Gordon, M., 'Meyerhold's Biomechanics', in *The Drama Review*, vol. 18, No. 3, New York 1974.

Goorney, H., *The Theatre Workshop Story*, London 1981.

Gyseghem, A. van, *Theatre in Soviet Russia*, London 1943.

Hedgbeth, L., 'Meyerhold's "D.E." ', in *The Drama Review*, vol. 19, No. 2, New York 1975.

Hobsbawm, E., 'Confronting Defeat: the German Communist Party', in *New Left Review*, No. 61, London 1970.

Hoffmann, L., *Theater der Kollektive*, Proletarisch-revolutionäres Berufstheater in Deutschland 1928–1933, Berlin 1980.

Kommissarzhevsky, V., *Moscow Theatres*, Moscow 1959.

Kotzioulas, G., *Theatre of the Mountains*, (in Greek) Athens 1976.

Lammel, I., *Das Arbeiterlied*, Leipzig, 1970.

Lammel, I., *Lieder der Agitprop-Truppen vor 1945*, Leipzig 1959.

Lammel, I., *Lieder des Roten Frontkämpferbundes*, Leipzig 1961.

Lenin, V. I., *On Culture and Cultural Revolution*, Moscow 1970.

Lenin, V. I., *On Literature and Art*, Moscow 1970.

Loveman, J., 'Workers' Theatre: Personal Recollections of political theatre in Greenwich during the 1920s and 1930s', in *Red Letters*, No. 13, London 1982.

Lunacharsky, A., *Die Kulturaufgaben der Arbeiterklasse*, Frankfurt am Main 1971.

Lunacharsky, A., *Die Revolution und die Kunst*, Dresden 1962.

Lunacharsky, A., *Theatre et Revolution*, Paris 1971.

Lunacharsky, A., *Vom Proletkult zum sozialistischen Realismus*, Berlin 1981.

Luxemburg, R., *Schriften über Kunst und Literatur*, Dresden 1972.

Märten, L., *Wesen und Veränderung der Formen/Künste*, 1924.

Marcuse, H., 'Art as Form of Reality', in *New Left Review*, No. 74, London 1972.

Marx, Engels, Lenin, *Über Kultur, Ästhetik, Literatur*, Leipzig 1981.

Mayakovsky, V., *The Complete Plays of Mayakovsky*, New York 1971.

McCreery, K., Proltet: Yiddish Theatre in the 1930s', in *Race and Class*, vol. XX, No. 3, London 1979.

Mehring, F., *Aufsätze zur deutschen Literaturgeschichte*, Leipzig 1972.

Mehring, F., 'Naturalismus und Proletarischer Klassenkampf', in Buch, H., *Parteilichkeit der Literatur oder Parteiliteratur*, Reinbek 1977.

Poole, P., 'The Workers' Theatre Movement', in *Red Letters*, No. 10, London 1980.

Schneider, H., *Exiltheater in der Tschechoslowakei 1933–1938*, Berlin 1979.

Skelley, J., *The General Strike 1926*, London 1976.

Suvin, D., 'The Mirror and the Dynamo: On Brecht's Aesthetic Point of View', in *The Drama Review*, vol. 12, No. 1, New York 1967.

Thalheimer, A., 'Proletariat und Kunst', in *Zur Literaturgeschichte von Calderon bis Heine*, Berlin 1929.

'Theater in der Weimarer Republik', in *Weimarer Republik*, Catalogue for the exhibition, published by Kunstamt Kreuzberg, Berlin und dem Institut für Theaterwissenschaft der Universität Köln, Berlin (West) and Hamburg, 1977.

Thompson, E. P., *The Making of the English Working Class*, London 1968.

Tretyakov, S., *Die Arbeit des Schriftstellers*, Reinbek 1972.

Trotsky, L., *Literature and Revolution*, University of Michigan 1968.

Trotsky, L., *On Literature and Art*, New York 1970.

Tuckett, A., 'The People's Theatre in Bristol', in *Our History*, No. 72, London 1978.

Willett, J., *The New Sobriety 1917–1933: Art and Politics in the Weimar Period*, London 1978.

Willett, J., *The Theatre of Erwin Piscator*, London 1978.

Index of theatre groups, plays, songs and sketches

(See also Appendix 1–3)

Key
Theatre groups are capitalized: BATTERSEA PLAYERS
Plays are in italics: *Adding Machine, The*
Sketches are in inverted commas: 'About Comrade Kollontai'
Songs are indicated by (song)

General Index